Peak

Performance

SUCCESS
IN COLLEGE
AND
BEYOND

seventh edition

Peak

Performance

seventh edition

SUCCESS
IN COLLEGE
AND
BEYOND

Sharon K. Ferrett, Ph.D.

Humboldt State University

Baker College Custom Edition

 Learning Solutions

Boston   Burr Ridge, IL   Dubuque, IA   New York   San Francisco
St. Louis   Bangkok   Bogotá   Caracas   Lisbon   London   Madrid
Mexico City   Milan   New Delhi   Seoul   Singapore   Sydney   Taipei   Toronto

PEAK PERFORMANCE: SUCCESS IN COLLEGE AND BEYOND, Seventh Edition
Baker College Custom Edition

1 2 3 4 5 6 7 8 9 0 EUS EUS 0 9

ISBN-13: 978-0-07-736884-5
ISBN-10: 0-07-736884-3

Learning Solutions Manager: Melani Theis
Learning Solutions Representative: Nada Mraovic
Production Editor: Susan Culbertson
Printer/Binder: Quebecor World

Brief Table of Contents

Table of Contents

3 Manage Your Time 81

> PART TWO
> ## Basic Skills and Strategies

4 Listen and Take Effective Notes 123

5 Actively Read   153

6 Improve Your Memory Skills   189

7 Excel at Taking Tests 221

PART THREE
Application

8 Become a Critical Thinker and Creative Problem Solver 255

Preface to the Instructor

Why I Wrote This Book

I have spent more than 30 years working with students as a college professor, an advisor, and a dean and more than 20 years as a management consultant. I began my research into personal productivity and human relations early in my teaching career and began compiling data from years of teaching classes in organizational behavior and giving hundreds of workshops to managers and executives. I have always been interested in transitions, which led me to teaching classes to help students successfully make the transition from high school to college and from college to the world of work.

It is apparent that there is a strong connection between the world of college and the world of work, yet college is often viewed as separate from the real world. This text, more than any other, presents the relationship of college with the larger systems of work and life. It focuses on responsibility and the consequences of one's decisions and actions. It goes further and shows how decisions and actions can affect others and the larger world.

I contend that it is the nature of people to love learning and to strive for peak performance. As educators, we have the unique opportunity to provide our students with the knowledge and skills they will use in their journey to becoming a peak performer. This book provides the strategies, personal qualities, and habits that will help students put knowledge into action.

As I have developed this edition, I have kept a number of definite goals at the forefront. Essentially, to be successful, students need to

- **Learn how they learn best—and incorporate new ways to learn.** Throughout this text, students are given the opportunity to explore learning styles and to develop personal strategies that work for them. Features throughout the text reinforce the core principles and give students the opportunity to practice their critical thinking skills.

- **Maximize their available resources and seek out new opportunities.** Often, students overlook what is already available to them. Thus, throughout the text we provide strategies for making the most of surrounding resources and tips for seeking out new resources and opportunities.

- **Relate what they are exploring and learning now to future success on the job.** Students are more motivated when they can make the connection between school and job success. Throughout this text, we provide numerous examples and features that directly tie the knowledge, skills, and habits learned in class today to what they will experience in their career.

- **Be challenged to strive to become the best individuals they can be.** Our hope is not only that students become successes in the business world but also that they are productive contributors to their communities. Throughout this text, we focus on the key personal qualities, habits, and strategies that will help students become peak performers in all facets of life.

Additionally, it is critical that we

● **Provide you, the instructor, with the most useful and practical teaching tools possible.** The goals of your course may vary and you may be dealing with a variety of students—from incoming freshmen straight out of high school, to **returning students** coming from the workforce, **to transferring students coming from other schools.** Thus, we have developed a number of teaching tools to suit your situation and your ultimate goals.

New to the Seventh Edition

The seventh edition of *Peak Performance: Success in College and Beyond* has been thoroughly updated and refined based on the many helpful comments and suggestions of adopters and reviewers of the previous edition. This new edition provides even more specific "how-to" information, including how to use the latest technologies to your advantage. Revised with our main objectives in mind, following are just some of the revised features and new material. (For a complete list of all the text's chapter-by-chapter changes, please see the Instructor's Resource Manual that accompanies this text.)

1. **Many new *hot topics and current issues* have been added to demonstrate the relevance of the material to today's student.**
   - Material on **using laptops** in class has been added to the note-taking strategies. (Chapter 4, page 137)
   - A new section devoted to **reading difficulties,** including a discussion of dyslexia, decoding, and helpful strategies, has been added. (Chapter 5, page 172)
   - A new introduction in Chapter 6 mentions how **technology** has changed our use of "personal memory." (Chapter 6, page 190)

2. **More *"how-to" information* is provided to help the student put the material into practice.**
   - A new feature entitled **"Starting Today"** appears at the end of each chapter and asks the student to choose a strategy to immediately implement and how he or she plans to incorporate it into his or her daily routine. (Chapter 1, page 38)
   - A new box entitled **"How to Say No"** gives readers specific dialog to use in situations in order to manage their time by also maintaining positive relationships. (Chapter 3, page 101)
   - A new box shows how to manage your time effectively when **taking online courses.** (Chapter 3, page 103)
   - A new box entitled **"Getting the Most Out of a Class Lecture"** gives students specific tips on how to excel when an instructor's teaching style may present certain challenges. (Chapter 4, page 135)
   - A new section is devoted to strategies for **reading manuals.** (Chapter 5, page 169)
   - A new box provides specific strategies for **taking online exams.** (Chapter 7, page 226)
   - A new box entitled **"Asking Questions"** provides tips on how to frame questions. (Chapter 8, page 262)

3. **New and revised *illustrations* help visual learners understand key theories and concepts and provide more applications.**
   - A new illustration of the **Adult Learning Cycle** shows how to move through the steps and the importance of practice and repetition. (Chapter 1, page 30)
   - A revised illustration of **Maslow's Hierarchy of Needs** includes examples of needs at each level. (Chapter 2, page 56)
   - A new **goal-setting** illustration helps students map out their learning goals. (Chapter 2, page 61)

- Revised **time log charts** clarify how to fill them out and more effectively support the narrative. (Chapter 3, page 85)
- Revised **note-taking illustrations** more effectively demonstrate how to take notes using these systems. (Chapter 4, pages 131, 133)
- A new illustration of the **Ebbinghaus Curve of Forgetting** reinforces the importance of reviewing notes directly after lecture. (Chapter 4, page 138)
- A new illustration on **how to take notes on a page** gives students the opportunity to practice taking notes and examples of possible note-taking styles. (Chapter 5, page 165)
- A new figure shows examples of **different illustrations** and what to look for when reading graphs. (Chapter 5, page 170)
- A new figure shows how to **sketch out a math problem.** (Chapter 7, page 228)
- A new illustration of **Bloom's Taxonomy** further explains the critical thinking skills. (Chapter 8, page 257)

4. *Statistics* have been updated and/or added throughout to support the material. Also, many *examples* have been added or revised to encourage application and personal reflection.
   - A new exercise entitled **"Am I a Positive Person?"** asks students to assess their overall attitude to life in general and how they approach every day. (Chapter 1, page 4)
   - Specific examples of **negative thinking** have been added. (Chapter 1, page 7)
   - A revised **mission statement** relates to the reader's experiences. (Chapter 1, page 9)
   - The **Peak Self-Assessment Test** now includes examples of skills for reference. (Chapter 1, page 11)
   - Material on **reading for different courses** includes additional examples of courses in sociology, psychology, and anthropology. (Chapter 5, page 161)

- Examples of **prefixes and suffixes** for certain fields of study have been added to the section on building vocabulary. (Chapter 5, page 166)
- An exercise on creating your own **acronyms and acrostics,** including examples, has been added. (Chapter 6, page 201)
- A new box entitled **"Think It Through"** reinforces that one must think of the consequences when making decisions. (Chapter 8, page 259)
- A new box on **inductive versus deductive reasoning** provides examples of each and gives the reader the opportunity to create his or her own statements. (Chapter 8, page 264)

5. **The narrative has been revised throughout for** *clarity and streamlining of the material,* **focusing on key content and strategies.**
   - The **ABC Method of Self-Management** has been revised from five to three steps, making the process more palatable and easier to understand and apply. (Chapter 1, page 7)
   - **Chapter 2 has been reorganized** into two main sections: Emotional Intelligence and Maturity, and A Positive Attitude and Personal Motivation. Topics within the latter section have been further organized and condensed for ease of understanding. (Chapter 2, page 45)
   - The material on **discretionary time and urgent and important priorities** has been revised for further clarity. (Chapter 3, page 86)
   - The section on **assessing and reviewing your notes** includes creating a timeline for reviewing. (Chapter 4, page 139)
   - **Part 4** of the Five-Part Reading System has been retitled to "Process Information" to better describe the purpose and tasks for that step. (Chapter 5, page 155)
   - Definitions of **problem solving and decision making** have been added. (Chapter 8, page 256)

- A revised section on **math and science anxiety** includes the most relevant strategies. (Chapter 8, page 278)
- Many **references to historical and trade authors** are available in the AIE version under "Further Reading." (Chapter 1, page 8)

Successful Features

A number of features throughout this text reinforce learning, critical thinking, and the main goals of the text, and all continue to be fine-tuned to support the chapter material more succinctly.

- **Student preface.** This unique introduction not only walks the student through the numerous beneficial features that reinforce the text's goals but also includes "As You Get Started in Your New School: What You Need to Know and Should Not Be Afraid to Ask." This section helps students explore the reasons they are attending college, provides a checklist of the tasks to accomplish the first week of school, and gives the critical questions that they should get answers to in their situation and school (including the top questions asked advisors). It also includes information on topics such as graduation requirements, registering, adding and dropping classes, incomplete grades, taking a leave of absence, and transferring. Also included are the top 50 strategies for success in college.

- **The ABC Method of Self-Management.** Introduced in Chapter 1, the ABC Method of Self-Management will help students manage thoughts, feelings, and behaviors, so that they create positive results and achieve goals. This three-step process (A = Actual event; B = Beliefs; C = Challenge) uses visualization to show the connection among thoughts, feelings, and actions and empowers the reader to dispel negative thoughts and replace them with realistic and positive thoughts and behaviors. Each chapter begins with a "Self-Management" exercise, which includes a scenario that students can relate to. The student is then given the opportunity to reflect on personal experiences in the follow-up journal entry. A chapter worksheet is provided to record the journal entry and helps the student practice critical thinking by using the ABC Method of Self-Management to work through difficult situations and determine positive solutions. A Self-Management Workbook is also available on the text's Web site (www.mhhe.com/ferrett7e) to give the student further practice applying the model.

- **The Adult Learning Cycle.** Introduced in Chapter 1 and carried throughout each chapter, the Adult Learning Cycle is a five-step process that demonstrates that learning comes from repetition, practice, and recall. This process offers a critical fifth stage not included in other learning theories: (1) relate, (2) observe, (3) reflect, (4) do, and (5) teach. Each chapter provides the reader an opportunity to apply the chapter material to the Adult Learning Cycle within a Peak Progress box.

- **Secretary's Commission on Achieving Necessary Skills (SCANS).** Found on pages xix–xx and introduced in Chapter 1, this is the list of the competencies employees need to be able to demonstrate on the job. Included in this handy chart are the corresponding chapters in this text. The many exercises, strategies, case studies, and guidelines throughout the text correlate with several SCANS requirements, as well as systems thinking, diversity, and critical thinking.

- **Academic honesty.** An ever-increasing issue on college campuses, academic honesty continues to be thoroughly addressed, including discussions on the topics of cheating, plagiarism, the citing of sources, and paraphrasing.

- **"Active" titles.** All chapter titles include active verbs, reinforcing that the content needs to be put into action in order to be effective.

- **Learning Objectives.** Written in an active voice, clear and concise objectives at the beginning of each chapter identify the chapter's key concepts.

- **Self-Management and Journal Entry.** Each chapter begins with a Self-Management scenario that students can relate to. The reader is then given the opportunity to reflect on personal experiences in the follow-up Journal Entry. An end-of-chapter worksheet is provided to record the journal entry.

- **Success Principle.** Each chapter begins with a Success Principle that succinctly communicates the important lesson to be learned from the chapter. These provide the student with a quick and meaningful take-away message.

- **Words to Succeed.** Found throughout the text, these quotes provide insight, motivation, and food for thought and are tied to the chapter's content. Many quotes are included that are from pioneers and personalities the student will quickly recognize.

- **Personal Evaluation Notebook.** Appearing in every chapter, these exercises provide opportunities to practice critical thinking and decision-making skills. Many have been revised to provide more specific instructions and to avoid closed questions (simple yes/no answers). Spaces are provided for recording answers and thoughts directly within the activity.

- **Peak Progress.** The Peak Progress boxed feature demonstrates the themes and concepts of each chapter and includes helpful suggestions to accelerate and assess progress.

- **Key terminology.** Key terms are boldfaced at their first discussion, and all terms appear in the end-of-text glossary.

- **Summary.** Every chapter concludes with a summary of the main points presented in the chapter. Written as "I" statements, they reinforce that the chapter presents a number of potential strategies to implement and master.

- **Performance Strategies.** Included in every chapter is a recap of the top 10 strategies for success in applying the chapter's concepts.

- **Tech for Success.** This feature offers tips for making the most out of technology applications in school and on the job.

- **Study Team Notes.** The benefits of a study group are presented throughout the text. This provides a convenient and consistent place to record notes and tips.

- **Career in Focus.** This feature provides real-world career profiles that illustrate examples of the relationship between the study skills necessary for college success and the skills needed for career success.

- **Peak Performer Profile.** Each chapter presents a noted person in the area of business, education, the arts, or public service. These peak performers have overcome obstacles and challenges to become successful. Each profile includes an updated "Check It Out" section, with Web sites related to the profiled individual or his or her profession or personal cause.

- **Starting Today.** This new feature asks the student to choose a strategy to implement immediately and to record how he or she plans to incorporate it into his or her daily routine.

- **Review Questions.** Each chapter includes five basic application and critical thinking questions to help the student review the chapter's main concepts. Space is included for students to write their responses or include key terms.

- **Case Study.** Each chapter includes a Case Study activity that presents college students dealing with real-life situations that reflect the chapter's concepts.

- **Worksheet activities.** Each chapter concludes with numerous activities that are perforated and thumb-tabbed for ease of use. New worksheets are included to offer more critical thinking opportunities as well as handy planning forms. Scoring and/or explanations have been provided where applicable. Many of the useful forms are also available on the book's Web site, www.mhhe.com/ferrett7e, so they can be customized.

- **Career Development Portfolio worksheet.** Found at the end of every chapter, the Career Development Portfolio gives the student the opportunity to track and showcase skills, competencies, accomplishments, and work.

Ancillaries

We have designed an extensive and convenient ancillary package that focuses on course goals, allows you to maximize your time with students, and helps students understand, retain, and apply the main principles.

- **Annotated Instructor's Edition (AIE) (0-07-722771-9).** The AIE contains the full text of the student edition of the text, along with instructional strategies that reinforce and enhance the core concepts. Notes and tips in the margin provide topics for discussion, teaching tips for hands-on and group activities, and references to materials provided in the Instructor's Resource Manual and the Online Learning Center Web site.

- **Instructor's Resource Manual, Test Bank, and Student Retention Kit (0-07-722772-7).** Included in this extensive resource are chapter goals and outlines, teaching tips, additional activities, and essay exercises. Also provided is an extensive section on course planning, with sample syllabi. The extensive test bank includes matching, multiple choice, true/false, and short answer questions. The test bank is also available in an electronic format that can be downloaded from the text's Web site. The kit also includes unique resource guides that give instructors and administrators the tools to retain students and maximize the success of the course, using topics and principles that last a lifetime. Specialized sections include
  - Facilitator's Guide
  - Tools for Time Management
  - Establishing Peer Support Groups
  - Developing a Career Portfolio
  - Involving the Faculty Strategy
  - Capitalizing on Your School's Graduates

- **Implementing a Student Success Course CD-ROM (0-07-310690-9).** This innovative CD assists you in developing and sustaining your Student Success course. The features include a "how-to" guide for designing and proposing a new course, with easy-to-use templates for determining budget needs and resources. Examples of model programs are provided from two-year, four-year, and career schools. The CD explores course goals, such as orientation and retention, and provides research data to support your proposal. Also included are materials to help sustain your course, such as faculty development programs and online resources.

- **Online Learning Center Web site (www.mhhe. com/ferrett7e).** The book's Web site includes features for both instructors and students—downloadable ancillaries, Web links, student quizzing, additional information on topics of interest, and much more. Access to the Web site is provided free to students.

- **PageOut, WebCT, Blackboard, and more.** The Online Learning Center content of *Peak Performance* is supported by WebCT, eCollege.com, and Blackboard. Additionally, our PageOut service, free to qualified adopters, is available to get you and your course up and running online in a matter of hours! To find out more, contact your McGraw-Hill representative or visit www.pageout.net.

- **Customized text options.** *Peak Performance* can be customized to suit your needs. The text can be abbreviated for shorter courses or can be expanded to include semester schedules, campus maps, additional essays, activities, or exercises, along with other materials specific to your curriculum or situation. Contact your McGraw-Hill sales representative for more information or:

  Canada: 1-905-430-5034

  United States: 1-800-446-8979

  E-mail: FYE@mcgraw-hill.com

- **Additional support.** Consult your McGraw-Hill sales representative for the latest video and workshop support available for faculty development and course preparation.

More Resources for Teaching and Learning

- **LASSI: Learning and Study Strategies Inventory.** The LASSI is a 10-scale, 80-item assessment of students' awareness about and use of learning and study strategies related to skill, will, and self-regulation components of strategic learning. The focus is on both the covert and the overt thoughts, behaviors, attitudes, and beliefs that relate to successful learning and that can be altered through educational interventions. Research has repeatedly demonstrated that these factors contribute significantly to success in college and that they can be learned or enhanced through educational interventions, such as learning and study skills courses.

The LASSI provides standardized scores and national norms for 10 different scales. The LASSI is both diagnostic and prescriptive. It provides students with a diagnosis of their strengths and weaknesses, compared with other college students in the areas covered by the 10 scales, and it is prescriptive in that it provides feedback about areas where students may be weak and need to improve their knowledge, attitudes, beliefs, and skills.

The LASSI student assessment is available in print and packaged with *Peak Performance*. Please contact your local McGraw-Hill sales representative for details.

- **Student Planner.** Updated annually, this convenient organizational tool is available as a stand-alone or with the student text. The planner provides daily tips for success, time-management techniques, a daily calendar, and contact information. Contact your McGraw-Hill sales representative for the latest order information.
- **Study Smart: Study Skills for Students 2.0 (Online at www.mhhe.com/studymart2 or CD-ROM 0-07-245515-2).** Developed by Andrea Bonner and Mieke Schipper of Sir Sanford Fleming College, this innovative study skills tutorial teaches students essential note-taking methods, test-taking strategies, and time-management secrets. Study Smart can be ordered free when packaged with new copies of *Peak Performance*.
- **Random House Webster's College Dictionary (0-07-240011-0).** Updated for the twenty-first century, this dictionary is available for a nominal cost when packaged with the text.

Acknowledgments

We would like to thank the many instructors whose insightful comments and suggestions provided us with inspiration and the ideas that were incorporated into this new edition:

Peg Adams	Northern Kentucky University
Gabriel Adona	San Diego Mesa College
Jennifer Bebergal	Florida Atlantic University
Jeanette Berger	University of Akron
Castell Burton	Valencia Community College
Robert Busha	The Art Institute of Ohio
Robin Hanson	Minnesota Community and Technical College
Sheryl Hartman	Miami Dade College
Amy Hickman	Collins College
Beverly Hixon	Houston Community College Southeast
Robbie Ludy	Buena Vista University
Diana Lurz	Rogers State University
Judith Lynch	Kansas State University
Claudia McDade	Jacksonville State University
Susan Regan	Cloud County Community College
Katie Scott	Miami-Jacobs Career College
Anna Slaski	International Institute of the Americas
Holly Susi	Community College of Rhode Island
Karla Thompson	New Mexico State University–Carlsbad
Tammy Thone	Arkansas Tech University

Additionally, we would like to thank a number of instructors and students from the following schools who participated in insightful focus group discussions and provided us valuable feedback on the needs of today's students:

American Intercontinental University

Broward College

ECPI College of Technology

International Institute of the Americas

Herzing College

Medical Careers Institute

Remington College

Sanford-Brown College

Southwest Florida College

University of South Florida

Virginia College

Webster College

Also, I would like to gratefully acknowledge the contributions of the McGraw-Hill editorial staff—specifically, Vicki Malinee, for her considerable effort, suggestions, ideas, and insights.

Dedication

To the memory of my father, Albert Lawrence Ferrett, for setting the highest standards.

To my mother, Velma Mary Hollenbeck Ferrett, for her seamless expression of love.

To my husband, Sam, and my daughters, Jennifer Katherine and Sarah Angela, for making it all worthwhile.

—Sharon K. Ferrett

SCANS: Secretary's Commision on Achieving Necessary Skills

Competency Chart

Competencies and Foundations	Peak Performance Chapters That Address SCANS Competencies
Resources: Identifies, Organizes, Plans, and Allocates Resources	
• Managing time	Chapter 3
• Managing money	Chapter 4
• Managing space	Chapter 3
• Managing materials	Chapters 3, 4, 5
• Managing facilities	Chapter 4
Information: Acquires and Uses Information	
• Acquiring information	Chapters 4, 5
• Evaluating information	Chapters 6, 7
• Organizing and maintaining information	Chapters 3, 6, 7, 8
Systems: Understands Complex Interrelationships	
• Understanding systems	All chapters
• Designing systems	Chapters 6, 7
• Monitoring systems	Chapters 3, 4, 5
• Correcting systems	Chapters 3, 4, 8
Interpersonal Skills: Works with Others	
• Positive attitudes	Chapter 2
• Self-control	Chapter 2
• Goal setting	Chapters 1, 2, 3
• Teamwork	Chapter 2
• Responsibility	Chapter 2
Technology: Works with a Variety of Technologies	
• Solving problems	Chapter 8

SCANS: Secretary's Commision on Achieving Necessary Skills *(concluded)*

Competencies and Foundations	Peak Performance Chapters That Address SCANS Competencies
Personal Qualities	
• Responsibility, character, integrity, positive habits, self-management, self-esteem, sociability	Chapter 2
Basic Skills	
• Reading—locates, understands, and interprets written information in prose and in documents, such as manuals, graphs, and schedules	Chapter 5
• Arithmetic/mathematics—performs basic computations and approaches practical problems by choosing appropriately from a variety of mathematical techniques	Chapter 8
• Listening—receives, attends to, interprets, and responds to verbal messages and other cues	Chapter 4
Thinking Skills	
• Creative thinking—generates new ideas	Chapter 8, Personal Evaluation Notebooks
• Decision making—specifies goals and constraints, generates alternatives, considers risks, and evaluates and chooses best alternative	Chapter 8, Case Study, Personal Evaluation Notebooks
• Listening—receives, attends to, interprets, and responds to verbal messages and other cues	Chapter 4
• Seeing things in the mind's eye—organizes and processes symbols, pictures, graphs, objects, and other information	All chapters, with a strong emphasis in Chapter 8
• Knowing how to learn—uses efficient learning techniques to acquire and apply new knowledge and skills	Chapter 1
• Reasoning—discovers a rule or principle underlying the relationship between two or more objects and applies it when solving a problem	Chapter 8

Preface to the Student

Getting the Most Out of This Book

Congratulations! You are about to start or restart an amazing journey of opportunity, growth, and adventure. You may be at this point in your life for a number of reasons: You may be furthering your education right after high school; you may be focusing on a specific career or trade and want to acquire the appropriate skills or certification; or you may be returning to school after years in the workforce, needing additional skills or just looking for a change.

Whatever your reasons, this is an opportunity for you to learn new things, meet new people, acquire new skills, and better equip yourself both professionally and personally for the years ahead. This book is designed to get you started on that journey by helping you (1) learn how you learn best—and incorporate new ways to learn; (2) maximize available resources and seek out new opportunities; (3) relate what you are exploring now to future success on the job; and (4) strive to become the best person you can be.

Learn How You Learn Best—and Incorporate New Ways to Learn

We Learn

Ten percent of what we read

Twenty percent of what we hear

Thirty percent of what we see

Fifty percent of what we see and hear

Seventy percent of what we discuss with others

Eighty percent of what we do and experience

Ninety-five percent of what we teach others

In this text, you will find a number of features and discussion topics that will help you become a better learner:

- **Exploration of learning styles and personality types.** As you will discover in Chapter 1, each person has a preferred learning style and dominant personality type(s). However, the truly successful learner not only maximizes current preferences but also incorporates other styles and applications, thus becoming a more well-rounded learner. As you complete the exercises in this chapter, you will discover how you learn best and what strategies you can incorporate to maximize your learning efforts and environment.

- **The Adult Learning Cycle.** This is introduced in Chapter 1 and carried throughout each chapter. This is a five-step process that demonstrates that learning comes from repetition, practice, and recall: (1) Relate, (2) Observe, (3) Reflect,

(4) Do, and (5) Teach. You can apply this method to any new skill or information you want to learn and master. In each chapter, you will find a Peak Progress box that helps you see how the Adult Learning Cycle applies the chapter's content. This exercise will help you increase your awareness of how you learn best and how to explore and practice other learning styles. It will also help you overcome obstacles to learning in many different settings by giving hands-on, practical examples.

- **Critical thinking and creative problem solving.** Introduced in Chapter 1, critical thinking is more than just an educational buzzword—it is an important skill you will use and practice in situations in life. Chapter 8 further explores how to solve problems creatively, including extended examples and applications to use in relation to math and science concepts. You will learn to overcome any anxieties you may have in these course areas by focusing on problem-solving techniques.

- **Personal Evaluation Notebook.** The Personal Evaluation Notebook exercises that appear in every chapter give you opportunities to practice your critical thinking and decision-making skills. You are asked to observe, evaluate, and apply chapter concepts to your life. Spaces are provided for you to record your answers and thoughts directly within the activity.

- **Chapter Objectives.** Clear and concise objectives at the beginning of each chapter aid you in identifying and mastering each chapter's key concepts.

- **Peak Progress.** In every chapter, the Peak Progress boxes demonstrate the themes and concepts of the chapter and include helpful suggestions to accelerate and assess your progress.

- **Summary.** Every chapter concludes with a summary of the main points presented in the chapter. Written as "I" statements, they reinforce that the chapter presents a number of potential strategies for you to implement and master.

- **Review Questions.** Each chapter includes five basic questions to help you review the chapter's main concepts.

- **Worksheet activities.** Each chapter concludes with numerous activities that help you apply what you have learned to other classes and situations. The worksheets are perforated and thumb-tabbed for ease of use. Many of the useful forms are also available on the book's Web site, **www.mhhe.com/ferrett7e,** so you can customize them and make multiple copies.

Maximize Available Resources and Seek Out New Opportunities

Often, we overlook the obvious resources and opportunities available to us. Some areas of the text that will guide you in maximizing your resources and seeking out new ones include

- **Time is money and vice versa.** In Chapter 3, you will explore time management, prioritizing, and where your time is spent—and where it should be spent. Also included is a discussion of how to use your short- and long-term goals to determine your priorities.

- **Web site for this text.** The book's Web site, **www. mhhe.com\ferrett7e,** offers a number of activities and resources for mastering and applying each chapter's content and for further study and exploration. Access to the Web site is provided free with the text.

- **Tech for Success.** The Tech for Success feature appears in every chapter and has been updated to offer tips for making the most out of technology applications for both school and job.

Relate What You Are Exploring Now to Future Success on the Job

Chances are, one of your main reasons for attending college is to better your career opportunities. Throughout this text, you will find numerous features and examples that directly relate your experiences in college to your future success on the job. Just a few examples include

- **Secretary's Commission on Achieving Necessary Skills (SCANS).** Found on pages xix–xx and introduced in Chapter 1, this is a list of the ideal competencies you will need to be able to demonstrate on the job and the corresponding chapters in this text. The many exercises, strategies, case studies, and guidelines throughout the text correlate with several SCANS requirements, as well as systems thinking, diversity, and critical thinking.

- **Career Development Portfolio worksheet.** Found at the end of every chapter, the Career Development Portfolio presents the best of your skills, competencies, accomplishments, and work. When completed, the portfolio will contain sections on self-analysis, an inventory of skills and competencies, goals, educational and career plans, an inventory of interests, cover letters, resumés, and samples of work. You can use the portfolio to create and update your resumé, to help you prepare for an interview, and to advance your career. The portfolio will give you the opportunity to assess your strengths, set goals, and possess an organized system of important documents. It will also help you explore possible majors and careers.

- **Career in Focus.** This feature provides real-world career profiles that illustrate examples of the relationship between the study skills necessary for college success and the skills you will need for career success. Work situations that directly call on chapter skills are highlighted, so that you can see the interrelationships.

- **Case Study.** Each chapter includes a Case Study activity that presents college students dealing with real-life situations that reflect the chapter's concepts. This feature stresses that the same issues that you deal with in school also exist in the workplace; the same skills and strategies that you use in the classroom can be adapted to your job.

Additional case study opportunities are provided on the text's Web site.

Strive to Become the Best Person You Can Be

In this text, you are introduced to the concept of a "peak performer" (Chapter 1) and are provided strategies for maximizing your success in school, career, and life. Our hope is that you are empowered to "walk the talk" and put these strategies and perspectives into practice, starting today. To be successful, you must not only adapt to college and the larger community but also acquire the necessary skills, personal qualities, habits, and motivation to face the challenges of tomorrow's workplace and the tremendous opportunities provided by a world that is increasingly rich in its demographic and cultural diversity.

This preface includes a number of features that provide you with handy guides for future success (such as the "Best Strategies for Success in School"). Additional features in the text include

- **The essential personal qualities.** Chapter 2 explores Emotional Intelligence and focuses on character first, stressing that good character, integrity, and ethics are the hallmarks of truly successful leaders in both business and the community.

- **The ABC Method of Self-Management.** Introduced in Chapter 1, the ABC Method of Self-Management will help you manage your thoughts, feelings, and behavior, so that you create the results you want and achieve your goals. This five-step process (A = Actual event; B = Beliefs; C = Challenge) helps you see the connection among your thoughts, feelings, and actions and empowers you to dispel negative thoughts and replace them with realistic and positive thoughts and behaviors.

- **Self-Management exercise.** As discussed in Chapter 1, self-management involves using many powerful tools you can use, such as self-assessment, critical thinking, visualization, affirmations, and reflection, to imagine your success and critically think through difficult situations. A scenario is presented at the beginning of every chapter that asks you to think about your own experiences. A worksheet is provided at the end of the chapter to record your thoughts and help you practice the ABC Method of Self-Management.

- **Success Principle.** Each chapter begins with a Success Principle that succinctly communicates the important lesson to be learned from the chapter. The Success Principles in total provide a unique and powerful guide to striving for success in school, career, and life.

- **Peak Performer Profile.** Each chapter presents a noted person in the area of business, education, the arts, or public service. These peak performers have overcome obstacles and challenges to become successful. You will see that having a positive attitude and perseverance is important for success. Each profile includes a "Check It Out" section, with Web sites related to the profiled individual or his or her profession or personal cause.

- **Words to Succeed.** Found throughout the text, these quotes provide you with insights, motivation, and food for thought and are tied to the chapter's content.

- **Performance Strategies.** Included in every chapter is a recap of the top 10 strategies for success in applying the chapter's concepts.

- **Starting Today.** This feature at the end of each chapter encourages you to determine at least one new strategy you want to try out and how you will put it into action—today!

As You Get Started in Your New School: What You Need to Know and Should Not Be Afraid to Ask

Now that you have your book in hand, you are ready to get started. Or are you really ready? What else should you be aware of at this point? You may have already attended a basic orientation session, offered by most schools, which reviews school and community resources and program requirements. Going through orientation, meeting with your advisor, and reviewing your catalog will help you get oriented. Additionally, the quick review provided in this text is designed to outline the essentials that you will want to know, so that you not only survive but also make your first year a success. **Peak Progress 1** provides a handy checklist for the essential tasks you need to consider and accomplish the first week of school. Add to this list any tasks that are unique to your situation or school.

Why Are You Here?

College success begins with determining your goals and mapping out a plan. A good place to start is to have you reflect on why you are in college and what is expected of you. You will be more motivated if you clarify your interests and values concerning college. You will read in Chapter 2 the reasons students don't graduate from college, including poor study skills and habits and a lack of preparation, motivation, and effort. College is a commitment of many precious resources you can't afford to waste—time, money, and mental energies. Consider the following statements and your reasons for being in college, and share this in your study team or with students you meet the first few weeks of class:

- I value education and want to be a well-educated person.
- I want to get a good job that leads to a well-paying career.
- I want to learn new ideas and skills and grow as a person.
- I want to get away from home and be independent.
- I want to make new friends.
- I want to have new experiences and stretch myself.
- I want to fulfill my goal of being a college-educated person.

Peak Progress

Tasks to Accomplish the First Week of School

- Attend orientation and meet with an advisor. Ask questions and determine available resources. (See **Peak Progress 2** for questions to ask.)
- Register and pay fees on time.
- Set up an e-mail account.
- Check deadlines and procedures. *Never* just quit going to class.
- Buy books and keep receipts. Establish a record-keeping system.
- Find out the location of classrooms, parking, and campus resources.
- Know expectations and requirements. Get a syllabus for each class. E-mail instructors for clarification.
- Create an organized study area. Post instructors' names, office locations, and hours, as well as important deadlines.
- Form study teams and exchange e-mails and phone numbers. Get to know instructors and other students.
- Explore resources, such as the library, learning skills center, health center, and advising center.
- Go to all classes on time and sit in the front row.

Jot down what you want from college and why you're motivated to get it.

List four values that are most important to you and how college will help you achieve them.

1. _____
2. _____
3. _____
4. _____

What Should You Be Asking?

You don't want to learn the hard way that you need one more class to graduate, only to find it's offered only once a year (and you just missed it). Make your time with your advisor productive by getting answers to important questions that will help you map out your coursework. **Peak Progress 2** provides a handy checklist of common questions to get you started.

What Do You Need to Do to Graduate?

You will be more motivated and confident if you understand graduation requirements. If you are a transfer student, requirements vary among schools. Don't rely on the advice of friends. Go to orientation and meet with your advisor early and often. Check out the catalog and make certain you know what is required to graduate. Fill in the following (or go to **www.mhhe.com/ferrett7e** and print out the form):

GRADUATION REQUIREMENTS

- Number of units required:
- General education requirements:
- Curriculum requirements:
- Residency at the school:
- Departmental major requirements:
- Cumulative GPA required:
- Other requirements, such as special writing tests and classes:

Peak Progress

2

The Most Common Questions Students Ask Advisors

1. What classes do I need to take for general education?
2. Can a course satisfy both a general education and a major requirement?
3. Can I take general elective (GE) courses for Credit/No Credit if I also want to count them for my major?
4. How can I remove an *F* grade from my record?
5. What is the deadline for dropping courses?
6. Can I drop a course after the deadline?
7. What is an "educational leave"?
8. What is the difference between a withdrawal and a drop?
9. Do I need to take any placement tests?
10. Are there other graduation requirements, such as a writing exam?
11. Where do I find out about financial aid?
12. Is there a particular order in which I should take certain courses?
13. Are there courses in which I must earn a *C–* or better?
14. How do I change my major?
15. Which of my transfer courses will count?
16. What is the minimum residency requirement for a bachelor's degree?
17. Is there a GPA requirement for the major?
18. Is there a tutoring program available?
19. If I go on exchange, how do I make sure that courses I take at another university will apply toward my degree here?
20. What is a major contract and when should I get one?
21. When do I need to apply for graduation?
22. How do I apply for graduation?
23. What is a degree check?
24. What is the policy for incomplete grades?
25. Can I take major courses at another school and transfer them here?
26. As a nonresident, how can I establish residency in this state?
27. How do I petition to substitute a class?
28. Once I complete my major, are there other graduation requirements?
29. What is academic probation?
30. Is there any employment assistance available?
31. Is there a mentor program available in my major department?
32. Are there any internships or community service opportunities related to my major?

How to Register for Classes

Find out if you have an access code and the earliest date you can register. Meet with your advisor, carefully select classes, and review general education and major requirements. Add electives that help keep you active and interested, such as an exercise or a weight-training class. Make certain that you understand why you are taking each class and double-check with your advisor that it is meeting certain requirements.

Many colleges have a purge date and, if you miss the deadline to pay your fees, your class schedule is canceled. You may not be able to get into classes and may have to pay a late fee.

Know the Grading System

Learn the minimum grade point average (GPA) that you need to maintain good standing. If your GPA falls below 2.0, you may be placed on academic probation. The GPA is calculated according to the number of credit hours each course represents and your grade in the course. In the traditional system, $A = 4$ points, $B = 3$ points, $C = 2$ points, $D = 1$ point, and $F = 0$ points (your school may have a different system, so ask to be sure). To calculate your GPA, first determine your total number of points. Following is an example:

Course	Grade Achieved	Number of Credit Hours	Points
Political Science	C	2	$2 \times 2 = 4$
Psychology	B	3	$3 \times 3 = 9$
English	A	3	$4 \times 3 = 12$
Personal Finance	A	1	$4 \times 1 = 4$
TOTAL		9	29

Then, to arrive at your GPA, you must divide your total points by your total number of credit hours:

GPA = Total points divided by total number of credit hours

Thus, in this example,

GPA = 29 divided by 9 = 3.22

Monitor your progress and meet with your instructors often, but especially at midterm and before final exams. Ask what you can do to improve your grade.

Adding or Dropping Classes

Make certain that you know the deadlines for adding and dropping classes. This is generally done in the first few weeks of classes. A withdrawal after the deadline could result in a failing grade. Also make certain before you drop the class that

- You will not fall below the required units for financial aid.
- You will not fall below the required units for playing sports.
- If required, the class is offered again before you plan to graduate.
- You don't need the class or units to meet graduation requirements.
- You are meeting important deadlines.
- You talk with the instructor first.
- You talk with your advisor.

If you choose to withdraw from all your classes, take an academic leave. Don't just walk away from your classes. Remember, it is your responsibility to drop or withdraw from a class. The instructor will not drop you, nor will you be dropped automatically if you stop going to class at any time during the semester. You must complete required forms.

An Incomplete Grade

If you miss class due to illness or an emergency, you may be able to take an incomplete if you can't finish a project or miss a test. Check out this option with your instructor before you drop a class. Make certain you have a written agreement to finish the work at a specific time and that you stay in touch with the instructor through e-mail and phone.

Withdrawing or Taking a Leave of Absence

Some students withdraw because they don't have the money, they can't take time off from work, they lack child care, or they are having difficulty in classes. Before you drop out of college, talk with your advisor and see if you can get the support and motivation to succeed. If you want to take a leave to travel, want to explore other schools, are ill, or just need to take a break, make certain that you take a leave of absence for a semester, a year, or longer. Taking a leave means that you do not have to reapply for admission, and generally you fall under the same category as when you entered school.

Transferring

Before you transfer to another school, make certain you understand the requirements, which courses are transferable, and if there is a residency requirement. If you plan to transfer from a two-year school to a four-year school, your advisor will help you clarify the requirements.

Expectations of Instructors

Most instructors will hand out a syllabus that will outline their expectations for the class. Make certain you understand and clarify expectations and have a good understanding of the course requirements. **Worksheet 1** on page xxxiii is a convenient guide to complete when checking your progress with your instructor.

The Best Strategies for Success in School

In this text, we will focus on a number of strategies that will help you determine and achieve your goals. **The Best Strategies for Success in School** provides a comprehensive list of the proven strategies you will find woven throughout this text. Apply these to your efforts in school now and through your course of study. You will find that not only are they key to your progress in school, but also they will help you develop skills, behaviors, and habits that are directly related to success on the job and in life in general.

The Best Strategies for Success in School

1. **Attend every class.** Going to every class engages you with the subject, the instructor, and other students. Think of the tuition you are paying and what it costs to cut a class.

2. **Be an active participant.** Show that you are engaged and interested by being on time, sitting in front, participating, asking questions, and being alert.

3. **Go to class prepared.** Preview all reading assignments. Highlight key ideas and main concepts and put question marks next to anything you don't understand.

4. **Write a summary.** After you preview the chapter, close the book and write a short summary. Go back and fill in with more details. Do this after each reading.

5. **Know your instructors.** Choose the best instructors, call them by their preferred names and titles, e-mail them, and visit them during office hours. Arrive early for class and get to know them better.

6. **Know expectations.** Read the syllabus for each course and clarify the expectations and requirements, such as tests, papers, extra credit, and attendance.

7. **Join a study team.** You will learn more by studying with others than by reading alone. Make up tests, give summaries, and teach others.

8. **Organize your study space.** Create a quiet space, with a place for school documents, books, catalogs, a dictionary, a computer, notes, pens, and a calendar. Eliminate distractions by closing the door and focus on the task at hand.

9. **Map out your day, week, and semester.** Write down all assignments, upcoming tests, meetings, daily goals, and priorities on your calendar. Review your calendar and goals each day. Do not socialize until your top priorities are completed.

10. **Get help early.** Know and use all available campus resources. Go to the learning center, counseling center, and health center; get a tutor; and talk with your advisor and instructors about concerns. Get help at the first sign of trouble.

11. **Give school your best effort.** Commit yourself to being extra disciplined the first three weeks—buy your textbooks early; take them to class; get to class early; keep up on your reading; start your projects, papers, and speeches early; and make school a top priority.

12. **Use note cards.** Jot down formulas and key words. Carry them with you and review them during waiting time and right before class.

13. **Review often.** Review and fill in notes immediately after class and again within 24 hours. Active reading, note taking, and reviewing are the steps that improve recall.

14. **Study everywhere.** Review your note cards before class, while you wait for class to begin, while waiting in line, before bed, and so on. Studying for short periods of time is more effective than cramming late at night.

15. **Summarize out loud.** Summarize chapters and class notes out loud to your study team. This is an excellent way to learn.

16. **Organize material.** You cannot remember information if it isn't organized. Logical notes help you understand and remember. Use a mind map for outlining key facts and supporting material.

(continued)

The Best Strategies for Success in School *(continued)*

17. **Dig out information.** Focus on main ideas, key words, and overall understanding. Make questions out of chapter headings, review chapter questions, and always read summaries.

18. **Look for associations.** Improve memory by connecting patterns and by linking concepts and relationships. Define, describe, compare, classify, and contrast concepts.

19. **Ask questions.** What is the obvious? What needs to be determined? How can you illustrate the concept? What information is the same and what is different? How does the lecture relate to the textbook?

20. **Pretest yourself.** This will serve as practice and reduces anxiety. This is most effective in your study team.

21. **Study when you are most alert.** Know your energy level and learning preference. Maximize reviewing during daytime hours.

22. **Turn in all assignments on time.** Give yourself an extra few days to review papers and practice speeches.

23. **Make learning physical.** Read difficult textbooks out loud and standing up. Draw pictures, write on a chalkboard, and use visuals. Tape lectures and go on field trips. Integrate learning styles.

24. **Review first drafts with your instructor.** Ask for suggestions and follow them to the letter.

25. **Pay attention to neatness.** Focus on details and turn in all assignments on time. Use your study team to read and exchange term papers. Proofread several times.

26. **Practice!** Nothing beats effort. Practice speeches until you are comfortable and confident and visualize yourself being successful.

27. **Recite and explain.** Pretend that you are the instructor and recite main concepts. What questions would you put on a test? Give a summary to others in your study group. Make up sample test questions in your group.

28. **Take responsibility.** Don't make excuses about missing class or assignments or about earning failing grades. Be honest and take responsibility for your choices and mistakes and learn from them.

29. **Ask for feedback.** When you receive a grade, be reflective and ask questions: "What have I learned from this?" "How did I prepare for this?" "How could I improve this grade?" "Did I put in enough effort?" Based on what you learn, what new goals will you set for yourself?

30. **Negotiate for a better grade before grades are sent in.** Find out how you are doing at midterm and ask what you can do to raise your grade. Offer to do extra projects or retake tests.

31. **Always do extra credit.** Raise your grade by doing more than is required or *expected*. Immerse yourself in the subject and find meaning and understanding.

32. **Take responsibility for your education.** You can do well in a class even if your instructor is boring or insensitive. Ask yourself what you can do to make the class more effective (study team, tutoring, active participation). Be flexible and adapt to your instructor's teaching style.

(continued)

The Best Strategies for Success in School (continued)

33. **Develop positive qualities.** Think about the personal qualities that you need most to overcome obstacles and work on developing them each day.

34. **Stay healthy.** You cannot do well in school or in life if you are ill. Invest time in exercising, eating healthy, and getting enough sleep and avoid alcohol, cigarettes, and drugs.

35. **Dispute negative thinking.** Replace it with positive, realistic, helpful self-talk and focus on your successes. Don't be a perfectionist. Reward yourself when you make small steps toward achieving goals.

36. **Organize your life.** Hang up your keys in the same place, file important material, and establish routines that make your life less stressful.

37. **Break down projects.** Overcome procrastination by breaking overwhelming projects into manageable chunks. Choose a topic, do a rough draft, write a summary, preview a chapter, do a mind map, and organize the tools you need (notes, books, outline).

38. **Make school your top priority.** Working too many hours can cut into study time. Learn to balance school, your social life, and work, so that you're effective.

39. **Meet with your advisor to review goals and progress.** Ask questions about requirements, and don't drop and add classes without checking on the consequences. Develop a good relationship with your advisor and your instructors.

40. **Be persistent.** Whenever you get discouraged, just keep following positive habits and strategies and you will succeed. Success comes in small, consistent steps. Be patient and keep plugging away.

41. **Spend less than you make.** Don't go into debt for new clothes, a car, CDs, gifts, travel, or other things you can do without. Education is the best investment in future happiness and job success that you can make. Learn to save.

42. **Use critical thinking and think about the consequences of your decisions.** Don't be impulsive about money, sex, smoking, or drugs. Don't start a family until you are emotionally and financially secure. Practice impulse control by imagining how you would feel after making certain choices.

43. **Don't get addicted.** Addictions are a tragic waste of time. Ask yourself if you've ever known anyone whose life was better for being addicted. Do you know anyone whose life has been destroyed by alcohol and other drugs? This one decision will affect your life forever.

44. **Know who you are and what you want.** Visit the career center and talk with a career counselor about your interests, values, goals, strengths, personality, learning style, and career possibilities. Respect your style and set up conditions that create results.

45. **Use creative problem solving.** Think about what went right and what went wrong this semester. What could you have done that would have helped you be more successful? What are new goals you want to set for next semester? What are some creative ways to overcome obstacles? How can you solve problems instead of letting them persist?

(continued)

The Best Strategies for Success in School *(concluded)*

46. **Contribute.** Look for opportunities to contribute your time and talents. What could you do outside of class that would complement your education and serve others?

47. **Take advantage of your texts' resources.** Many textbooks have accompanying Web sites, CDs, and study materials designed to help you succeed in class. Visit this book's Web site at **www.mhhe.com/ferrett7e.**

48. **Respect yourself and others.** Be supportive, tolerant, and respectful of people who are different from you. Look for ways to learn about other cultures and different views; and to expand your friendships. *Respect yourself.* Surround yourself with people who are positive and successful, who value learning, and who are supportive and respectful of you and your goals.

49. **Focus on gratitude.** Look at the abundance in your life—your health, family, friends, and opportunities. You have so much going for you to help you succeed.

50. **Just do it.** Newton's first law of motion says that things in motion tend to stay in motion, so get started and keep working on your goals!

Progress Assessment

Course: _____

Instructor: _____

Office: _____   Office hours: _____

Phone: _____   E-mail: _____

1. How am I doing in this class?

_____

_____

_____

2. What grades have you recorded for me thus far?

_____

_____

_____

3. Are there any adjustments that I should make?

_____

_____

_____

4. Am I missing any assignments?

_____

_____

_____

5. Do you have any suggestions as to how I can improve my performance or excel in your class?

_____

_____

_____

1

Be a Lifelong Learner

LEARNING OBJECTIVES

In this chapter, you will learn to

1.1 List the characteristics of a peak performer

1.2 Use self-management techniques for academic, job, and personal achievement

1.3 Use critical thinking skills in self-assessment

1.4 Apply visualization and affirmations to help you focus on positive outcomes

1.5 Create a personal mission statement

1.6 Identify skills and competencies for school and job success

1.7 Integrate learning styles and personality types

1.8 Describe the Adult Learning Cycle

SELF-MANAGEMENT

It's the first day of class and I'm already overwhelmed. How will I manage all this?

Are you feeling like this? Are you afraid you will never achieve your goals, or do you even know what your goals are? Instead of focusing on negative feelings, channel your energies into positive results and envision yourself being successful. In this chapter, you will learn about "self-management" and many tools—such as self-assessment, critical thinking, visualization, and reflection—you can use to become a success in all facets of life.

JOURNAL ENTRY What are you hoping to gain from your college experience? How does earning a college degree help you both personally and professionally? Consider answering the question "Why am I here?" Is your answer part of a bigger life plan? In **Worksheet 1.1** on page 40, take a stab at answering those questions. Think about the obstacles you may have faced to get to this point and what you did to overcome them. In this chapter, you'll discover that successful, lifelong learning begins with learning about yourself.

LEARNING IS A LIFELONG JOURNEY. People who are successful—peak performers—are on this journey. They are lifelong learners. We are constantly faced with many types of changes—economic, technological, societal, and so on. To meet these challenges, you will need to continually learn new skills in school, on your job, and throughout your life. You will meet these challenges through your study and learning strategies, in your methods of performing work-related tasks, and even in the way you view your personal life and lifestyle.

Lately, you may have been asking yourself, "Who am I?" "What course of study should I take?" "What kind of job do I want?" "Where should I go to school?" or "What should I do with my life?" These are all important questions. Some you may have already answered—and some of those answers may change by tomorrow, next week, or next year. And that's OK. This is all part of the learning process—learning about yourself and what you want out of life.

Throughout this book, as you journey on the road to becoming a peak performer, you will discover methods that will help you master self-management, set goals, and achieve personal success. One of the first steps is self-assessment. Self-assessment requires seeing yourself objectively. This helps you determine where you are now and where you want to go. Then by assessing how you learn—including your learning and personality styles—you will discover how to maximize your learning potential.

The many exercises, journal entries, and portfolio worksheets throughout this text support one of the major themes of this book—that success in school and success in your career are definitely connected! The skills, competencies, and behaviors you learn and practice today will guide your marketability and flexibility throughout your career, and they will promote success in your personal life as well.

What Is a "Peak Performer"?

Peak performers come from all lifestyles, ages, cultures, and genders. Some are famous, such as many of the people profiled in this book. However, anyone can become a peak performer by setting goals and developing appropriate attitudes and behaviors to achieve desired results. Peak performers become masters at creating excellence by focusing on results. They know how to change their negative thoughts into positive and realistic affirmations. They focus on their long-term goals and know how to break down goals into daily action steps. They are not perfect or successful overnight. They learn to face the fear of making mistakes and working through them. They use the whole of their intelligence and abilities.

Every day, thousands of individuals quietly overcome incredible setbacks, climb over huge obstacles, and reach within themselves to find inner strength. Many are neither rich nor famous, nor have they reached the top of their careers. They are successful because they know that they possess the personal power to produce results in their lives and find passion in what they contribute to life. They are masters, not victims, of life's situations. They control the quality of their lives. In short, they are their own best friend.

Peak performers

- Take responsibility for their actions, behaviors, and decisions
- Know their learning styles and preferences and how to maximize their learning
- Take risks and move beyond secure comfort zones
- Use critical thinking to solve problems creatively
- Make sound judgments and decisions
- Are effective at time management and self-management
- Involve themselves in supportive relationships
- Continually acquire new skills and competencies
- Remain confident and resilient
- Are motivated to overcome barriers
- Take small, consistent steps that lead to long-term goals

Self-Management: The Key to Reaching Your Peak

What is a primary strength of every peak performer? A positive attitude! First and foremost, peak performers have a positive attitude toward their studies, their work, and virtually everything they do in their lives. This fundamental inclination to view life optimistically as a series of opportunities is a key to their success. Does this describe how you approach each day? Take a quick check of your attitude by completing **Personal Evaluation Notebook 1.1** on page 4.

Having a positive attitude involves more than positive thinking. It also includes clear and critical thinking. The good news is that anyone can develop the attitude of a peak performer, and it is not even difficult. It simply involves a restructuring of thought patterns. Instead of dwelling on problems, you can create options and alternatives to keep you on track. Redirecting your thought patterns in this way will not only give you more drive but will also make every task you approach seem more meaningful and less daunting.

A positive attitude is one of the many components of **self-management.** Are you responsible for your own success? Do you believe you can control your own destiny? Think of self-management as a toolkit filled with many techniques and skills you can use to keep you focused, overcome obstacles, and help you succeed.

Along with a positive attitude (which we will discuss further in Chapter 2), some very important techniques in this toolkit that we will begin to explore in this chapter are self-assessment, critical thinking, visualization, and reflection.

Self-Assessment

One of the first steps in becoming a peak performer is **self-assessment.** Out of self-assessment comes recognition of the need to learn new tasks and subjects,

Personal Evaluation Notebook 1.1

Am I a Positive Person?

Having a positive attitude is key to effective self-management. Most people believe they are generally positive but often are not truly aware of their negative self-talk or behavior. Answer the following questions to determine your overall outlook. After you have answered the questions, ask a friend, co-worker, or family member to answer the questions about you. Were your answers the same?

	Mostly True	Sometimes True	Rarely True
I tend to look for the good in everyone.			
I look for the positive in each situation.			
I do not take offense easily.			
I welcome constructive criticism and use it to improve.			
I am not easily irritated.			
I am not easily discouraged.			
I do not take everything personally.			
I take responsibility and face problems, even when it is not comfortable.			
I don't dwell on personal mistakes.			
I don't look for perfection in myself.			
I don't look for perfection in others.			
I do not depend on others to make me happy.			
I can forgive and move on.			
I do not become overly involved or disturbed by others' problems.			
I do not make snap judgments about people.			
I praise others for their accomplishments.			
I don't start conversations with something negative.			
I view mistakes as learning experiences.			
I know that, if Plan A doesn't work, Plan B will.			
I look forward to—not worry about—what tomorrow will bring.			

relate more effectively with others, set goals, manage time and stress, and create a balanced and productive life. Self-assessment requires facing the truth and seeing yourself objectively. For example, it is not easy to admit that you procrastinate or lack certain skills. Even when talking about your strengths, you may feel embarrassed. However, honest self-assessment is the foundation for making positive changes in your life.

Self-assessment can help you

- Understand how you learn best
- Work with your strengths and natural preferences
- Balance and integrate your preferred learning style with other styles
- Use critical thinking and reasoning
- Make sound and creative decisions about school and work
- Change ineffective patterns of thinking and behaving
- Create a positive and motivated state of mind
- Work more effectively with diverse groups of people
- Handle stress and conflict
- Achieve better grades
- Determine and capitalize on your strengths
- Recognize irrational and negative thoughts and behavior
- Most important, focus on self-management and develop strategies that maximize your energies and resources. The world is full of people who believe that, if only the other person would change, everything would be fine. This book is not for them. Change is possible if you take responsibility for your thoughts and behaviors and are willing to practice new ways of thinking and behaving.

Self-assessment is very important for job success. Self-assessment and feedback are tools for self-discovery and positive change. Keep a portfolio of your awards, letters of appreciation, and training program certificates, as well as the projects you have completed. Assess your expectations in terms of the results achieved and set goals for improvement. At the end of each chapter in this text, you will find a Career Development Portfolio worksheet, which will help you begin to relate current activities to future job success. This portfolio will furnish you with a lifelong assessment tool for learning where you are and where you want to go and with a place for documenting the results. This portfolio of skills and competencies will become your guide for remaining marketable and flexible throughout your career.

Critical Thinking Skills

Throughout this book, you will be asked to apply critical thinking skills to help you with college courses and life situations. Self-management involves using your critical thinking skills to make the best choices and decisions and to solve problems. What exactly is critical thinking? **Critical thinking** is a logical, rational, systematic thought process that is necessary in understanding, analyzing, and evaluating information in order to solve a problem or situation. Since critical thinking determines the quality of the decisions that you make in all areas of your life, it is an important theme throughout this book. Chapter 8 is entirely devoted to honing your critical thinking skills and practicing creative problem solving. However, it's obvious that you need to use critical thinking every day—from analyzing and determining your learning styles to communicating effectively with family members, classmates, or co-workers.

To fine-tune your critical thinking skills, make a habit of assessing your thinking skills regularly. Use the following guidelines in your journey to becoming a more critical thinker:

- Suspend judgment until you have gathered facts and reflected on them.
- Look for evidence that supports or contradicts your initial assumptions, opinions, and beliefs.
- Adjust your opinions as new information and facts are known.
- Ask questions, look for proof, and examine the problem closely.
- Reject incorrect or irrelevant information.
- Consider the source of the information.
- Recognize and dispute irrational thinking.

Make sure to complete the exercises and activities throughout this book, including the **Personal Evaluation Notebook** exercises and the end-of-chapter **Worksheets.** You will also enhance your critical thinking skills by practicing visualization and reflection.

Visualization and Affirmations

Visualization and affirmations are powerful self-management tools that help you focus on positive action and outcomes. **Visualization** is using your imagination to see your goals clearly and to envision yourself successfully engaging in new, positive behavior. **Affirmations** are the positive self-talk—the internal dialogue—you carry on with yourself. Affirmations counter self-defeating patterns of thought with more positive, hopeful, and realistic thoughts.

Using visualization and affirmations can help you relax, boost your confidence, change your habits, and perform better on exams, in speeches, or in sports. They can be used to rehearse for an upcoming event, and you can practice coping with obstacles. Visualization and affirmations are even part of the curriculum at the U.S. Olympic training campus.

Through self-management, you demonstrate that you are not a victim or passive spectator; you are responsible for your self-talk, images, thoughts, and behaviors. When you observe and dispute negative thoughts and replace them with positive, appropriate, and realistic thoughts, images, and behaviors, you are practicing your critical thinking and creativity skills. You are taking charge of your life, focusing on what you can change, and working toward your goals.

You can practice visualization anytime and anywhere throughout the day. For example, between classes, find a quiet place and close your eyes. It helps to use relaxation techniques, such as taking several deep breaths and seeing yourself calm, centered, and focused on your goals. This is especially effective when your mind starts to chatter and you feel overwhelmed, discouraged, or stressed. Visualize yourself graduating and walking across the stage to receive your diploma. See yourself achieving your goals. Say to yourself, "I am calm and centered. I am taking action to meet my goals. I will use all available resources to be successful."

Reflection

Reflection is an important self-management tool, whether you consider yourself a reflective person or not. To reflect is to think about something in a purposeful way, with the intention of making connections, exploring options, and creating new meaning. Sometimes the process causes us to reconsider our previous knowledge and to explore new alternatives and ideas.

Don't confuse reflection with daydreaming—the two have little in common. Reflection is a conscious, focused, purposeful activity; it is not simply letting your mind wander. When you reflect, you direct your thoughts and use imagination. Think of your mind as an ultra-powerful database. To reflect on a new experience is to search through this vast mental database in an effort to discover—or create—relationships between experiences: new and old, new and new, old and old. Reflection, then, is the process of reorganizing countless experiences stored in your mental database. As you do so, your mind's database becomes more complex, more sophisticated, and ultimately more useful. This ongoing reorganization is a key component of your intellectual development; it integrates critical thinking, creative problem solving, and visualization.

A convenient way to reflect is simply to write down your thoughts, such as in a journal or on your computer. In this text is ample opportunity to practice reflection and critical thinking, including a **Journal Entry** exercise at the beginning of each chapter, with a follow-up **Worksheet** at the end of each chapter.

Throughout the text, we'll explore additional self-management techniques that focus on certain aspects of your schoolwork, employment, and personal life. See which techniques work best for you. **Peak Progress 1.1** explores the ABC Method of Self-Management, a unique process to help you work through difficult situations and achieve positive results. It uses skills such as critical thinking, visualization, and reflection to find positive outcomes.

Peak Progress **1.1**

The ABC Method of Self-Management

Earlier in this chapter you answered some questions to determine if you approached everyday life with a positive attitude. Researchers believe that positive thinking improves your skills for coping with difficult challenges, which may also benefit your overall health and minimize the effects of stress.

What does "negative thinking" mean? If you are negative, you may tend to

- Filter out and eliminate all the good things that happen and focus on one bad thing
- Blame yourself (or someone else) automatically when something bad happens
- Always anticipate the very worst that could happen
- See things as only good or bad—there's no middle ground
- Criticize yourself—either aloud or internally—in a way you would never do to someone else
- Waste time complaining, criticizing, reliving, and making up excuses—rather than creating solutions and moving on

(continued)

> " It's not the load that breaks you down, it's the way you carry it. "
>
> LOU HOLTZ
> *College football coach*

WORDS TO SUCCEED

The ABC Method of Self-Management *(concluded)*

The good news is that anyone can become a positive thinker. First, you need to become aware of patterns of defeating thoughts that are keeping you from achieving your goals. Then you can challenge and dispute these negative and irrational thoughts. You can be calm and centered in any situation. Learn to take a deep breath and give yourself the space to choose positive thoughts and actions.

Clear thinking will lead to positive emotions. Let's say you have to give a speech in a class and speaking in public has caused you a lot of anxiety in the past. You might be saying to yourself, "I am terrified. I just hate getting up in front of people. I just can't do this. I might as well drop the class." These negative beliefs and irrational thoughts can cause severe anxiety and are not based on clear thinking. You can direct your thoughts with positive statements that will dispel anxiety: "Public speaking is a skill that can be learned with practice and effort. I will not crumble from criticism and, even if I don't do well, I can learn with practice and from constructive feedback. I will explore all the resources available to help me and I'll do well in this class." Self-management can be as easy as ABC. These simple steps help you manage your thoughts, feelings, and behaviors, so that you can create the results you want.

A = Actual event: State the actual situation that affected your emotions.

B = Beliefs: Describe your thoughts and beliefs about the situation that created these emotions and behavior.

C = Challenge: Dispute the negative thoughts and replace them with accurate and positive statements.

Let's use another example. When you read the quote on page 1 of this chapter, you may have felt the same way—overwhelmed. You are in a new situation, with many new expectations—of you and by you. Let's apply the ABC method to focus your energies on developing a positive outcome. For example, you might say,

A = Actual event: "I'm feeling overwhelmed and depressed. I'm panicking and totally stressed out."

B = Beliefs: "It is only the first week and I already have an overload of information from this class. What if I fail? What if I can't keep it all straight—learning styles, personalities, temperaments? These other people are probably a lot smarter than me. Maybe I should drop out."

C = Challenge: "Stop these negative thoughts! Going to college is a big change, but I have handled new and stressful situations before. I know how to overcome feeling overwhelmed by breaking big jobs into small tasks. Everyone tells me I'm hardworking, and I know I'm talented and smart in many different ways. I know that going to college is a very good idea and I want to graduate. I've handled transitions in the past and I can handle these changes, too."

When you challenge negative thoughts and replace them with positive thinking, you feel energized and your thoughts spiral upward: "I'm excited about discovering my learning and personality styles and how I can use them to my advantage. There are so many resources available to me—my instructor, my classmates, the book's Web site, and so on. I will get to know at least one person in each of my classes, and I will take a few minutes to explore at least one resource at school that can provide support. I see myself confident and energized and achieving my goals."

In the end-of-chapter **Worksheets** throughout this text, you will find opportunities to practice the ABC Method of Self-Management, as well as the self-management exercises at **www.mhhe.com/ferrett7e.**

Draft a Personal Mission Statement

At the beginning of the chapter, you were asked to write about why you're in school and how it relates to your life plan. In the Preface to the Student, you also explored many reasons you are attending college, such as to learn new skills, to get a well-paying job, and to make new friends. (If you haven't read the Preface to the Student, now is the perfect time to do so.) Thinking about the answers to these and related questions gets you started on creating and writing your mission statement.

A mission statement looks at the "big picture" of your life, from which your goals and priorities will flow. This written statement (which can be one sentence or a number of sentences) focuses on the contributions you want to make based on your values, philosophy, and principles. When you have a sense of purpose and direction, you will be more focused and your life will have more meaning.

In one sense, what you are doing is looking at the end result of your life. What kind of a person do you want to be when you're 95? What legacy do you want to leave? What do you want to be remembered for as a person? What do you think will be most important to you?

Here is one example of a mission statement: "I want to thrive in a career that allows me to use my creativity, grow in knowledge from mentors and colleagues, advance into leadership positions, make a positive impact on my profession, and provide an effective balance with personal interests, including having a family, traveling, and participating in team sports. I plan to model respect—for others, our environment, and my health—so that my children will learn tolerance, responsibility, and the importance of making healthy decisions. I view each day as another opportunity to learn how to be a better contributor to my partner, my family, my employer, and my community."

You will want your mission statement to reflect your individuality. You may want to think about how a college education will help you fulfill your mission in life. If you have chosen a profession (for example, nursing or teaching) you may want to include the aspects of the career that interested you (such as helping others achieve healthy lifestyles or educating and nurturing young children). It does not need to be lengthy and detailed. Focusing on your mission statement will help you overcome obstacles that will inevitably challenge you.

To write your mission statement, begin by answering these (or similar) questions:

1. What do I value most in life? (List those things.)

2. What is my life's purpose?

3. What legacy do I want to leave?

Now, considering the answers to those questions, draft a personal mission statement.

My mission statement:

In Chapter 2, we will discuss how you can use your personal goals to motivate you. Then, in Chapter 3, we will explore how your mission statement and personal goals will guide you to use your time effectively. You will also be asked to review your mission statement at the end of this text. Over the years, you will want to review and update your mission statement as you change and grow personally and professionally.

Skills for School and Job Success

Have you ever asked yourself, "What does it take to be successful in a job?" Many of the skills and competencies that characterize a successful student can also apply to a successful employee. Becoming aware of the connection between school success and job success helps you see how the skills you learn in the classroom will eventually apply to the skills you will need in the workplace.

Over the years, employers have told educators what skills they want employees to have. In 1990, Elizabeth Dole, who was then the Secretary of Labor, created the Secretary's Commission on Achieving Necessary Skills (SCANS), which included business and industry leaders, human resource personnel, and other top advisors in labor and education. **Figure 1.1** illustrates the skills and competencies that are necessary not only for job success but also for school success. You can apply and practice them now by completing the Peak Performance Self-Assessment Test in **Personal Evaluation Notebook 1.2** on page 11. Be honest and use critical thinking skills as you complete the assessment.

Figure 1.1
Peak Performance Competency Wheel

SCANS recommends these skills and competencies for job success. *Which of these skills have you been acquiring?*

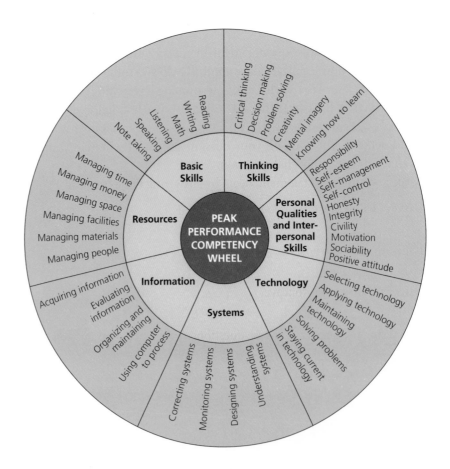

Personal Evaluation Notebook

Peak Performance Self-Assessment Test

Assess your skills on a scale of 1 to 5 by placing a check mark. Examples are given for each. Review your answers to discover your strongest skills and weakest skills.

Area	Excellent 5	4	OK 3	2	Poor 1
1. Reading (i.e., comprehending; summarizing key points; reading for pleasure)	____	____	____	____	____
2. Writing (i.e., using correct grammar; presenting information clearly and concisely; documenting accurately)	____	____	____	____	____
3. Speaking (i.e., expressing main points in an interesting manner; controlling anxiety)	____	____	____	____	____
4. Mathematics (i.e., understanding basic principles and formulas; showing work)	____	____	____	____	____
5. Listening and note taking (i.e., staying focused and attentive; recording key points)	____	____	____	____	____
6. Critical thinking and reasoning (i.e., assessing facts; making decisions; linking material)	____	____	____	____	____
7. Creative problem solving (i.e., developing options; weighing alternatives)	____	____	____	____	____
8. Positive visualization (i.e., creating mental images to support goals)	____	____	____	____	____
9. Knowing how you learn (i.e., recognizing preferred learning style; integrating all styles)	____	____	____	____	____
10. Honesty and integrity (i.e., doing the right thing; telling the truth; presenting original work)	____	____	____	____	____
11. Positive attitude and motivation (i.e., being optimistic; identifying personal motivators; establishing goals)	____	____	____	____	____
12. Responsibility (i.e., keeping commitments; not blaming others)	____	____	____	____	____

(continued)

Personal Evaluation Notebook

1.2

Peak Performance Self-Assessment Test *(concluded)*

Area	Excellent 5	4	OK 3	2	Poor 1
13. Flexibility/ability to adapt to change (i.e., being open to new ideas; seeing the "big picture")	____	____	____	____	____
14. Self-management and emotional control (i.e., taking ownership of thoughts and behaviors)	____	____	____	____	____
15. Self-esteem and confidence (i.e., focusing on strengths; maintaining a positive self-image)	____	____	____	____	____
16. Time management (i.e., setting priorities; planning; accomplishing tasks)	____	____	____	____	____
17. Money management (i.e., budgeting; minimizing debt; saving)	____	____	____	____	____
18. Management and leadership of people (i.e., inspiring; communicating; delegating; training)	____	____	____	____	____
19. Interpersonal and communication skills (i.e., building rapport; listening; being an effective team member)	____	____	____	____	____
20. Ability to work well with culturally diverse groups (i.e., respecting and celebrating differences)	____	____	____	____	____
21. Organization and evaluation of information (i.e., assembling key points and ideas; summarizing; documenting)	____	____	____	____	____
22. Understanding technology (i.e., using essential programs; troubleshooting basic problems)	____	____	____	____	____
23. Commitment and effort (i.e., being persistent; working consistently toward goals)	____	____	____	____	____

Discover Your Learning Style

As a lifelong learner, you need to know how to learn to maximize your learning potential. Everyone processes information differently and not everyone learns the same way. There is no single right way to learn, but knowing your preferred learning style can increase your effectiveness in school or at work and can enhance your self-esteem. Knowing how you learn best can help you reduce frustration, focus on your strengths, and integrate various styles.

Integrate Both Sides of the Brain

Do you use both sides of your brain? "I use my whole brain!" you might answer—and, indeed, you do. However, you have a preference for using the left or right side of the brain for many mental and physical functions. In the 1960s, Dr. Roger Sperry and his colleagues discovered that the left and right sides of the brain specialize in different modes of thinking and perception. Dominant brain function may play a significant role in how you learn.

Studies show that the brain has two systems by which it classifies information. One is linguistic and factual (left brain), and one is visual and intuitive (right brain). Although they are interconnected, one is usually more dominant. For example, if you are left-brain dominant, you probably like facts and order and think in a concrete manner. You use a logical, rational, and detailed thought process. If you are right-brain dominant, you are more inclined to use an intuitive and insightful approach to solving problems and processing new information. You are more comfortable with feelings and hunches and like to think abstractly and intuitively. **Figure 1.2** lists a number of traits that are considered either left-brain or right-brain dominant.

Although you may find that you favor one side of your brain, definitely the key is to use all your brain power and integrate a variety of learning styles (which you will explore next). By doing this, you enhance learning, memory, and recall.

Left-Brain Dominant	Right-Brain Dominant
Feels more comfortable with facts	Feels more comfortable with feelings
Thinks rationally based on reason and logic	Thinks intuitively based on hunches and feelings
Uses concrete thinking	Uses abstract thinking
Likes a sense of order	Likes a sense of space
Uses linear, step-by-step thinking	Uses holistic, visual thinking
Uses speech and words	Uses pictures and drawings
Is more "cerebral"	Is more "physical"
Makes lists and notes	Uses visuals and colors
Is concerned about time	Lives in the moment
Analyzes parts of the whole	Looks at the whole for patterns
Likes traditional outlines	Likes mind maps or creative outlines
Likes well-organized lectures	Likes group work and open-ended class discussion

Figure 1.2

Left-Brain versus Right-Brain Traits

Put a check mark next to the descriptions that apply to you. *Would you consider yourself more of a left-brain dominant person or a right-brain dominant person?*

Are You a Reader, a Listener, or a Doer?

Your brain allows you to experience the world through your many senses. One way to explore how you learn best is to ask yourself if you are a reader, a listener, or a doer. Do you get more information from reading and seeing, talking and listening, or doing? Of course, you do all these things, but your learning strength, or preferred style, may be in one of these areas. For example, you may organize information visually, favoring right-brain activities. Although such classifications may oversimplify complex brain activity and are not meant to put you in a box or category, the goal is to help you be more aware of your natural tendencies and habits and how you can use these preferences and learn new ways to enhance your success.

A person who learns better by reading possesses a visual learning style. Someone who learns better by listening is considered an auditory learner. A kinesthetic learner learns by touch and physical activity. **Personal Evaluation Notebook 1.3** on pages 15 and 16 has a Learning Style Inventory that will help you discover your learning style.

VISUAL LEARNERS

Visual learners prefer to see information and read material. They learn most effectively with pictures, graphs, illustrations, diagrams, time lines, photos, pie charts, and visual design. They like to contemplate concepts, reflect, and summarize information in writing. They might use arrows, pictures, and bullets to highlight points. Visual learners are often holistic in that they see pictures in their minds that create feelings and emotion. They often use visual descriptions in their speech, such as "It is clear . . . ," "Picture this . . . ," or "See what I mean?" Visual learners tend to

- Be right-brain dominant
- Remember what they see better than what they hear
- Like to see charts and pictures
- Try to sit close to the instructor
- Prefer to have written directions they can read
- Learn better when someone shows them rather than tells them
- Like to read, highlight, and take notes
- Keep a list of things to do when planning the week
- Be fast thinkers and gesture frequently while talking
- Communicate clearly and concisely and watch facial expressions
- Like to read for pleasure and to learn

Visual learners may enjoy being an interior designer, a drafter, a proofreader, a writer, or an artist.

AUDITORY LEARNERS

Auditory learners prefer to rely on their hearing sense. They like tapes and music, and they prefer to listen to information, such as lectures. They like to talk, recite, and summarize information aloud. Auditory learners may create rhymes out of words and play music that helps them concentrate. When they take study breaks, they listen to music or chat with a friend. They are usually good listeners but are easily

Personal Evaluation Notebook

Learning Style Inventory

Determine your learning preference. Complete each sentence by checking a, b, or c. No answer is correct or better than another.

1. I learn best when I
   - _____ **a.** see information.
   - _____ **b.** hear information.
   - ✓ **c.** have hands-on experience.

2. I like
   - _____ **a.** pictures and illustrations.
   - _____ **b.** listening to tapes and stories.
   - ✓ **c.** working with people and going on field trips.

3. For pleasure and relaxation, I love to
   - ✓ **a.** read.
   - _____ **b.** listen to music and tapes.
   - _____ **c.** garden or play sports.

4. I tend to be
   - _____ **a.** contemplative.
   - _____ **b.** talkative.
   - ✓ **c.** a doer.

5. To remember a zip code, I like to
   - ✓ **a.** write it down several times.
   - _____ **b.** say it out loud several times.
   - _____ **c.** doodle and draw it on any available paper.

6. In a classroom, I learn best when
   - _____ **a.** I have a good textbook, visual aids, and written information.
   - _____ **b.** the instructor is interesting and clear.
   - ✓ **c.** I am involved in doing activities.

7. When I study for a test, I
   - ✓ **a.** read my notes and write a summary.
   - _____ **b.** review my notes aloud and talk to others.
   - _____ **c.** like to study in a group and use models and charts.

8. I have
   - _____ **a.** a strong fashion sense and pay attention to visual details.
   - _____ **b.** fun telling stories and jokes.
   - ✓ **c.** a great time building things and being active.

(continued)

Personal Evaluation Notebook

1.3

Learning Style Inventory *(concluded)*

9. I plan the upcoming week by
   - ✓ **a.** making a list and keeping a detailed calendar.
   - _____ **b.** talking it through with someone.
   - _____ **c.** creating a computer calendar or using a project board.

10. When preparing for a math test, I like to
    - _____ **a.** write formulas on note cards or use pictures.
    - ✓ **b.** memorize formulas or talk aloud.
    - _____ **c.** use marbles, LEGO® blocks, or three-dimensional models.

11. I often
    - ✓ **a.** remember faces but not names.
    - _____ **b.** remember names but not faces.
    - _____ **c.** remember events but not names or faces.

12. I remember best
    - _____ **a.** when I read instructions and use visual images to remember.
    - _____ **b.** when I listen to instructions and use rhyming words to remember.
    - ✓ **c.** with hands-on activities and trial and error.

13. When I give directions, I might say,
    - _____ **a.** "Turn right at the yellow house and left when you see the large oak tree. Do you see what I mean?"
    - ✓ **b.** "Turn right. Go three blocks. Turn left onto Buttermilk Lane. OK? Got that? Do you hear what I'm saying?"
    - _____ **c.** "Follow me," after giving directions by using gestures.

14. When driving in a new city, I prefer to
    - ✓ **a.** get a map and find my own way.
    - _____ **b.** stop and get directions from someone.
    - _____ **c.** drive around and figure it out by myself.

Score: Count the number of check marks for all your choices:

Total a choices ___6___ (visual learning style)

Total b choices ___2___ (auditory learning style)

Total c choices ___4___ (kinesthetic learning style)

The highest total indicates your dominant learning style. You may find that you are a combination and that's good. It means you are integrating styles already.

distracted by noise. They often use auditory descriptions when communicating, such as "This rings true . . . ," "It's clear as a bell . . . ," or "Do you hear what you're saying?"

Auditory learners tend to

- Be left-brain dominant
- Remember what they hear better than what they see
- Prefer to listen to instructions
- Like lectures organized in a logical sequence
- Like to listen to music and talk on the telephone
- Plan the week by talking it through with someone
- Use rhyming words to remember
- Learn best when they hear an assignment as well as see it

Auditory learners may enjoy being a disc jockey, trial lawyer, counselor, or musician.

KINESTHETIC LEARNERS

Kinesthetic learners are usually well coordinated, like to touch things, and learn best by doing. They like to collect samples, write out information, spend time outdoors, and relate to the material they are learning. They like to connect abstract material to something concrete. They are good at hands-on tasks. They often use phrases such as "I am getting a handle on . . . ," "I have a gut feeling that . . . ," and "I get a sense that . . ."

Kinesthetic learners tend to

Know How You Learn
Everyone has his or her own way of learning. *What type of learning style do you think best suits this person?*

- Be right-brain dominant
- Create an experience
- Use hands-on activities
- Build things and put things together
- Use models and physical activity
- Write down information
- Apply information to real-life situations
- Draw, doodle, use games and puzzles, and play computer games
- Take field trips and collect samples
- Relate abstract information to something concrete

Kinesthetic learners may enjoy being a chef, a surgeon, a medical technician, a nurse, an automobile mechanic, an electrician, an engineer, a forest ranger, a police officer, or a dancer.

Redefining Intelligence: Other Learning Styles

Because each of us has our own unique set of abilities, perceptions, needs, and ways of processing information, learning styles vary widely. Besides visual, auditory, and kinesthetic learning styles, there are other, more specific styles, and some people have more than one learning style.

Plus, intelligence has been redefined. We used to think of intelligence as measured by an IQ test. Many schools measure and reward linguistic and logical/mathematical modes of intelligence; however, Thomas Armstrong, author of *7 Kinds of Smart: Identifying and Developing Your Many Intelligences,* and Howard Gardner, who wrote *Frames of Mind: The Theory of Multiple Intelligences,* illustrated that we all possess many different intelligences. (See **Personal Evaluation Notebook 1.4,** which includes a number of traits associated with each "intelligence.").

1. **Verbal/linguistic.** Some people are **word smart.** They have verbal/linguistic intelligence and like to read, talk, and write information. They have the ability to argue, persuade, entertain, and teach with words. Many become journalists, writers, or lawyers. **To learn best:** Talk, read, or write about it.

2. **Logical/mathematical.** Some people are **logic smart.** They have logical/mathematical intelligence and like numbers, puzzles, and logic. They have the ability to reason, solve problems, create hypotheses, think in terms of cause and effect, and explore patterns and relationships. Many become scientists, accountants, or computer programmers. **To learn best:** Conceptualize, quantify, or think critically about it.

3. **Spatial.** Some people are **picture smart.** They have spatial intelligence and like to draw, sketch, and visualize information. They have the ability to perceive in three-dimensional space and re-create various aspects of the visual world. Many become architects, photographers, artists, or engineers. **To learn best:** Draw, sketch, or visualize it.

4. **Musical.** Some people are **music smart.** They have rhythm and melody intelligence. They have the ability to appreciate, perceive, and produce rhythms and to keep time to music. Many become composers, singers, or instrumentalists. **To learn best:** Sing, chant, rap, or play music.

5. **Bodily/kinesthetic.** Some people are **body smart.** They have physical and kinesthetic intelligence. They have the ability to understand and control their bodies; they have tactile sensitivity, like movement, and handle objects skillfully. Many become dancers, carpenters, physical education teachers, or coaches and enjoy outdoor activities and sports. **To learn best:** Build a model, dance, use note cards, or do hands-on activities.

6. **Environmental.** Some people are **outdoor smart.** They have environmental intelligence. They are good at measuring, charting, and observing plants and animals. They like to keep journals, to collect and classify, and to participate in outdoor activities. Many become park and forest rangers, surveyors, gardeners, landscape architects, outdoor guides, wildlife experts, or environmentalists. **To learn best:** Go on field trips, collect samples, go for walks, and apply what you are learning to real life.

7. **Intrapersonal.** Some people are **self smart.** They have intrapersonal, inner, intelligence. They have the ability to be contemplative, self-disciplined, and introspective. They like to work alone and pursue their own interests. Many become writers, counselors, theologians, or self-employed businesspeople. **To learn best:** Relate information to your feelings or personal experiences or find inner expression.

8. **Interpersonal.** Some people are **people smart.** They have interpersonal intelligence. They like to talk and work with people, join groups, and solve problems

Personal Evaluation Notebook ✓ 1.4

Multiple Intelligences

Put a check mark on the line next to the statement that is most often true for you. Consider what interests you or what you believe you are good at doing.

Verbal/ Linguistic	Logical/ Mathematical	Spatial	Musical	Bodily/ Kinesthetic	Environmental	Intrapersonal	Interpersonal
"Word Smart"	"Logic Smart"	"Picture Smart"	"Music Smart"	"Body Smart"	"Outdoor Smart"	"Self Smart"	"People Smart"
I like to	I like to	I like to	I like to	I like to	I like to	I like to	I like to
—Tell stories —Read —Talk and express myself clearly —Persuade, argue, or negotiate —Teach or discuss topics with others —Write	—Use logic to solve problems —Explore mathematics —Explore science —Observe and question how things work —Figure out how to fix things —Use logic to solve problems	—Draw or sketch —Visualize —Add color —Build models —Create illustrations —Use space and spatial relationships	—Use rhythms —Respond to music —Sing —Recognize and remember melodies and chords —Use songs to help me remember —Relax with music	—Experience physical movement —Act things out —Use note cards and models to learn —Work with others —Touch and feel material —Be active and enjoy sports	—Be outdoors —Camp and hike —Work in the earth —Collect samples —Take field trips —Appreciate nature	—Be independent and work on my own —Reflect on ideas —Read and contemplate new thoughts —Go off and think through a situation alone —Be self-disciplined and set individual goals —Use personal experiences and inner expression	—Inspire and lead others —Learn through discussions —Work with a group of people —"Read" other people —Hear another person's point of view —Be compassionate and helpful

Multiple Intelligences

Your goal is to try new strategies and create learning opportunities in line with each category.
What are some strategies you could easily incorporate?

For more information, see

Frames of Mind: The Theory of Multiple Intelligences by Howard Gardner, Basic Books, 1983.

Their Own Way: Discovering and Encouraging Your Child's Personal Learning Style by Thomas Armstrong, Tarcher/Putnam, 1987.

as part of a team. They have the ability to work with and understand people, as well as to perceive and be responsive to the moods, intentions, and desires of other people. Many become mediators, negotiators, social directors, social workers, motivational speakers, or teachers. **To learn best:** Join a group, get a study partner, or discuss with others.

Discover Your Personality Type

Your learning style is often associated with your personality type—your "temperament." The concepts of learning styles, personality, and temperament are not new. Early writings from ancient Greece, India, the Middle East, and China addressed various temperaments and personality types. The ancient Greek founder of modern medicine, Hippocrates, identified four basic body types and the personality type associated with each body type. Several personality typing systems grew out of this ancient view of body/mind typing.

Carl Jung's Typology System

In 1921, psychologist Carl Jung proposed, in his book *Psychological Types,* that people are fundamentally different but also fundamentally alike. He identified three main attitudes/psychological functions people have, each with two types of personalities:

1. First, Jung classified *how people relate to the external or internal world.* **Extroverts** are energized and recharged by people, tending to be outgoing and social. They tend to be optimistic and are often uncomfortable with being alone. **Introverts** are energized by time alone, solitude, and reflection, preferring the world of ideas and thoughts. They tend to have a small but close set of friends and are more prone to self-doubt.

2. Next, Jung developed an assessment of *how people perceive and gather information.* **Sensors** learn best from their senses and feel comfortable with facts and concrete data. They like to organize information systematically. **Intuitives** feel

more comfortable with theories, abstraction, imagination, and speculation. They respond to their intuition and rely on hunches and nonverbal perceptions.

3. Then, Jung characterized *how people prefer to make decisions.* **Thinkers** like to analyze problems with facts, rational logic, and analysis. They tend to be unemotional and use a systematic evaluation of data and facts for problem solving. **Feelers** are sensitive to the concerns and feelings of others, value harmony, and dislike creating conflict.

Jung suggested that differences and similarities among people can be understood by combining these types. Although people are not exclusively one of these types, he maintained that they have basic preferences or tendencies.

The Myers-Briggs Type Indicator

Jung's work inspired Katherine Briggs and her daughter, Isabel Briggs Myers, to design a personality test, called the Myers-Briggs Type Indicator (MBTI), which has become the most widely used typological instrument. They added a fourth attitude/psychological function (judgment/perception), which they felt was implied in Jung's writings, focusing on *how people live.* **Judgers** prefer orderly, planned, structured learning and working environments. They like control and closure. **Perceivers** prefer flexibility and spontaneity and like to allow life to unfold. Thus, with the four attitudes/psychological functions (extroverts vs. introverts, sensors vs. intuitives, thinkers vs. feelers, and judgers vs. perceivers), the MBTI provides 16 possible personality combinations. Although we may have all 8 preferences, 1 in each pair tends to be more developed. (See **Figure 1.3** on page 22, which lists many characteristics of extroverts, introverts, sensors, intuitives, thinkers, feelers, judgers, and perceivers.)

● **Understanding Personality Types**
Psychologists have developed a variety of categories to identify how people function best. *What personality type or types might apply to the person in this photograph?*

Connect Learning Styles and Personality Types: The Four-Temperament Profile

You now are aware of your preferred learning styles and have a sense of your personality type. How are these connected? How can you use this information to improve your learning skills and participate in productive group and team situations?

The simple Four-Temperament Profile demonstrates how learning styles and personality types are interrelated. **Personal Evaluation Notebook 1.5** on page 23 includes a number of questions that will help you determine your dominant temperament.

The following descriptions elaborate on the four temperaments in Personal Evaluation Notebook 1.5. Which is your dominant temperament: analyzer, creator, supporter, or director? Did the answer surprise you? Please keep in mind that inventories provide only clues. People change over time and react differently in different situations. However, use this knowledge to discover your strengths and to become a

Figure 1.3

Characteristics of Personality Types

This chart reflects information influenced by psychologists Carl Jung and Myers and Briggs. *How can understanding your own personality and temperament help you succeed in school and life?*

Extroverts (E) vs. Introverts (I)		Sensors (S) vs. Intuitives (iN)	
Gregarious	Quiet	Practical	Speculative
Active, talkative	Reflective	Experience	Use hunches
Speak, then think	Think, then speak	See details	See the big picture
Outgoing, social	Fewer, closer friends	Sequential, work steadily	Work in burst of energy
Energized by people	Energized by self	Feet on the ground	Head in the clouds
Like to speak	Like to read	Concrete	Abstract
Like variety and action	Like quiet for concentration	Realistic	See possibilities
Interested in results	Interested in ideas	Sensible and hardworking	Imaginative and inspired
Do not mind interruptions	Dislike interruptions	Good and precise work	Dislike precise work

Thinkers (T) vs. Feelers (F)		Judgers (J) vs. Perceivers (P)	
Analytical	Harmonious	Decisive	Tentative
Objective	Subjective	Closure	Open-minded
Impersonal	Personal	Plan ahead	Flexible
Factual	Sympathetic	Urgency	Open time frame
Want fairness	Want recognition	Organized	Spontaneous
Detached	Involved	Deliberate	Go with the flow
Rule	Circumstances	Set goals	Let life unfold
Things, not people	People, not things	Meet deadlines	Procrastinate
Lineal	Whole	Just the facts	Interested and curious

well-rounded and balanced learner. Peak performers know not only their dominant style but also the way to integrate other styles when appropriate.

Analyzers

Analyzers tend to be logical, thoughtful, loyal, exact, dedicated, steady, and organized. They like following direction and work at a steady pace. The key word for analyzers is *thinking*. (See **Figure 1.4** on page 25.)

Strengths: Creating concepts and models and thinking things through

Goal: Intellectual recognition; analyzers are knowledge seekers

Classroom style: Analyzers relate to instructors who are organized, know their facts, and present information logically and precisely. They dislike the ambiguity of subjects that do not have right or wrong answers. They tend to be left-brained and seem more concerned with facts, abstract ideas, and concepts than with people.

Learning style: Analyzers often perceive information abstractly and process it reflectively. They learn best by observing and thinking through ideas. They like models, lectures, textbooks, and solitary work. They like to work with things and analyze how things work. They evaluate and come to a precise conclusion.

Personal Evaluation Notebook

1.5

The Four-Temperament Profile

The following statements indicate your preference in working with others, making decisions, and learning new information. Read each statement, with its four possible choices. Mark 4 next to the choice MOST like you, 3 next to the choice ALMOST ALWAYS like you, 2 next to the choice SOMEWHAT like you, and 1 next to the choice LEAST like you.

1. I learn best when I

_____ **a.** rely on logical thinking and facts.

_____ **b.** am personally involved.

_____ **c.** can look for new patterns through trial and error.

_____ **d.** use hands-on activities and practical applications.

2. When I'm at my best, I'm described as

_____ **a.** dependable, accurate, logical, and objective.

_____ **b.** understanding, loyal, cooperative, and harmonious.

_____ **c.** imaginative, flexible, open-minded, and creative.

_____ **d.** confident, assertive, practical, and results-oriented.

3. I respond best to instructors and bosses who

_____ **a.** are factual and to the point.

_____ **b.** show appreciation and are friendly.

_____ **c.** encourage creativity and flexibility.

_____ **d.** expect me to be involved, be active, and get results.

4. When working in a group, I tend to value

_____ **a.** objectivity and correctness.

_____ **b.** consensus and harmony.

_____ **c.** originality and risk taking.

_____ **d.** efficiency and results.

5. I am most comfortable with people who are

_____ **a.** informed, serious, and accurate.

_____ **b.** supportive, appreciative, and friendly.

_____ **c.** creative, unique, and idealistic.

_____ **d.** productive, realistic, and dependable.

6. Generally, I am

_____ **a.** methodical, efficient, trustworthy, and accurate.

_____ **b.** cooperative, genuine, gentle, and modest.

_____ **c.** high-spirited, spontaneous, easily bored, and dramatic.

_____ **d.** straightforward, conservative, responsible, and decisive.

7. When making a decision, I'm generally concerned with

_____ **a.** collecting information and facts to determine the right solution.

_____ **b.** finding the solution that pleases others and myself.

_____ **c.** brainstorming creative solutions that feel right.

_____ **d.** quickly choosing the most practical and realistic solution.

(continued)

Personal Evaluation Notebook

The Four-Temperament Profile *(concluded)*

8. You could describe me in one word as

   _____ **a.** analytical.

   _____ **b.** caring.

   _____ **c.** innovative.

   _____ **d.** productive.

9. I excel at

   _____ **a.** reaching accurate and logical conclusions.

   _____ **b.** being cooperative and respecting people's feelings.

   _____ **c.** finding hidden connections and creative outcomes.

   _____ **d.** making realistic, practical, and timely decisions.

10. When learning at school or on the job, I enjoy

   _____ **a.** gathering facts and technical information and being objective.

   _____ **b.** making personal connections, being supportive, and working in groups.

   _____ **c.** exploring new possibilities, tackling creative tasks, and being flexible.

   _____ **d.** producing results, solving problems, and making decisions.

Score: To determine your style, mark the choices you made in each column below. Then add the column totals. Highest number in

- Column a, you are an analyzer
- Column b, you are supporter
- Column c, you are a creator
- Column d, you are a director

	Choice a	Choice b	Choice c	Choice d
1.	_____	_____	_____	_____
2.	_____	_____	_____	_____
3.	_____	_____	_____	_____
4.	_____	_____	_____	_____
5.	_____	_____	_____	_____
6.	_____	_____	_____	_____
7.	_____	_____	_____	_____
8.	_____	_____	_____	_____
9.	_____	_____	_____	_____
10.	_____	_____	_____	_____
Total	_____	_____	_____	_____
	Analyzer	**Supporter**	**Creator**	**Director**

Effective Traits	Ineffective Traits	Possible Majors	Possible Careers	How to Relate to Analyzers
Objective	Too cautious	Accounting	Computer programmer	Be factual
Logical	Abrupt	Bookkeeping	Accountant	Be logical
Thorough	Unemotional	Mathematics	Bookkeeper	Be formal and thorough
Precise	Aloof	Computer science	Drafter	Be organized, detached, and calm
Detail-oriented	Indecisive	Drafting	Electrician	Be accurate and use critical thinking
Disciplined	Unimaginative	Electronics	Engineer	State facts briefly and concisely
		Auto mechanics	Auto mechanic	
			Technician	
			Librarian	

Figure 1.4
Profile of an Analyzer

Analyzers want things done right. Their favorite question is "What?" *Do you recognize any analyzer traits in yourself?*

Supporters

People who are supporters tend to be cooperative, honest, sensitive, warm, and understanding. They relate well to others. They value harmony and are informal, approachable, and tactful. In business, they place emphasis on people and are concerned with the feelings and values of those around them. The key word for supporters is *feeling*. (See **Figure 1.5**.)

Strengths: Clarifying values, creating harmony, and being a loyal team player
Goal: To create harmony, meaning, and cooperation; they are identity seekers
Classroom style: Supporters tend to learn best when they like an instructor and feel accepted and respected. They are easily hurt by criticism. They like to integrate course concepts with their own experiences. They relate to instructors who are

Effective Traits	Ineffective Traits	Possible Majors	Possible Careers	How to Relate to Supporters
Understanding	Overly compliant	Counseling or therapy	Elementary teacher	Be friendly
Gentle	Passive	Social work	Physical therapist	Be positive
Loyal	Slow to act	Family and consumer science	Social worker	Be sincere and build trust
Cooperative	Naive	Nursing	Therapist	Listen actively
Diplomatic	Unprofessional	Medical assisting	Counselor	Focus on people
Appreciative	Can be overly sensitive	Physical therapy	Nurse	Focus on personal values
		Education	Medical assistant	Create a comfortable, relaxed climate
				Create an experience they can relate to

Figure 1.5
Profile of a Supporter

Supporters want things done harmoniously and want to be personally involved. Their favorite question is "Why?" *Do you recognize any supporter traits in yourself?*

Figure 1.6

Profile of a Creator

Creators want things done with a sense of drama and style. Their favorite question is *"What if?"* *Do you recognize any creator traits in yourself?*

Effective Traits	Ineffective Traits	Possible Majors	Possible Careers	How to Relate to Creators
Imaginative	Unrealistic	Art	Writer	Be enthusiastic
Creative	Unreliable	English	Politician	Be involved
Visionary	Inconsistent	Music	Travel agent	Be flexible
Idealistic	Hasty	Design	Hotel manager	Be accepting of change
Enthusiastic	Impulsive	Hospitality	Cartoonist	Focus on creative ideas
Innovative	Impatient	Travel	Musician	Talk about dreams and possibilities
	Fragmented	Theater	Composer	
		Communications	Artist	
			Journalist	
			Craftsperson	
			Florist	
			Costume designer	
			Salesperson	
			Scientist	

warm and sociable, tell interesting stories, use visuals, and are approachable. They learn best by listening, sharing ideas and feelings, and working in teams.

Learning style: Supporters perceive information through intuition and process it reflectively. They like to deal with their feelings. They prefer learning information that has personal meaning, and they are patient and likeable. They are insightful; they are imaginative thinkers and need to be personally involved.

Creators

Creators are innovative, flexible, spontaneous, creative, and idealistic. Creators are risk takers; they love drama, style, and imaginative design. They like fresh ideas and are passionate about their work. The key word for creators is *experience*. (See **Figure 1.6**.)

Strengths: Creating visions that inspire people

Goal: To make things happen by turning ideas into action; they are experience seekers

Classroom style: Creators learn best in innovative and active classrooms. They relate to instructors who have a passion for their work; who are challenging, imaginative, and flexible; who present interesting ideas; and who make the topic exciting.

Learning style: Creators learn by doing and being involved in active experiments. They perceive information concretely and process it actively. They like games, role-playing, stories, plays, music, illustrations, drawings, and other visual stimuli. They ask questions and enjoy acting on ideas. They are usually good public speakers. They are future-oriented and good at seeing whole systems.

Directors

Directors are dependable, self-directed, conscientious, efficient, decisive, and results-oriented. They like to be the leader of groups and respond to other people's ideas when they are logical and reasonable. Their strength is in the practical

Effective Traits	Ineffective Traits	Possible Majors	Possible Careers	How to Relate to Directors
Confident	Aggressive	Business	Lawyer	Set deadlines
Assertive	Pushy	Law enforcement	Police officer	Be responsible for your actions
Active	Insistent	Construction	Detective	Focus on results
Decisive	Overpowering	Woodworking	Consultant	Focus on achievements
Forceful	Dominating	Carpentry	Banker	Do not try to take control
Effective leader		Business management	Park ranger	Do not make excuses
Results-oriented		Wildlife conservation	Forest ranger	Have a direction
		Forestry	Administrator for outdoor recreation	Make known time or other changes in schedule

Figure 1.7

Profile of a Director

Directors want to produce results in a practical manner. Their favorite question is "How?" *Do you recognize any director traits in yourself?*

application of ideas. Because of this ability, they can excel in a variety of careers, such as law enforcement, banking, and legal professions. The key word for directors is *results*. (See **Figure 1.7**.)

Strengths: Integrating theory with practical solutions

Goal: To find practical solutions to problems; they are security seekers

Classroom style: Directors relate to instructors who are organized, clear, to the point, punctual, and results-oriented. They prefer field trips and hands-on activities.

Learning style: Directors learn by hands-on, direct experience. They learn best by practical application. They like classes that are relevant. They work hard to get things done.

Integrate Styles to Maximize Learning

Just as there is no best way to learn, there is no one instrument, assessment, or inventory that can categorize how you learn best. There are many theories about learning styles, and none of them should be regarded as air-tight explanations. Any learning style assessment or theory is, at best, a guide.

The assessment instruments discussed in this text have been adapted from various sources and are based on many years of research. They are simple, yet they provide valuable clues and strategies for determining how you learn, process information, and relate to others. They also provide you with clues for possible college majors and careers that fit your personality and style. Ask your instructor or learning center if there are certain assessments they recommend.

As mentioned, the purpose of these inventories is to provide a guide, not to categorize you into a specific box. Note how all learning styles are connected and that we use all of them, depending on the situation, task, and people involved. The goals are to develop positive strategies based on your natural talents and abilities and to expand your effectiveness by integrating all learning styles.

Figure 1.8

Integrated Brain Power

Integrating both sides of the brain boosts learning, memory, and recall. *Do you think you are left- or right-brain dominant?*

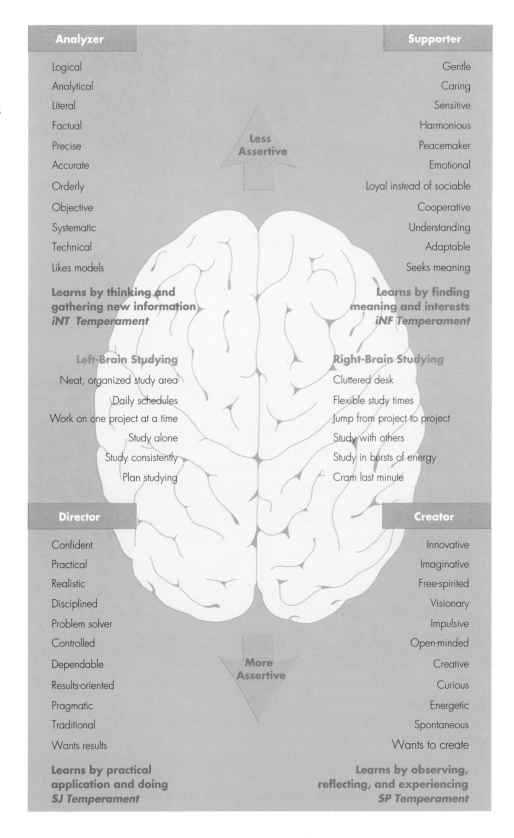

Analyzer

Logical
Analytical
Literal
Factual
Precise
Accurate
Orderly
Objective
Systematic
Technical
Likes models

Learns by thinking and gathering new information
iNT Temperament

Left-Brain Studying

Neat, organized study area
Daily schedules
Work on one project at a time
Study alone
Study consistently
Plan studying

Supporter

Gentle
Caring
Sensitive
Harmonious
Peacemaker
Emotional
Loyal instead of sociable
Cooperative
Understanding
Adaptable
Seeks meaning

Learns by finding meaning and interests
iNF Temperament

Right-Brain Studying

Cluttered desk
Flexible study times
Jump from project to project
Study with others
Study in bursts of energy
Cram last minute

Less Assertive

Director

Confident
Practical
Realistic
Disciplined
Problem solver
Controlled
Dependable
Results-oriented
Pragmatic
Traditional
Wants results

Learns by practical application and doing
SJ Temperament

Creator

Innovative
Imaginative
Free-spirited
Visionary
Impulsive
Open-minded
Creative
Curious
Energetic
Spontaneous
Wants to create

Learns by observing, reflecting, and experiencing
SP Temperament

More Assertive

Psychologist William James believed that people use less than 5 percent of their potential. Think of what you could accomplish if you could learn to work in alignment with your natural preferences and integrate various learning styles and techniques. **Figure 1.8** illustrates how the many learning styles and personality types

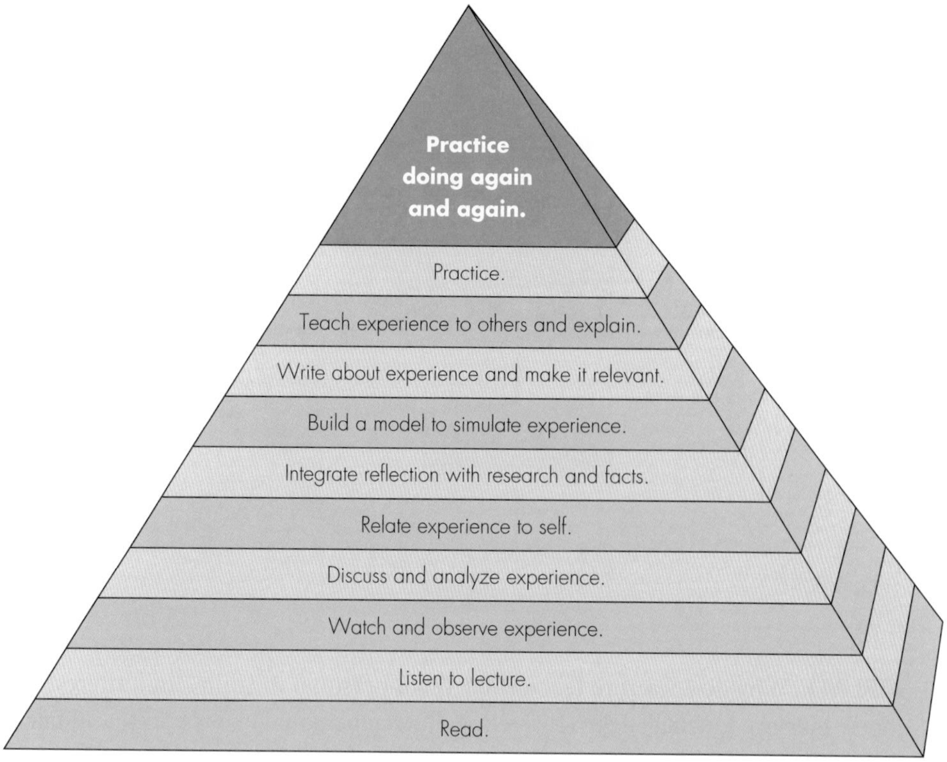
Practice doing again and again.
Practice.
Teach experience to others and explain.
Write about experience and make it relevant.
Build a model to simulate experience.
Integrate reflection with research and facts.
Relate experience to self.
Discuss and analyze experience.
Watch and observe experience.
Listen to lecture.
Read.

Figure 1.9
Peak Performance Learning Pyramid
Maximize your effectiveness by integrating various learning styles and skills as you move up the pyramid. *What additional skills and learning styles would enhance your learning ability?*

come together. **Figure 1.9** then explores the Peak Performance Learning Pyramid, which illustrates how you can maximize your effectiveness by integrating learning styles. Now that you have assessed how you learn best—as well as new ways to learn—let's explore how learning is a never-ending cycle.

The Adult Learning Cycle

You can become a more effective learner, problem solver, and decision maker when you understand how you learn best and when you integrate all the learning and personality styles. David Kolb, a professor at Case Western Reserve University, developed an inventory that categorizes learners based on how they process information:

1. Concrete experience: learn by feeling and personal experience
2. Reflective observation: learn by observing and reflecting
3. Abstract conceptualization: learn by thinking and gathering information
4. Active experimentation: learn by doing and hands-on activities

Kolb's theory about learning styles is similar to Carl Jung's four attitudes/psychological functions (feeling, intuition, thinking, and sensation). The crux of Kolb's theory is that you learn by practice, repetition, and recognition. Thus, do it, do it again, and then do it again.

The following Adult Learning Cycle is an adaptation of both Kolb's and Jung's theories. It includes a fifth stage and illustrates how they are complementary to one another. (See **Figure 1.10**.)

Figure 1.10

The Adult Learning Cycle

The key to learning is practice and repetition. *Why is "Teach" an essential, unique step?*

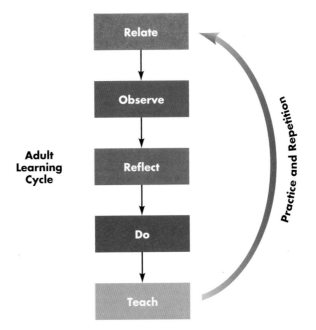

1. **RELATE. Why do I want to learn this?** What personal meaning and interest does this have for me? I learn by feeling, having personal experiences, and talking with others.

2. **OBSERVE. How does this work?** I learn by watching, listening, and experiencing.

3. **REFLECT. What does this mean?** I learn by thinking, gathering information, and reflecting.

4. **DO. What can I do with this?** I learn by doing, finding practical applications, and defining procedures.

5. **TEACH. How can I relay this information to others?** I learn by demonstrating and explaining, as well as by acknowledging and rewarding positive outcomes.

Depending on your learning style, the information to be learned, and the situation, you may find yourself starting the Adult Learning Cycle at different stages. *The key to learning is practice and repetition.* As you repeat the stages, meaning and recall are strengthened. To make learning long-lasting, you need to find ways to make learning meaningful and physical. For example, let's say you are taking a computer class:

1. **RELATE personal meaning, interests, and relevance.** Why do you want to use the computer? What are the benefits to you, your coursework, and your career? How does this relate to what you already know, such as typing skills? In what programs or skills would you like to become proficient? Think about the opportunities and talk with other people about the practical uses of a computer. Study and learn in a group.

2. **OBSERVE your instructor and watch other people using the computer.** Listen and ask questions. Talk, read, and write about your experiences. What is new and different? Jot down instructions, draw, sketch, and add color to your notes. Find music to illustrate ideas or use background music as you learn. Experience doing a task as your instructor or a friend helps you.

3. **REFLECT on problems critically and in sequence.** Build on information and qualify it. What works and doesn't work? Test new ways of doing things. Ask people when you get stuck. Find new ways to solve problems. Relate what you know to new information. Review instructions when you are stumped.

4. **DO it and learn by trial and error.** Jump in and try new tasks. Learning to use a computer is a great example of hands-on learning. Find new applications.

5. **TEACH it to others.** Demonstrate to someone else what you have learned. Answer questions and ask for feedback.

Then return to Stage 1 and reaffirm the benefits of learning this valuable new skill. Here's another example. Susan owns a bed and breakfast inn, which has a combination lock on the front door. Her guests need to learn how to use the lock:

1. **RELATE:** "I don't want to get locked out!" Guests have a personal interest in learning the combination, since that will be how they get in and out of the inn. It is important and relevant information.

2. **OBSERVE:** "Here's how it works." Susan shows them how to use the combination lock and talks to them as she demonstrates. They watch and gather information. Often, they repeat what she has said.

3. **REFLECT:** "Did I get it?" They integrate information and Susan offers an overview: "Don't forget to turn the knob all the way to the right."

4. **DO:** "Now I'll try it." They practice learning by doing it, and Susan offers instruction as they are doing it. "Press the 5 button four times and turn all the way to the right."

5. **TEACH:** "Let me show you." They may teach it to their spouse or practice it again while they say the combination out loud.

You can adapt the Adult Learning Cycle to fit your preference, but you will be most effective if you integrate all the learning styles and make learning physical and meaningful.

In each chapter, we will explore practical examples of the Adult Learning Cycle.

.

Overcome Obstacles

On your journey to success, more than likely you will run into stumbling blocks (or even big boulders). As mentioned before, maintain a positive attitude and make sure you are using your self-management tools.

Adjust Your Learning Style to Your Instructor's Teaching Style

Just as we all have different learning styles, your instructors will have a variety of teaching styles. Rather than being resistant, find ways to adapt by maximizing the ways you learn best and by incorporating other techniques. For example, if you prefer a highly structured lecture, focusing on facts and taking notes, you may not feel comfortable in a student-centered course where ideas and class discussion are key and you work in small groups with little structure. The following are some strategies to help you succeed in this type of course:

- Ask questions and clarify expectations.
- Be flexible and willing to try new approaches.
- Be an active participant in class and go to every class.
- Get to know other students and form study teams.
- Be interested in other points of view.
- See exercises and class discussions as learning opportunities.
- Be friendly yet respectful and visit your instructor during office hours.
- Ask your instructor what you can do to improve.
- Do any extra credit projects that are offered.
- Try looking at the whole of a concept before breaking it into parts.
- If the instructor jumps around a lot in a lecture, or digresses, ask for main points.
- Find or ask for the theme or key points of each class.
- Focus on the learning process, not just the final product.

Let's say you prefer warm relationships and a nonstructured class. You find yourself in a traditional, content-centered, straight lecture class with few visuals or class discussion. Here are a few suggestions for adapting:

- Read the syllabus and know expectations.
- Listen attentively and take detailed notes.
- Clarify the weight of each test, paper, or project.
- Make certain you know and meet each deadline.
- Anticipate the lecture and be prepared.
- Focus on the lecture and avoid talking to others during class.
- Work in a study team, discuss lecture concepts, and predict test questions.
- Ask questions and ask for examples from the instructor and study team.
- Take advantage of the logical sequence of material and take notes accordingly.
- Add color, supporting examples, and drawings to your notes.
- Connect lectures to drawings, photographs, and diagrams in the textbook.
- Ask the instructor for visuals that help illustrate the points made in class.
- Have your questions ready when talking to your instructor during office hours.
- Use analytical thinking and focus on facts and logic.
- Be precise in definitions and descriptions.

If absolutely necessary, you can drop the class and sign up for a class with an instructor who has a teaching style that is similar to your learning style. However, since in the workplace you will be interacting with colleagues and employers with a variety of personality types and learning styles, it's important for you to learn coping and adapting skills now to help you maximize your success.

Use Critical Thinking

A barrier to success is a lack of critical thinking, which keeps you from facing reality. Look honestly at all areas of your life. Use critical thinking to assess your performance and plan new ways to overcome discouragement and setbacks. For example, you may have discovered in your assessment exercises that you tend to be late for class or work. Create ways to help you become punctual, such as setting your clock 10 minutes early and getting organized the night before. Positive habits help you overcome counterproductive behavior. Do not get discouraged. Acknowledge and work on your shortcomings and focus on your successes. Realize that everyone gets off course sometimes, so don't dwell on mistakes. Focus on your strengths and positive habits to get back on track.

" I have not failed. I've just found 10,000 ways that won't work. "

THOMAS EDISON
Inventor

TAKING CHARGE

Summary

In this chapter I learned to:

- **Strive to become a peak performer.** Peak performers come from all walks of life, maximize their abilities and resources, and focus on positive results.

- **Practice self-management.** I know that I am responsible for my own success, and there are a number of self-management techniques and behaviors that I can practice that will make me successful.

- **Self-assess.** Assessing and objectively seeing myself will help me recognize my need to learn new skills, relate more effectively with others, set goals, manage time and stress, and create a balanced and productive life.

- **Use my critical thinking skills.** Critical thinking is a logical, rational, and systematic thought process I can use to think through a problem or situation to make sound choices and good decisions.

- **Visualize success.** Visualization is a self-management tool I can use to see myself being successful. I will also use affirmations (positive self-talk) to focus on what's important.

- **Reflect on information.** I will think about how experiences are related and what I can learn from them, including keeping a written (or online) journal to record my thoughts.

- **Create a personal mission statement.** Drafting a mission statement will help me determine my values and interests and focus on my long-term goals.

- **Make connections between skills for school and job success.** The Secretary's Commission on Achieving Necessary Skills (SCANS) outlines skills and competencies that are critical to success in school as well as the job market.

- **Determine my learning style.** By knowing my preferred learning style, such as visual, auditory, or kinesthetic, I know how I learn best and how to incorporate features of other learning styles in order to maximize my learning opportunities.

- **Explore various personality types.** Although personality typing has been around for centuries, Jung identified extroverts vs. introverts, sensors vs. intuitives, and thinkers vs. feelers. Myers and Briggs added judgers and perceivers and developed the Myers-Briggs Type Indicator.

- **Integrate learning styles and personality types.** Once I understand my learning style(s) and personality type(s), I can incorporate features of other styles to maximize my learning. Although I tend to be either left-brain dominant (linguistic) or right-brain dominant (visual), the goal is to use all my brain power to learn new skills and information.

- **Apply the Adult Learning Cycle.** This five-step process (relate, observe, reflect, do, and teach) demonstrates that learning comes from repetition, practice, and recall.

- **Adjust to my instructor's teaching style.** If my learning style is different from my instructor's teaching style, I will try new strategies that will maximize my learning in that class.

Performance Strategies

Following are the top 10 strategies for becoming a life-long learner.

- Strive to become a peak performer in all aspects of your life.
- Practice self-management to create the results you want.
- Use critical thinking and honesty in self-assessment.
- Practice visualization and state affirmations that focus on positive outcomes.
- Create a personal mission statement.
- Make the connection between school and job success.
- Discover your learning and personality styles.
- Integrate all learning styles.
- Apply the Adult Learning Cycle to maximize your learning.
- Focus on strengths and successes.

Tech for Success

Take advantage of the text's Web site at **www.mhhe.com/ferrett7e** for additional study aids, useful forms, and convenient and applicable resources.

- **Electronic journal.** Sometimes critical thinking is easier when you write down your responses. Keeping an electronic reflection and self-assessment journal allows for easy updating and gathering of information, which can be pulled into your career portfolio later.

- **Mission statement business cards.** To keep yourself motivated and focused, print your mission statement on business cards, carry them with you, and share them with family and friends. Consider chipping in with another student or your study group and buying prescored printer paper, or simply print on a heavier paper stock and cut the cards apart.

- **Online self-assessments.** A number of online assessments can help you determine the best careers to fit your personality. Talk with your instructor, as your school may already have some available in your career center, such as the Learning and Study Strategies Inventory (LASSI).

Study Team Notes

Career *in* focus

Louis Parker
ACCOUNTANT AND FINANCIAL PLANNER

Related Majors: Accounting, Business Administration, Economics, Finance

Setting Business Goals

Louis Parker is a certified public accountant (CPA) and financial planner. In 1994, he started his own business, Parker Inc., by offering accounting services. Louis prepares taxes, financial reports, and payroll, and he does bookkeeping for individuals and small businesses. He employs three full-time and one part-time assistant but needs five full-time workers to help during peak tax season (January–April).

To get feedback on his services, Louis occasionally does a survey of his clients. The survey shows whether his clients are getting the services they want at prices they believe are reasonable. Louis uses the results of the survey to set goals and plan for the future.

Another of Louis's goals is to continually increase business, as Louis believes that, without marketing and growth, his business will decline. Louis has used telemarketing services to help him set up appointments with prospective clients.

A few years ago, Louis decided to add financial planning because his clients were continually asking for his advice in financial areas. Financial planners help clients attain financial goals, such as retirement or a college education for their children. Louis was able to get certified in financial planning. Because he is affiliated with a financial services organization, he sometimes helps clients invest in the stock market, mainly in mutual funds. Currently, financial planning is only 10 percent of his business, but Louis's goal is to eventually increase that amount to 30 percent.

CRITICAL THINKING How might a survey of his clients help Louis assess his personal strengths and weaknesses? What strategies should he put in place to follow up on client feedback? How can he incorporate the feedback into his long-term goals?

Peak Performer

PROFILE

Christy Haubegger

At first glance, the glossy magazine looks like many others on the newsstands. The front cover offers a snapshot of the current issue: a profile of a famous celebrity, beauty and fashion tips, and a self-help article to improve the inner being. The big, bold letters across the top, however, spell the difference. This is *Latina*, the first bilingual magazine targeted at Hispanic-American women and the inspiration of founder Christy Haubegger. More than 2 million bilingual, bicultural women are avid readers of this popular magazine.

Born in Houston, Texas, in 1968, Haubegger has described herself as a "chubby Mexican-American baby adopted by parents who were tall, thin, and blond." As a teenager during the mega-media 1980s, she was especially sensitive to the lack of Hispanic role models in women's magazines. It was a void waiting to be filled. At the age of 20, Haubegger received a bachelor's degree in philosophy from the University of Texas. At 23, she earned her law degree from Stanford, where she joined the editorial staff of the *Law Review,* rising to the position of senior editor: "My experience as senior editor gave me a start in the worlds of journalism and publishing."

Haubegger also took a course in marketing. In that class, she had to write a business plan for a favorite

enterprise. *Latina* magazine was born. As one of the best-known publications for Hispanic-American women, *Latina* covers issues such as health, politics, family, and finance, as well as beauty and entertainment. *Latina* provides Hispanic women a voice and reminds them that they are part of the American Dream.

PERFORMANCE THINKING If you were assessing the characteristics that make Christy Haubegger a successful entrepreneur, which would you say are the most important?

CHECK IT OUT Go to **www.latina.com** to see the numerous online features the magazine offers of interest to the U.S. Latin community.

Starting Today

At least one strategy I learned in this chapter that I plan to try right away is:

_____

_____

_____

What changes must I make in order for this strategy to be effective?

_____

_____

_____

Review Questions

Based on what you have learned in this chapter, write your answers to the following questions:

1. What is a peak performer? List at least three potential characteristics.

_____

_____

2. Define visualization and how and when you can practice this self-management tool.

_____

_____

3. Explain the differences among the three types of learners (visual, auditory, kinesthetic).

_____

_____

4. Why is it important to know your learning style and personality type?

_____

_____

5. How does critical thinking help you overcome barriers to self-assessment?

_____

_____

Making a Commitment

In the Classroom

Eric Silver is a freshman in college. He doesn't know what major to choose and isn't even sure if he wants to continue going to college. His parents are urging him to pursue his college career, but Eric wants to go to work instead. In high school, he never settled on a favorite subject, though he did briefly consider becoming a private investigator after reading a detective novel. His peers seem more committed to college and have better study habits. Eric prefers a hands-on approach to learning, and he finds it difficult to concentrate while studying or listening to a lecture. However, he enjoys the outdoors and is creative. Once he gets involved in a project he finds interesting, he is very committed.

1. What strategies from this chapter would be most useful to help Eric understand himself better and gain a sense of commitment?

   _____

   _____

2. What would you suggest to Eric to help him find direction?

   _____

   _____

In the Workplace

Eric has taken a job as a law enforcement officer. He feels more comfortable in this job than he did in school, since he knows he performs best when actively learning. He enjoys teamwork and the exchange of ideas with his co-workers. Eric also realizes that, in order to advance in his work, he needs to continue his education. He is concerned about balancing his work, school, and family life. He does admit that he did not excel in subjects he was less interested in. Eric never learned effective study habits but realizes that he must be disciplined when returning to college.

3. What suggestions would you give Eric to help him do better in school?

   _____

   _____

4. Under what category of learning style does Eric fall and what are the ineffective traits of this style that he needs to work on most?

   _____

   _____

Applying the ABC Method of Self-Management

In the Journal Entry on page 1 of this chapter, you were asked to think about what you are hoping to gain from your college experience. How does earning a college degree help you both personally and professionally? Essentially, "Why are you here?" On the lines provided, indicate your answers to those questions.

_____

_____

_____

Now think about the obstacles you may have faced to get to this point and what you did to overcome them. State at least one of those obstacles:

_____

_____

_____

Now apply the ABC method to one of the obstacles.

A = Actual event:

B = Beliefs:

C = Challenge:

Did you use this or a similar thought process when you first encountered the obstacle? Was the obstacle not really as big as it first seemed?

PRACTICE SELF-MANAGEMENT

For more examples of learning how to manage difficult situations, see the "Self-Management Workbook" section of the Online Learning Center Web site at **www.mhhe.com/ferrett7e.**

Assessing and Applying Learning Styles, Personality Types, and Temperaments

LEARNING STYLES

I am a(n) (circle one):

Visual learner

Auditory learner

Kinesthetic learner

The following learning habits make me most like this learning style:

What features of the two other learning styles should I incorporate to make me a well-rounded learner?

PERSONALITY TYPES

I am a(n) (circle one for each):

Extrovert or introvert

Sensor or intuitive

Thinker or feeler

The following characteristics make me most like these personality types:

How can I incorporate positive features of the opposite personality types?

TEMPERAMENTS

I am a(n) (circle one):

Analyzer

Supporter

Creator

Director

The following characteristics make me most like this temperament:

What positive behaviors/traits can I incorporate from the other three temperaments?

(continued)

CREATING THE IDEAL TEAM

In school and at work, you will often be a member of a project team. In most cases, you do not have the opportunity to select your team members but, instead, need to learn how to maximize each other's strengths.

Let's pretend, however, that you have the opportunity to select a four-person team to tackle an assignment. Now that you know your preferences, indicate the characteristics of three potential teammates who would be complementary. Indicate why you think each person would be an asset to the team.

PERSON #1

Learning style:

Personality type:

Temperament:

What this person will add to the team:

PERSON #2

Learning style:

Personality type:

Temperament:

What this person will add to the team:

PERSON #3

Learning style:

Personality type:

Temperament:

What this person will add to the team:

AND ME

What I add to the team:

Applying the Four-Temperament Profile

You've explored your temperament and discovered your preferred learning style and personality type. Apply this knowledge by associating with people who have various styles and find ways to relate to and work more effectively with different people.

For example, let's say that you are assigned to a five-person team that will present a serious public health issue to your personal health class. You are a supporter type, and you find yourself having a conflict with Joe, a director type. You are in your first meeting, and Joe is ready to choose a topic for the group project, even though one team member is absent.

Apply the ABC Method of Self-Management to focus your energies on building rapport and understanding:

A = Actual event: "Joe wants to choose a topic for the group project, even though one person isn't here to voice her opinion."

B = Beliefs: "I think that we are not taking the time to be sensitive to the needs of all the team members. Everyone should be present before we make a decision. Joe is trying to take control of the group and is just impatient. I'm worried that the absent group member will not like the decision or may even be hurt that she wasn't involved. I resent being rushed and I'm afraid that conflict will result. Maybe this person will even quit the group."

C = Challenge: "What is the worst thing that could happen if we choose a topic today? We can always refocus later if we find this topic doesn't fit our goals. Chances are the absent member would agree with the topic in question, anyhow. Joe is probably not impatient—he just wants to make a decision and get us moving. I'm glad our group is made up of different strengths and personalities. I'm psyched that our team members have complementary strengths and can respect and work well with each other. I know that Joe will keep us moving forward and that he will be sensitive to my concerns that we listen to each other and respect each other's feelings."

Are you experiencing a similar situation or conflict in your school, work, or personal life? If so, use the ABC method to visualize a positive solution:

A = Actual event:

B = Beliefs:

C = Challenge:

Autobiography

The purpose of this exercise is to look back and assess how you learned skills and competencies. Write down the turning points, major events, and significant experiences of your life. This autobiography, or chronological record, will note events that helped you make decisions, set goals, or discover something about yourself. Record both negative and positive experiences and what you learned from them. Add this page to your Career Development Portfolio—for example,

Year/Event	Learned Experience
1997 Moved to Michigan.	Learned to make new friends and be flexible.
1998 First job baby-sitting.	Learned responsibility and critical thinking.
1999 Grandmother became ill.	Helped with care. Learned dependability, compassion.

Year/Event	Learned Experience

2

Expand Your Emotional Intelligence

LEARNING OBJECTIVES

In this chapter, you will learn to

2.1 Describe emotional intelligence and the key personal qualities

2.2 Explain the importance of good character, including integrity, civility, and ethics

2.3 Display responsibility, self-management, and self-control

2.4 Develop self-esteem and confidence

2.5 Incorporate a positive attitude and motivation

2.6 Use goal setting as a motivational tool

2.7 List the benefits of a higher education

2.8 Overcome the obstacles to staying positive and motivated

SELF-MANAGEMENT

On my commute to class, a car cut me off. I was furious and yelled at the driver. I was fuming and distracted during classes, and later I blew up at a co-worker. This just ruined my entire day. How can I handle my angry feelings in a more constructive way?

Have you ever had a similar experience? Are you easily offended by what others do or say? Have you said things in anger that have caused a rift in a relationship? In this chapter, you will learn how to control your emotions and create a positive and resourceful state of mind.

JOURNAL ENTRY In **Worksheet 2.1** on page 76, describe a time when you were angry and lost control of your emotions. How did you feel? How did others react to your outburst? What would you do differently? Visualize yourself calm and in control and realize that you have a choice in how you interpret events.

THERE IS A TENDENCY TO DEFINE INTELLIGENCE AS A SCORE ON AN IQ TEST OR THE SAT OR AS SCHOOL GRADES. Educators have tried to predict who will succeed in college and have found that high school grades, achievement test scores, and ability are only part of the picture. Emotional intelligence and maturity have more effect on school and job success than traditional scholastic measures. In fact, research has indicated that persistence and perseverance are major predictors of college success. A landmark study by the American College Test (ACT) indicated that the primary reasons for first-year students' dropping out of college were not academic but, rather, were emotional difficulties, such as feelings of inadequacy, depression, loneliness, and a lack of motivation or purpose.

Employers also list a positive attitude, motivation, honesty, the ability to get along with others, and the willingness to learn as more important to job success than a college degree or specific skills. In Chapter 1, you learned that SCANS identifies many personal qualities as important competencies for success in the workplace. These qualities and competencies are also essential for building and maintaining strong, healthy relationships throughout life. Essential personal qualities should be viewed as a foundation on which to build skills, experience, and knowledge.

In this chapter, you will learn the importance of emotional intelligence and why character is so important for school and job success. You will also develop personal strategies for maintaining a positive attitude and becoming self-motivated. You may realize that you are smarter than you think. You are smarter than your test scores or grades. Success in your personal life, school, and career is more dependent on a positive attitude, motivation, responsibility, self-control, and effort than on inborn abilities or a high IQ. Peak performers use the whole of their intelligence—and so can you.

Emotional Intelligence and Maturity

Emotional intelligence is the ability to understand and manage yourself and relate effectively to others. **Maturity** is the ability to control your impulses, to think beyond the moment, and to consider how your words and actions affect yourself and others before you act. Emotional intelligence has become a popular topic as we learn more about the importance of personal qualities, communication, the management of feelings, and social competence. Researchers have demonstrated that people who have developed a set of traits that adds to their maturity level increase their sense of well-being, help them get along with others, and enhance their school, job, and life success.

The ability to regulate emotions is vital for school and job success. Emotional maturity contributes to competent behavior, problem-solving ability, socially appropriate behavior, and good communication. Being unaware of or unable to control emotions often accompanies restlessness, a short attention span, negativism, impulsiveness, and distractibility. Clearly, having emotional intelligence distinguishes peak performers from mediocre ones. Becoming more emotionally mature involves three stages:

1. Self-awareness—tuning in to yourself
2. Empathy—tuning in to others
3. Change—tuning in to results

In Chapter 1, you explored many strategies to help you increase your self-awareness and tune in to yourself. You had an opportunity to assess many skills and personal qualities in the Peak Performance Self-Assessment Test on page 11. By learning personality types, you also began to tune in to others as well. The central theme of this book is that you can use this information to begin changing your thoughts, images, and behaviors to produce the results you want in every aspect of your life. Enhancing your emotional intelligence and focusing on positive personal qualities are key to achieving those successful results.

Character First: Integrity, Civility, and Ethics

Good **character** is an essential personal quality for true success in school, work, and life. A person of good character has a core set of principles that most of us accept as constant and relatively noncontroversial. These principles include fairness, honesty, respect, responsibility, caring, trustworthiness, and citizenship. Recent surveys of business leaders indicate that dishonesty, lying, and lack of respect are top reasons for on-the-job difficulties. If an employer believes that an employee lacks integrity, all of that person's positive qualities—from skill and experience to productivity and intelligence—are meaningless. Employers usually list honesty or good character as an essential personal quality, followed by the ability to relate to and get along with others. A number of books have been written by successful top executives who claim that good character, honesty, and a strong value system are what make you an effective leader. All the corporate scandals seen in the news lately are testimonials that business leaders with poor values will eventually meet their demise.

Following The Golden Rule (treating others as we want to be treated) is a simple way to weave integrity and civility into our everyday lives. The word *integrity* comes from the Latin word *integre,* meaning "wholeness." Integrity is the integration of your principles and actions. In a sense, people who have integrity "walk the talk." They consistently live up to their highest principles. Integrity is not adherence to a rigid code but, rather, an ongoing commitment to being consistent, caring, and true to doing what is right. Not only is integrity understanding what is right, but it is also the courage to do it even when it is difficult.

Civility is a set of tools for interacting with others with respect, kindness, and good manners, or etiquette. However, civility is more than good manners and politeness. It includes the many sacrifices we make each day in order to live together peacefully. **Empathy**—understanding and compassion for others—is essential for integrity and civility. You can practice civility in your classes by being on time, turning off your cell phone, staying for the entire class, and listening to the instructor and other students when they speak.

> 66 Character is like a tree and reputation like its shadow. The shadow is what we think of it; the tree is the real thing. 99
>
> ABRAHAM LINCOLN
> *U.S. president*

WORDS TO SUCCEED

Ethics are the principles of conduct that govern a group or society. Since a company's reputation is its most important asset, most organizations have a written code of ethics that deals with how people are expected to behave and treat others. It is your responsibility to know and understand the code of ethics at your place of employment and at school. Look in your school's catalog for statements regarding academic integrity, honesty, cheating, and plagiarism. **Cheating** is using or providing unauthorized help in test taking or on projects. **Plagiarism** is considered a form of cheating, since it is presenting someone else's ideas as if they were your own. Know the consequences of your behavior, which could result in an *F* grade, suspension, expulsion, or firing from a job. You always have the choice of telling the truth, being prepared, talking with the instructor, and being responsible for your own work.

Every day, you run into situations that test your character. **Personal Evaluation Notebook 2.1** includes a number of questions and situations to get you thinking critically about your experiences. While completing this exercise, consider the personal qualities that make you smarter than you think you are, such as positive attitude, motivation, dependability, and honesty—for example, "I was raised on a farm in Michigan. What personal quality makes me smarter than my IQ or test scores?" If you answer "hard work," you're right. That one personal quality—putting in extra effort—has helped many people be more successful in life.

Personal qualities, especially honesty, are very important to consider when you think of hiring someone to work for a business you own. Let's say that a candidate sends in an outstanding resume. She has a college degree, experience, and a great personality, and she is positive and motivated, but you find out that she stole from her last employer. No matter how bright or talented someone is, you may realize you cannot have a dishonest person working for you. Complete **Personal Evaluation Notebook 2.2** on page 50 to see what qualities you would look for in a potential employee and which of those qualities you possess.

There is no universal code of ethics, and many questions about ethical issues do not have clear-cut answers. For example, taking money out of a cash drawer is clearly dishonest, but what about coming in late to work, padding your expense account, or using someone else's words without giving credit?

You will be faced with situations in your personal, school, and business lives that will force you to make decisions that will be viewed as either ethical or unethical. Sometimes it is not easy. At one time or another, everyone is faced with situations that demand tough decisions. Consider the following situations.

Peggy Lyons has a midterm test to take. This test will determine 50 percent of her final grade. She has been very busy at home and has not attended class or her study group for the past week. She knows she probably won't do well on the test, but she needs a good grade. She knows the instructor is fair and has been asking about her. Someone Peggy met in the cafeteria tells her she can buy a copy of the test. She's tempted. What do you think she will do? What would you do?

While in college, Rey Armas has been working part-time at an electronics store. Rey's supervisor, Joe, has worked in the store for 10 years. Joe is 50 and has a family. This is his only means of support. Rey has discovered that Joe is stealing some of the electronics components to sell on the side. Rey likes Joe. What should Rey do? What would you do?

Tora Veda is up late, working on a term paper. She debates whether she should take the time to cite references. Her instructor warns the class about plagiarism, but,

Personal Evaluation Notebook 2.1

Character and Ethics

Integrity and honesty are essential qualities. It is important for you to assess and develop them as you would any skill. Use critical thinking to answer these questions.

1. What is the most difficult ethical dilemma you have faced in your life?

   _____

2. Do you have a code of ethics that helps guide you when making decisions? Explain.

   _____

3. When did you learn about honesty?

   _____

4. Who have you known that is a role model for displaying integrity and honesty?

   _____

5. Do you have a code of ethics at your college? Where did you find it? (Hint: Check your school's catalog or ask the dean of students for a copy.)

   _____

6. Does your company have a code of ethics? How do employees access it?

   _____

7. If you were the chief executive officer (CEO) or owner of a small company, what would you want to include in your code of ethics?

   _____

8. How would you make certain that employees understood and honored your company's code of ethics?

   _____

because some of her information came off the Internet, she doesn't think it should be a big deal. What should she do? What would you do?

Peggy, Rey, and Tora are all faced with tough decisions. Their final decisions will be viewed by others as either ethical or unethical and carry consequences, such as being fired, getting an *F* in the course, or even being suspended or expelled from school. They will have to call on their own personal code of ethics. When defining their code and their subsequent actions, they may find the following questions helpful. You, too, may find them helpful when developing a code of ethics.

- Is this action against the law?
- Is this action against company policy or code of behavior?

Personal Evaluation Notebook 2.2

Skills and Personal Qualities

1. Jot down the skills, personal qualities, and habits you are learning and demonstrating in each of your classes.

Skills	Personal Qualities	Habits
_____	_____	_____
_____	_____	_____
_____	_____	_____

2. Pretend that you own your own business. List the skills and personal qualities you would want in the employees you hire.

Type of business: _____

Employees' Skills	Employees' Personal Qualities
_____	_____
_____	_____
_____	_____

- How would this situation read if reported on the front page of the newspaper?
- How would you explain this to your mother? To your child?
- What might be the negative consequences?
- Are you causing unnecessary harm to someone?
- If unsure, have you asked a trusted associate outside of the situation?
- Are you treating others as you would want to be treated?

Remember, unethical behavior rarely goes unnoticed!

Responsibility

Peak performers take responsibility for their thoughts, state of mind, and behavior. They don't blame others for their problems but, rather, use their energy to solve them. They are persistent and patient. They know they must exert a consistent amount of high effort to achieve their goals. They keep their word and agreements. When they say they are going to do something, they keep their commitment. People can depend on them.

Examples of being responsible include showing up prepared and on time for work, meetings, study teams, and so on; paying bills and repaying loans on time; and cleaning up personal messes at home and elsewhere. Responsible people own up to

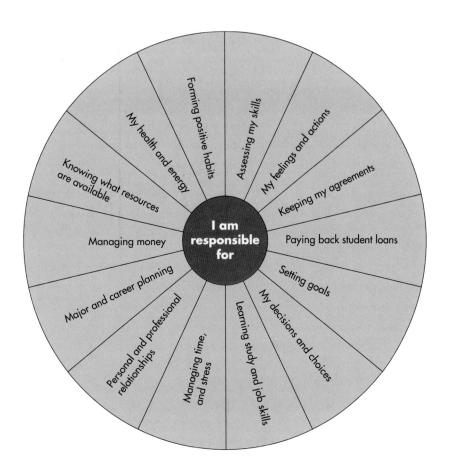

Figure 2.1

Personal Responsibilities

What you do or don't do in one area of life can affect other areas of your life and other people. *What one area of personal responsibility would you improve?*

Figure contents:

I am responsible for

- Assessing my skills
- My feelings and actions
- Keeping my agreements
- Paying back student loans
- Setting goals
- My decisions and choices
- Learning study and job skills
- Managing time, and stress
- Personal and professional relationships
- Major and career planning
- Managing money
- Knowing what resources are available
- My health and energy
- Forming positive habits

their mistakes and do what they can to correct them. The model in **Figure 2.1** illustrates many important interrelated personal responsibilities.

Other personal qualities related to responsibility include perseverance, punctuality, concentration, attention to details, follow-through, and high standards. What you do or don't do in one area of your life affects other areas of your life and other people.

Peak performers realize they are responsible for their attitudes and actions, and they know they have the power to change them. A negative attitude is sometimes the result of not coping effectively with change, conflict, and frustration. Emotional, physical, and social changes are part of the growing process at any age. Learning to adjust to frustration and discouragement can take many forms. Some people withdraw or become critical, cynical, shy, sarcastic, or unmotivated. Blame, excuses, justification, and criticism of others are devices for those who cannot accept personal responsibility for their behavior and state of mind. Acknowledge your feelings and attitudes. Decide if they support your goals; if they do not, choose a state of mind and actions that support you.

Being responsible creates a sense of integrity and a feeling of self-worth. For example, if you owe money to a friend, family member, or bank, take responsibility for repaying the loan. If you have a student loan, repay it on schedule or make new arrangements with the lender. Not repaying can result in years of guilt and embarrassment, as well as a poor credit rating. It is important to your self-worth to know you are a person who keeps commitments and assumes responsibility.

Self-Control

66 Holding on to anger is like grasping a hot coal with the intent of throwing it at someone else; you are the one who gets burned. 99

BUDDHA

If anger were a disease, there would be an epidemic in this country. Road rage, spousal and child abuse, and a lack of civility are just a few examples of anger. Emotionally mature people know how to control their thoughts and behaviors and how to resolve conflict. Conflict is an inevitable part of school and work, but it can be resolved in a positive way. Following are tips for trying to redirect and transform your anger:

1. **Calm down.** Step back from the situation and take a deep breath. Take the drama out of the situation and observe what is happening, what behavior is triggering angry emotions, and what options you have in responding in appropriate and positive ways. If you lash out without thinking and attack verbally, you may cause serious harm to your relationship. You cannot take back words once they are spoken. Resist the urge to overreact.

2. **Clarify and define.** Determine exactly with whom or what you are angry and why. What specific behavior in the other person is causing you to feel angry or frustrated? Determine whose problem it is. For example, your instructor may have an annoying tone and style of lecturing. If a behavior annoys only you, perhaps it is something you alone need to address.

3. **Listen with empathy and respect.** Empathy includes the ability to listen, understand, and respond to the feelings and needs of others. Take the tension out of the conflict by really listening and understanding the other person's point of view. Communicate that you have heard and understood by restating the other person's position. Respect yourself as well. Ask yourself how you feel. Are you tired, hot, hungry, frustrated, rushed, or ill? If so, you may not want to deal with your anger until you feel better. Sometimes getting a good night's sleep or having a good meal will put the situation into perspective, and your anger will dissolve.

4. **Use "I" statements.** Take ownership of your feelings. Using "I" statements— direct messages you deliver in a calm tone with supportive body language— can diffuse anger. You are not blaming another person but, rather, expressing how a situation affects you. For example, you can say, "Carlos, when I hear you clicking your pen and tapping it on the desk, I'm distracted from studying." This is usually received better than saying, "Carlos, you're so rude and inconsiderate. You must know that you're annoying me when you tap your pen."

5. **Focus on one problem.** Don't pounce on every annoying behavior you can think of to dump on the person. Let's continue with the example in Tip 4: "In addition to clicking your pen, Carlos, I don't like how you leave your dishes in the sink, drop your towels in the bathroom, and make that annoying little sound when you eat." Work to resolve only one behavior or conflict at a time.

6. **Focus on win-win solutions.** How can you both win? Restate the problem and jot down as many different creative solutions as possible that you can both agree on.

7. **Reward positive behavior.** As you use praise and reinforce positive behaviors, you will find that the person will exert less resistance. You can now be more direct about the specific behaviors and ask for a commitment: "Julie, if you could be here right at 8:00, we could get through this study session in 2 hours.

Can we agree on this?" Focus on behavior, not personality or name calling, which just angers you and antagonizes the other person. Don't let anger and conflict create more stress in your life and take a physical and emotional toll. You can learn to step back automatically from explosive situations and control them, rather than let your emotions control you. **Peak Progress 2.1** explores how you can use the Adult Learning Cycle to manage your emotions.

Self-Esteem and Confidence

Self-esteem is how you feel about yourself. Peak performers have developed self-respect and confidence and believe in themselves. They assess themselves honestly and focus on their strengths. They constantly learn new skills and competencies that build their confidence. They accept responsibility for their attitudes and behavior. They know that blame and anger do not solve problems.

Peak Progress 2.1

Applying the Adult Learning Cycle to Self-Control

The Adult Learning Cycle can help you increase your emotional intelligence. For example, you may have felt the same angry and frustrated feelings mentioned in the Self-Management exercise on the first page of this chapter. It could be because someone cut you off or you've lost your keys, you may have three papers due, or you are so overwhelmed with school, work, and family that your motivation dropped and you developed a negative attitude.

1. **RELATE. Why do I want to learn this?** What personal meaning and interest does controlling my anger have for me? Has it been a challenge for me? Has it hurt important relationships in my personal life or at school or work? How will controlling my anger help me in those situations?

2. **OBSERVE. How does this work?** I can learn a lot about anger management by watching, listening, and engaging in trial and error. Whom do I consider to be an emotionally mature person? Whom do I respect because of his or her patience, understanding, and ability to deal with stressful events? When I observe the problems that people around me have in their lives, how do they exhibit their emotional maturity in general and anger specifically?

3. **REFLECT. What does this mean?** Test new ways of behaving and break old patterns. Explore creative ways to solve problems rather than getting angry. Gather and assess information about anger management and reflect on what works and doesn't work.

4. **DO. What can I do with this?** Learn by doing and finding practical applications for anger management. Practice the seven steps outlined on pages 52–53. Apply the ABC Method of Self-Management to specific situations to determine positive outcomes.

5. **TEACH. Whom can I share this with?** Talk with others and share experiences. Demonstrate to and teach others the methods you've learned. Model by example.

Now return to Stage 1 and realize your accomplishment in taking steps to control your anger better.

People with a positive self-esteem have the confidence that allows them to be more open to new experiences and accepting of different people. They tend to be more optimistic. They are more willing to share their feelings and ideas with others and are willing to tolerate differences in others. Because they have a sense of self-worth, they do not find it necessary to put down or discriminate against others.

Confidence can develop from

- Focusing on your strengths and positive qualities and finding ways to bolster them. Be yourself and don't compare yourself with others.
- Learning to be resilient and bouncing back after disappointments and setbacks. Don't dwell on mistakes or limitations. Accept them, learn from them, and move on with your life.
- Using affirmations and visualizations to replace negative thoughts and images.
- Taking responsibility for your life instead of blaming others. You cannot control other people's behavior, but you have complete control over your own thoughts, emotions, words, and behavior.
- Learning skills and competencies that give you opportunities and confidence in your abilities. It is not enough to feel good about yourself; you must also be able to do what is required to demonstrate that you are a competent, honest, and responsible person. The more skills and personal qualities you acquire, the more competent and confident you will feel.
- Focusing on giving, not receiving, and make others feel valued and appreciated. You will increase your self-esteem when you make a contribution.
- Creating a support system by surrounding yourself with confident and kind people who feel good about themselves and who make you feel good about yourself.

If you want to change your outer world and experiences for the better, you must begin by looking at your thoughts, feelings, and beliefs about yourself. Assess your self-esteem at the end of the chapter in **Worksheet 2.3** on page 78.

A Positive Attitude and Personal Motivation

There is an old story about three men working on a project in a large city in France. A curious tourist asks them, "What are you three working on?" The first man says, "I'm hauling rocks." The second man says, "I'm laying a wall." The third man says with pride, "I'm building a cathedral." The third man has a sense of vision of the whole system. When college and work seem as tedious as hauling rocks, focus on the big picture.

A positive attitude is essential for achieving success in school, in your career, and in life. Your attitude, more than any other factor, influences the outcome of a task. **Motivation** is the inner drive that moves you to action. Even when you are discouraged or face setbacks, motivation can help you bounce back and keep on track. You may have skills, experience, intelligence, and talent, but you will accomplish little if you are not motivated to direct your energies toward specific goals.

A positive attitude results in enthusiasm, vitality, optimism, and a zest for living. When you have a positive attitude, you are more likely to be on time, alert in meetings and class, and able to work well even when you have an unpleasant assignment. A positive attitude encourages

- Higher productivity
- An openness to learning at school and on the job
- School and job satisfaction
- Creativity in solving problems and finding solutions
- The ability to work with diverse groups of people
- Enthusiasm and a "can do" outlook
- Confidence and higher self-esteem
- The ability to channel stress and increase energy
- A sense of purpose and direction

A negative attitude can drain you of enthusiasm and energy, and it can result in absenteeism, tardiness, and impaired mental and physical health. In addition, people who have a negative attitude may

- Feel that they are victims and are helpless to make a change
- Focus on the worst that can happen in a situation
- Blame external circumstances for their attitudes
- Focus on the negative in people and situations
- Look at adversity as something that will last forever
- Be angry and blame other people

As discussed in Chapter 1, peak performers display a positive attitude even when faced with adversity. **Peak Progress 2.2** on page 56 explores the seven positive attitudes of peak performers, explaining that having a positive attitude is more than simply seeing the glass as half full—it's a way of life.

How Needs and Desires Influence Attitudes and Motivation

One of the deepest needs in life is to become all that you can be by using all of your intelligence and potential. Abraham Maslow, a well-known psychologist, developed the theory of a hierarchy of needs. According to his theory, there are five levels of universal needs. **Figure 2.2** on the next page illustrates these levels, moving from the lower-order needs—physiological and safety and security needs—to the higher-order needs—the needs for self-esteem and self-actualization. The lower-order needs must be met first before satisfying the higher-order needs. For example, it may be difficult for you to participate in hobbies that foster your self-respect if you don't have enough money for food and rent. For some people, the lower-order needs include a sense of order, power, or independence. The higher levels, which address social and self-esteem factors, include the need for companionship, respect, and a sense of belonging.

As your lower-order needs are satisfied and cease to motivate you, you begin to direct your attention to the higher-order needs for motivation. As you go up the

Peak Progress

Seven Positive Attitudes of Peak Performers

1. A *flexible attitude* means that you are open to new ideas and situations. You are willing to learn new skills and are interested in continual growth.

2. A *mindful attitude* means that you are focused on lasting values. You are mindful of living in the moment, being a person of integrity and character, and acting with kindness and civility. Being is more important than acquiring or doing.

3. A *responsible attitude* means that you take an active role in school and work. You take responsibility for your life and don't rely on others to motivate you. You are a self-starter who takes the initiative to produce positive results.

4. A *supportive attitude* means that you encourage, listen to, show empathy for, and work well with others. You look for the best and are more concerned about understanding than persuading others. You look for win-win solutions and communicate clearly, concisely, and directly.

5. A *confident attitude* means that you have a balanced perspective about your strengths and limitations. You commit time and effort to grow and to renew yourself physically, mentally, emotionally, and spiritually. You are confident because you use the whole of your intelligence and you are self-disciplined.

6. A *follow-through attitude* means that you are aware of the big picture but are also attentive to details and follow through on essential steps. You see whole systems while attending to essential parts.

7. A *resourceful attitude* means that you are aware of all the resources available and use them to be more successful. You surround yourself with people who complement you and serve as models for becoming the best person you can be. Resourceful people ask for help and learn from others.

Figure 2.2
Maslow's Hierarchy of Needs

Maslow's theory states that most people need to satisfy the universal basic needs before considering the higher-order needs. *Which level of needs is motivating you right now?*

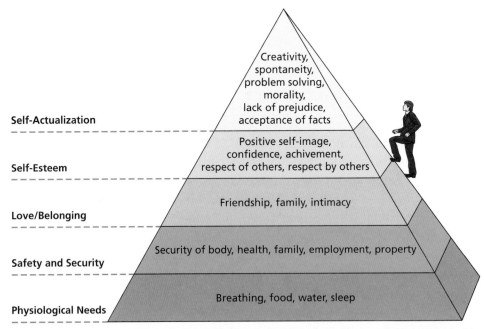

Source: "Hierarchy of Needs" from *Motivation and Personality,* 3rd ed., by Abraham H. Maslow. Revised by Robert Frager, James Fadiman, Cynthia McReynolds, and Ruth Cox. Copyright 1954, © 1987 by Harper & Row, Publishers, Inc. Copyright © 1970 by Abraham H. Maslow. Reprinted by permission of HarperCollins, Inc.

Personal Evaluation Notebook 2.3

Needs, Motivation, and Commitment

1. What needs motivate you at this time?

   _____

   _____

2. What do you think will motivate you in 20 years?

   _____

   _____

3. Complete this sentence in your own words: "For me to be more motivated, I need . . ."

   _____

   _____

4. Describe a time in your life when you were committed to something—such as a goal, a project, an event, or a relationship—that was important to you.

   _____

   _____

5. Regarding your answer to Question 4, what were the main factors that kept you motivated?

   _____

   _____

ladder of higher-order needs, you'll find that you're learning for the joy of new ideas and the confidence that comes from learning new skills and competencies. You have more energy and focus for defining and pursuing your dreams and goals. You want to discover and develop your full potential. You not only love learning new ideas but also value emotional maturity, character, and integrity. You are well on the path to self-actualization. According to Maslow, self-actualizing people embrace the realities of the world rather than deny or avoid them. They are creative problem solvers who make the most of their unique abilities to strive to be the best they can be. Complete **Personal Evaluation Notebook 2.3** to assess what motivates you.

The Motivation Cycle

The motivation cycle in **Figure 2.3** on page 58 amplifies what you learned in Chapter 1 about the power of visualization. It illustrates how your self-esteem influences what you say to yourself, which in turn influences your physical reactions—breathing,

Figure 2.3
The Motivation Cycle

Your emotions, body, and mind respond to what you say to yourself. *What positive message can you send to yourself?*

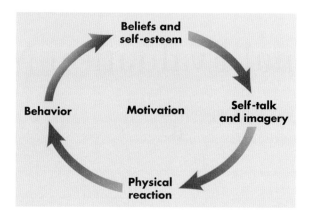

muscular tension, and posture. These physical reactions influence your behavior—both your verbal and your nonverbal responses. Isn't it amazing how the emotions, body, and mind are interrelated? You cannot change one part without changing the whole system. Try to remember how important affirmations and visualization are for creating a resourceful state of mind.

Motivational Strategies

Keeping yourself motivated isn't always easy with all the pressures you may be feeling from school, work, family, and so on. However, there are some key motivational strategies you can put into action:

1. **Act as if you were motivated.** Attitude can influence behavior, and behavior can influence attitude. The way you act every day can affect your self-esteem, and your self-esteem can affect the things you do. You can attempt to change your behavior anytime. You don't need to wait until your attitude changes or until you feel motivated to begin the positive behaviors. Act as if you were already motivated.

   For example, pretend you are performing in a movie. Your character is a positive, motivated student. How do you enter the room? Are you smiling? What are your breathing, posture, and muscle tension like? What kinds of gestures and facial expressions do you use to create this character? What kinds of friends does this person enjoy being with? Try acting out the part when you wake up in the morning and throughout the day. If you develop positive study and work habits and do them consistently, even when you don't feel like it, you'll be successful, and this will create a positive state of mind. You are what you do consistently. Positive habits create success.

2. **Use affirmations.** Any discussion of motivation must include your self-talk, what you say to yourself throughout the day. Once you start paying attention to your self-talk, you may be amazed at how much of it is negative. Throughout the day, countless thoughts, images, and phrases go through your brain almost unnoticed, but they have a tremendous influence on your mood and attitude. The first step, then, is to replace negative self-talk with affirmations or positive self-talk. For example, don't say, "I won't waste my time today." That just reminds you that you have a habit of wasting time. Instead, affirm, "I am setting goals and priorities and achieving the results I want. I have plenty of

Personal Evaluation Notebook 2.4

Self-Talk and Affirmations

Listen to your self-talk for a few days. Jot down the negative thoughts you say to yourself. For example, when you first wake up, do you say, "I don't want to go to class today"?

Do your thoughts and self-talk focus on lack of time, lack of money, or other problems? Observe when you are positive. How does this change your state of mind and your physical sense of well-being? List examples of your negative self-talk and positive affirmations:

Negative Self-Talk	Positive Affirmations
1. _____	1. _____
2. _____	2. _____
3. _____	3. _____

energy to accomplish all that I choose to do, and I feel good when I'm organized and centered." Complete **Personal Evaluation Notebook 2.4** to determine if your self-talk needs to become more positive.

3. **Use visualization.** As we explored in Chapter 1, visualization is seeing things in your mind's eye by organizing and processing information through pictures and symbols. You imagine yourself behaving in certain ways, so that behavior will become real. For example, businessman Calvin Payne knows the power of visualization. Before he graduated from college, he bought his graduation cap and gown and kept them in his room. He visualized himself crossing the stage in his gown to accept his diploma. This visual goal helped him when he suffered setbacks, frustration, and disappointments. He graduated with honors and now incorporates visualization techniques in his career.

   Most right-brain dominant people are visual and use imagery a great deal. They can see scenes in detail when they read or daydream. In fact, their imagery is like a movie of themselves, with scenes of how they will react in certain situations, or a replay of what has occurred in the past. These images are rich in detail, expansive, and ongoing. Left-brain dominant people tend to use imagery less, but using imagery is a technique that can be learned, developed, and practiced.

   Visualization will help you see problems through formulas; read a recipe and see and taste the finished food; read blueprints and visualize the building; and see scenes and characters through narratives. You can also use mental imagery to create a positive, calm, and motivated state of mind.

4. **Use goals as motivational tools.** Just as an athlete visualizes crossing the finish line, you, too, can visualize your final goal. Working toward your goal can be a great motivator; however, you first must know what your goal is. **Peak Progress 2.3** will help you distinguish the difference between a desire and a goal and between long-term and short-term goals.

Peak Progress

Setting Goals

There is an old saying: "If you don't know where you are going, any road will take you there." The key, then, is to figure out where you are going, and then you can determine the best way to get there. Goal setting will help you do that. But goals provide more than direction and a clear vision for the future. When appropriately understood and applied, they are very effective motivators.

It is helpful first to distinguish between goals and desires. Identifying what you want out of life (that is, creating your mission statement, as discussed in Chapter 1) is certainly an important step in developing effective goals, but the goals themselves are not mere desires; rather, they are specific, measurable prescriptions for action. For example, if you want to be financially secure, you should start by identifying the actions that will help you fulfill that desire. Knowing that financial security is tied to education, you might make college graduation your first long-term goal. However, be careful how you construct this goal. "My goal is to have a college degree" is passive and vague. On the other hand, "I will earn my Bachelor of Science degree in computer technology from State University by June 2011" prescribes a clear course of action that can be broken down easily into sequences of short-term goals, which then can be broken down into manageable daily tasks.

Note that your long-term goal always comes first. Discomfort with long-term commitment sometimes leads people to try to address short-term goals first. Do not fall into this trap. Remember that short-term goals are merely steps toward achieving the long-term goal. As such, they cannot even exist by themselves. To understand this better, try to imagine driving to an unfamiliar city and then using a road map without having first determined where you are going. It cannot be done. You must know where you are going before you can plan your route (as illustrated on the next page).

Peak performers have an internal **locus of control**—they believe that they have control over their lives and that their rewards or failures are a result of their behavior, choices, character, or efforts. They are able to delay gratification and cope effectively with stress. Many people who have less school and job success have an **external locus of control**—they credit outside influences, such as fate, luck, or other people, with their success or failure. They are impulsive about immediate pleasures and are easily swayed by the influences of others. If you practice responsibility and discipline every day in small ways, your internal locus of control will grow and you will be achieving your goals and writing your own life script, rather than living the script written by your parents, circumstances, or society. In Chapter 3, we will explore using your goals to plan how to use your time effectively.

The following are some points to remember:

- Desires are not goals.
- Goals prescribe action.
- Effective goals are specific.
- Goal setting always begins with a long-term goal.
- Short-term goals are the steps in achieving the long-term goal.
- Daily tasks are the many specific actions that fulfill short-term goals.

(continued)

Setting Goals *(concluded)*

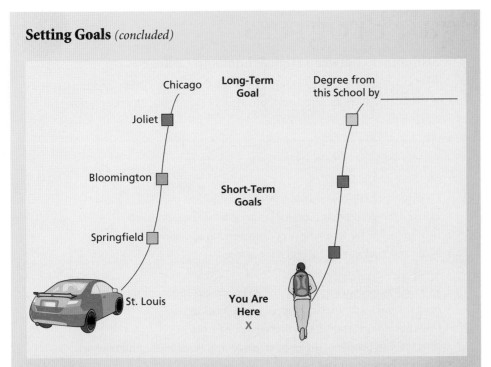

Goal Setting

Setting goals is just like planning a trip—first you need to know your destination (long-term goal) and then determine your best route to get there, including the milestones along the way (short-term goals). *If your long-term goal is to obtain your college degree, write in some of the short-term goals you need to accomplish (such as completing coursework, consulting with advisors and instructors, obtaining financial resources, and completing internships).*

Often, peak performers not only visualize goals but also write them down. Try keeping yours in your wallet, taping them on your bathroom mirror, or putting them on yellow sticky notes around your computer screen. Without a specific goal, it's not easy to find the motivation, effort, and focus required to go to classes and complete assignments. Make certain your goals are realistic. Achieving excellence doesn't mean attaining perfection or working compulsively toward impossible goals. If you try to be a perfectionist, you set yourself up for frustration, which can lead to decreased motivation, lowered productivity, increased stress, and failure.

5. **Understand expectations.** You will be more motivated to succeed if you understand what is expected of you in each class. Most instructors hand out a syllabus on the first day. Review it carefully and keep a copy in your class notebook. Review the syllabus with a study partner and clarify expectations with your instructor. Meet with your academic advisor to review general college and graduation requirements. College is different from high school and, the more you understand expectations, the more focused you'll be on reaching your goals. (See **Peak Progress 2.4.**)

Peak Progress

2.4

The Differences between High School and College

Accepting that entering college brings a new level of responsibility and expectations can be channeled into an effective motivator. For example, in college, you will be expected to

- Have more responsibilities and budget your time and money
- Express your opinions logically, not just give facts
- Motivate yourself
- Have more freedom and independence
- Have larger classes that meet for longer periods but less often
- Be responsible for knowing procedures and graduation requirements
- Write and read more than you have before
- Think critically and logically
- Receive less feedback and be tested less often but more comprehensively
- Have several textbooks and supplemental readings
- Have more work and turn in higher-quality work
- Interact with people of different values, cultures, interests, and religions
- Learn to be tolerant and respectful of diversity
- Be exposed to new ideas and critique these ideas in a thoughtful way
- Get involved in the community, school clubs, volunteer work, and internships related to your major

6. **Study in teams.** Success in the business world depends on team skills—the sharing of skills, knowledge, confidence, and decision-making abilities. The term *synergy* means that the whole is greater than the sum of the parts. It means seeing and using the whole system, not just isolated parts. You can increase your school and job success by learning, studying, and working in teams. You can also

- Teach each other material and outline main points
- Read and edit each other's reports
- Develop sample quizzes and test each other
- Learn to get along with and value different people

7. **Stay physically and mentally healthy.** It is difficult to motivate yourself if you don't feel well physically or emotionally. If you are ill, you will miss classes, fall behind in studying, or both. Falling behind can cause you to worry and feel stressed. Talk out your problems, eat well, get plenty of exercise and rest, and create a balance of work and play.

8. **Learn to reframe.** You don't have control over many situations or the actions of others, but you do have total control over your responses. **Reframing** is choosing to see a situation in a new way. For example, to pay for school, Joan

62   PART ONE   Building Foundation Skills

Bosch works at a fast-food hamburger place. She could have chosen to see this in a negative way; instead, she sees it in a positive way. She has reframed this work situation to focus on essential job skills. She is learning to be positive, dependable, hardworking, service-oriented, flexible, and tolerant.

9. **Reward yourself.** The simplest tasks can become discouraging without rewards for progress and for completion. Set up a system of appropriate rewards and consequences. Decide what your reward will be when you finish a project. For an easier task, the reward might be small, such as a snack, a hot shower, or a phone call to a friend. For a larger project, the reward might be going out to dinner, a movie, or a museum or throwing a small party. What are some rewards that would motivate you?

10. **Make learning relevant.** You will be more motivated if you understand the benefits of gaining knowledge and learning new skills in your coursework and the ways they will relate to your performance on the job. You may be attending college just because you love to learn and meet new people. However, it's more likely that you are enrolled to acquire or enhance your knowledge and skills, which will increase your marketability in the workforce.

The Benefits of Higher Education

As just mentioned, you will be more motivated in your schoolwork—and more likely to graduate and excel—if you understand how attending college benefits you both today and in the future.

HIGHER EDUCATION ENCOURAGES CRITICAL THINKING

Higher education has its roots in the liberal arts. Many years ago, being an educated person meant having a liberal arts education. *Liberal* comes from the Latin root word *liber,* which means "to free." A broad education is designed to free people to think and understand themselves and the world around them. The liberal arts include such areas as the arts, the humanities, the social sciences, mathematics, and the natural sciences. Classes in philosophy, history, language, art, and geography focus on how people think, behave, and express themselves in our culture and in the world. The liberal arts integrate many disciplines and provide a foundation for professional programs, such as criminal justice, electronics, computer systems, business, medicine, and law.

Technology is no longer a separate field of study from liberal arts but is an important tool for educated people. Employers want professionals who are creative problem solvers, have good critical thinking skills, can communicate and work well with others, can adapt to change, and understand our complex technical and social world. Liberal arts classes can help make a skilled professional a truly educated professional by providing an integration and understanding of history, culture, ourselves, and our world.

HIGHER EDUCATION IS A SMART FINANCIAL INVESTMENT

As mentioned earlier, you will be more motivated to put in long hours of studying when you feel the goal is worth it. Higher education is an excellent investment.

"Education's purpose is to replace an empty mind with an open one."

MALCOLM FORBES
Publisher

Figure 2.4

Annual Earnings and Education

Statistically, the level of your education is directly related to your income. These figures are average earnings for the U.S. population. Incomes vary within each category. *What other advantages, besides a good job and income, do you think education offers?*

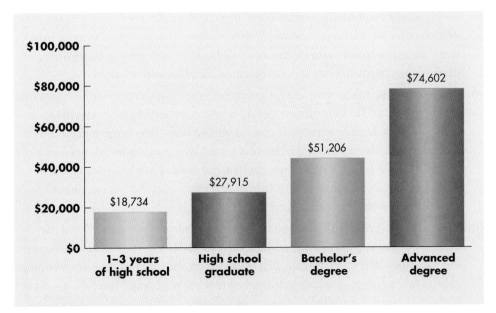

SOURCE: U.S. Census Bureau, U.S. Department of Commerce, 2005.

No one can take your education away from you, and it can pay large dividends. College graduates earn an average of well over $800,000 more in a lifetime than do high school graduates. (See **Figure 2.4**.) Although graduating from college or a career school won't guarantee you a great job, it pays off with more career opportunities, better salaries, more benefits, more job promotions, increased workplace flexibility, better workplace conditions, and greater job satisfaction. Many career centers at colleges make a commitment to help their students find employment.

Society and the workplace benefit when people improve their literacy. Various reports from the U.S. Department of Labor indicate that people who attend at least 2 years of college tend to

- Make better decisions
- Be willing to learn new skills
- Have more hobbies and leisure activities
- Have a longer life expectancy
- Be healthier
- Be more involved in the community
- Have more discipline and perseverance
- Have more self-confidence
- Learn to adapt to change

HIGHER EDUCATION PREPARES YOU FOR LIFE ON THE JOB

As you've no doubt noticed, the connection between school and job success is a major theme in this book. What you learn in school correlates directly with

Peak Progress

Skills for School and Career

Keep the following skills in mind as you see the connection between school and job success.

Skills	School Application	Career Application
Basic skills	Foundation for schoolwork	Foundation for work tasks
Motivation	Motivated to attend classes	Motivated to excel at work
Thinking skills	Solve case studies, equations	Solve work problems
Creativity	Creative experiments	Creative work solutions
Control of time	Homework first	Work priorities in order
Control of money	Personal budget	Departmental budgets
Writing	Writing papers	Writing reports, memos
Speeches	Classroom speeches	Presentations
Test taking	Tests in classes	Performance reviews
Information	Selecting class information	Selecting work information
Learning	Learning for classes	Learning job skills
Systems	Learning college system	Learning organization
Resources	Using college resources	Using work resources
Technology	Using computers for papers	Using computers for work

finding and keeping a job, as well as succeeding in a chosen career. As you go through school, think about how the skills, personal qualities, and habits you are learning and demonstrating in class are related to job and life success. **Peak Progress 2.5** includes a number of skills and qualities you are learning, practicing, and enhancing in your coursework and indicates how you will use them on the job.

As you develop your time- and stress-management skills, which we will explore in more detail later in this text, you will see improvement in your habits in school and on the job. Time management may help you show up for class on time and be prepared every day, thus leading to better grades. Punctuality in school will carry over to punctuality for work. Stress management may help you get along better with your roommates, instructors, or co-workers. Learning how to succeed in the school or college system can serve as a model for working effectively in organizational systems. Do you think you are maximizing your strengths, skills, and personal qualities? See **Peak Progress 2.6** on page 66 to determine what kind of student/worker you are and to determine what you need to do to improve your performance.

Peak Progress

What Kind of Student/Worker Are You?

A peak performer or an *A* student

- Is alert, actively involved, and eager to learn
- Consistently does more than required
- Consistently shows initiative and enthusiasm
- Is positive and engaged
- Can solve problems and make sound decisions
- Is dependable, prompt, neat, accurate, and thorough
- Attends work/class every day and is on time and prepared

A good worker or a *B* student

- Frequently does more than is required
- Is usually attentive, positive, and enthusiastic
- Completes most work accurately, neatly, and thoroughly
- Often uses critical thinking to solve problems and make decisions
- Attends work/class almost every day and is usually on time and prepared

An average worker or a *C* student

- Completes the tasks that are required
- Shows a willingness to follow instructions and learn
- Is generally involved, dependable, enthusiastic, and positive
- Provides work that is mostly thorough, accurate, and prompt
- Misses some work/classes

A problem worker or a *D* student

- Usually does the minimum of what is required
- Has irregular attendance, is often late, or is distracted
- Lacks a positive attitude or the ability to work well with others
- Often misunderstands assignments and deadlines
- Lacks thoroughness
- Misses many days of work/classes

An unacceptable worker or an *F* student

- Does not do the work that is required
- Is inattentive, bored, negative, and uninvolved
- Is undependable and turns in work that is incorrect and incomplete
- Misses a significant amount of work/classes

Overcome Obstacles

Don't Get Discouraged

Even peak performers sometimes feel discouraged and need help climbing out of life's valleys. Creating and maintaining a positive state of mind and learning self-management do not happen by reading a book, attending a lecture, or using a few strategies for a day or two. It takes time and effort. Everyone gets off course now and then, but the key is to realize that setbacks are part of life. Don't allow setbacks to make you feel as if you have failed and can no longer reach your goal. Find a formula that works for you to create a positive and resourceful mind.

Peak Progress 2.7 shows that a lack of personal qualities has a direct effect on the main reasons students don't graduate. If you think, "I'll be more motivated as soon as I graduate and get a real job," you may never develop the necessary qualities and skills to achieve that. Starting today, you should

- Focus on being motivated and positive
- Focus on your successes and accomplishments
- Surround yourself with positive, supportive, and encouraging friends
- Tell yourself, "This is a setback, not a failure"
- Learn self-control and self-management strategies
- Make certain you are physically renewed; get more rest, exercise more, and every day do something that you love

The Most Common Reasons Students Do Not Graduate

Between 30 and 50 percent of all college freshmen never graduate. The top reasons are

1. Poor study skills and habits
2. Lack of time-management skills
3. Lack of preparation for the demands and requirements of college
4. Inability to handle the freedom at college
5. Too much partying
6. Lack of motivation or purpose
7. Failure to attend class regularly
8. Failure to ask for help early
9. Lack of effort and time spent in studying
10. Failure to take responsibility for education (such as getting to know instructors, knowing expectations, setting goals, understanding deadlines, making up tests, redoing papers)

> 66 I've missed more than 9,000 shots in my career. I've lost almost 300 games. 26 times, I've been trusted to take the game winning shot and missed. I've failed over and over and over again in my life. And that is why I succeed. 99
>
> MICHAEL JORDAN
> *Professional basketball player*

- Replace negative and limiting thoughts and self-talk with affirmations and positive visualization
- Collect short stories about people who were discouraged, received negative messages, and bounced back

Create Positive Mind Shifts

Your beliefs and expectations about yourself can either limit or expand your success. Other people's expectations of you may cause you to redefine who you think you are and what you think you are capable of achieving. You may start to believe what you tell yourself or hear from others again and again, which may be limiting your thinking.

For example, Steve Delmay comes from a long line of lumber mill workers. Although they have lived for generations in a college town, his family has never had anything to do with the college. Steve was expected to go to work at the mill right after high school. He never thought about other options. However, during his senior year in high school, he attended Career Day. He met instructors and students from the local college who were friendly, supportive, and encouraging. His world opened up, and he saw opportunities he had never considered before. Steve experienced a major mind shift. Although he had to overcome a lack of support at home, he is now a successful college student with a bright future.

Creative problem solving can expand your mind and shift your thinking, so that you can see new possibilities and broader and more exciting horizons. College is an ideal time to develop your natural creativity and explore new ways of thinking. Try the following:

1. **Create a support system.** Without support and role models, you may question whether you can be successful. First-generation college students, women in technical programs, and men in nursing programs may feel uncomfortable and question whether they belong. Cultural minorities, veterans, and physically challenged or returning students may feel that they don't belong. Some students may be told that they are not college material. You can find encouragement with a support system of positive and accepting people. Join a variety of clubs. Make friends with diverse groups of students, instructors, and community leaders.

2. **Reprogram your mind.** Affirmations and visualization can create a self-fulfilling prophecy. If you think of yourself as a success and are willing to put in the effort, you will be successful. Focus on your successes and accomplishments and overcome limitations. For example, if you need to take a remedial math class, take it and don't label yourself as "dumb" or "math-impaired." Instead, focus on how improved your math skills will be.

3. **Use critical thinking.** Question limiting labels and beliefs. Where did they come from and are they accurate? Be mentally active and positive.

4. **Use creative thinking.** Ask yourself, "What if?" Explore creative ways of achieving your goals. Find out how you learn best and adopt positive habits.

5. **Take responsibility.** You are responsible for your thoughts, beliefs, and actions. You can question, think, and explore. You can achieve almost anything you dream.

6. **Learn new skills.** Focus on your strengths, but be willing to learn new skills and competencies continually. Feeling competent is empowering.

7. **Use the whole of your intelligence.** You definitely are smarter than you think you are. Use all your experiences and personal qualities to achieve your goals. Develop responsibility, self-control, dependability, sociability, character, manners, and all the other qualities necessary for school, job, and life success.

TAKING CHARGE

Summary

In this chapter I learned to:

- **Use the whole of my intelligence.** Developing emotional maturity and strong personal qualities is just as, if not more, important to my future success as learning new skills and information. Essential personal qualities include character, responsibility, self-management and self-control, self-esteem, confidence, attitude, and motivation.

- **Focus on character first.** Strong leaders are those who have an equally strong set of values. Having personal integrity gives me the courage to do the right thing, even when it is difficult. I display civility and empathy by interacting with family, friends, and colleagues with respect, kindness, good manners, empathy, and compassion. It's important for me to have a personal code of ethics that I follow in all facets of my life.

- **Take responsibility for my thoughts, actions, and behaviors.** I don't blame others for my setbacks, and I focus my energy on positive solutions. Others can depend on me to keep my commitments.

- **Manage and control my emotions, anger, and negative thoughts.** Conflict is an inevitable part of life, but it can be resolved in a positive way. Steps I can follow to redirect my negative thoughts and anger are (1) calm down; (2) clarify and define; (3) listen with empathy and respect; (4) use "I" statements; (5) focus on one problem; (6) focus on win-win solutions; and (7) reward positive behavior.

- **Develop self-esteem and confidence.** Through self-assessment, I understand my strengths and will continue to learn new skills and competencies that will build my confidence.

- **Maintain a positive attitude and keep myself motivated.** A positive attitude is essential for achieving success, and it influences the outcome of a task more than any other factor. Motivation is the inner drive that moves me to action. Working toward goals increases my motivation. Maslow's hierarchy of needs shows that I can fulfill my higher needs for self-esteem and self-actualization only when I have fulfilled my more basic needs first. The motivation cycle further demonstrates how affirmations, visualization, and self-talk affect my physical responses and behavior.

- **Realize the benefits of higher education.** Higher education has its roots in the liberal arts. Liberal arts classes can help make me a truly educated professional by providing an integration and understanding of history, culture, ourselves, and our world. My pursuit of a higher education should pay off with more career opportunities, a higher salary, more benefits, more job promotions, increased workplace flexibility, better workplace conditions, and greater job satisfaction. I will become more prepared for life on the job.

- **Overcome the barriers to staying positive and motivated.** Discouragement is the number one barrier to motivation. Setbacks will occur, but I will focus on my successes and accomplishments, surround myself with supportive and encouraging people, keep physically renewed, and replace negative self-talk with positive affirmations and visualization.

- **Create positive mind shifts and expand my comfort zone.** My beliefs and perceptions must be realistic. If they aren't, I must refocus my expectations in order to achieve my goals. I should not allow my beliefs to limit my potential, and I will use critical thinking techniques to expand my mind and comfort zone.

Performance Strategies

Following are the top 10 strategies for expanding your emotional intelligence and personal qualities:

- Cultivate character and integrity.
- Create a personal code of ethics.
- Take responsibility for your thoughts, actions, and behaviors.
- Practice self-control.
- Develop positive self-esteem and confidence.
- Determine personal motivators.
- Use goals as motivational tools.
- Reward yourself for making progress and strive for excellence, not perfection.
- Create positive mind shifts.
- Expand your comfort zone.

Tech for Success

Take advantage of the text's Web site at **www.mhhe.com/ferrett7e** for additional study aids, useful forms, and convenient and applicable resources.

- **Ethics information on the Web.** Search for articles on ethics, business etiquette, and codes of ethics.

  Check out different businesses, the military, government agencies, and colleges to find out if each has a code of ethics. Print some samples and bring them to class. What do all the codes of ethics have in common?

- **Online discussion groups.** When you are interested in a topic or goal, it's very motivating to interact with others who have the same interests. Join a discussion group or

listserv and share your knowledge, wisdom, and setbacks with others. You will learn their stories and strategies in return.

- **Goal-setting examples.** Although your goals should be personal, sometimes it helps to see how others have crafted theirs. This may inspire you to realize that setting goals isn't a difficult task—it just takes thinking critically about what you want out of life. A number of resources on the Web provide goal-setting ideas on everything from becoming more financially responsible to learning a second language.

Study Team Notes

Career *in* focus

Positive Attitudes at Work

Jacqui Williams
SALES REPRESENTATIVE

Related Majors: Business, Marketing, Public Relations

As a sales representative for a large medical company, Jacqui Williams sells equipment, such as X-ray and electrocardiograph (EKG) machines, to hospitals nationwide. Her job requires travel to prospective clients, where she meets with buyers to show her products and demonstrate their installation and use. Because Jacqui cannot take the large machines with her, she relies on printed materials and a laptop computer, from which she can point out the new aspects of the machines she sells. The sales process usually takes several months and requires more than one trip to the prospective client.

Jacqui works on commission, being paid only when she makes a sale. Because she travels frequently, Jacqui must be able to work independently without a lot of supervision. For this reason, being personally motivated is a strong requirement for her position. Jacqui has found that the best way to remain motivated is to believe in the products she sells. Jacqui keeps up on the latest in her field by reading technical information and keeping track of the competition. She sets sales goals and then rewards herself with a short vacation.

Because personal relations with buyers are so important, Jacqui is careful about her appearance. While traveling, she keeps a positive mind-set through affirmations, and she gets up early to eat a healthy breakfast and exercise in the hotel gym. She uses integrity by presenting accurate information and giving her best advice, even if it means not making a sale. Her clients would describe Jacqui as positive and helpful, someone whom they look forward to seeing and whose advice they trust.

CRITICAL THINKING In what way does having integrity, good character, and a code of ethics enhance a sales representative's business?

Peak Performer

PROFILE

Christiane Amanpour

"Amanpour is coming. Is something bad going to happen to us?"[1] That's how CNN's London-based chief international correspondent, Christiane Amanpour, says she's often greeted. Whether she appreciates the grim humor or not, Amanpour knows that her name and face have become linked in people's minds with war, famine, and death. But she has earned the respect of journalists and viewers around the world with her gutsy reporting from war-ravaged regions, such as Afghanistan, Iran, Israel, Pakistan, Somalia, Rwanda, and the Balkans.

Amanpour launched her career at CNN as an assistant on the international assignment desk in 1983, when some observers mockingly referred to the fledgling network as "Chicken Noodle News." "I arrived at CNN with a suitcase, my bicycle, and about 100 dollars,"[1] she recalls. Less than a decade later, Amanpour was covering Iraq's invasion of Kuwait, the U.S. combat operation in Somalia, and the breakup of the Soviet Union as these events unfolded.

Amanpour's globe trotting began early. Born in London, Amanpour soon moved with her family to Tehran, where her father was an Iranian airline executive. Her family fled the country and returned to England during the Islamic Revolution of 1979. After high school, Amanpour studied journalism at the University of Rhode Island. She took a job after college as an electronics graphic designer at a radio station in Providence. She worked at a second radio station as a reporter, an anchor, and a producer before joining CNN.[2]

"I thought that CNN would be my ticket to see the world and be at the center of history—on someone else's dime,"[1] she says, noting that she's logged more time at the front than most military units. Fear, she admits, is as much a part of her daily life as it is for the soldiers whose activities she chronicles: "I have spent almost every working day [since becoming a war correspondent] living in a state of repressed fear."[1]

Amanpour worries about the changes that have transformed the television news industry in recent years, as competition for ratings and profits has heated up.

But Amanpour remains optimistic. "If we the storytellers give up, then the bad guys certainly will win," she says. "Remember the movie *Field of Dreams* when the voice said 'Build it and they will come'? Well, somehow that dumb statement has always stuck in my mind. And I always say, 'If you tell a compelling story, they will watch.'"[1]

PERFORMANCE THINKING Christiane Amanpour demonstrates courage, integrity, and commitment. In what ways do you speak out for freedom, justice, and equality?

CHECK IT OUT The Committee to Protect Journalists indicates that 65 journalists were killed in 2007 because of their work. Visit **www.cpj.org** to see what's being done to safeguard the lives of journalists in the world's hotspots. Use the search field to find the manual "Journalist Safety Guide" to see what precautions journalists themselves must take in high-risk situations.

---

[1] AIDA International, 2000 Murrow Awards Ceremony Speech, September 13, 2000. **www.aidainternational.nl.**
[2] CNN Anchors and Reporters: Christiane Amanpour. **www.cnn.com/CNN/anchors_reporters/amanpour.Christiane.html.**

Starting Today

At least one strategy I learned in this chapter that I plan to try right away is:

_____

_____

_____

What changes must I make in order for this strategy to be effective?

_____

_____

_____

Review Questions

Based on what you have learned in this chapter, write your answers to the following questions:

1. What personal qualities are essential to success in school and work?

_____

_____

2. Give an example of a short-term goal versus a long-term goal.

_____

_____

3. List at least five motivational strategies.

_____

_____

4. Explain how affirmations and visualization affect the motivational cycle.

_____

_____

5. Explain what a mind shift is.

_____

_____

Getting Motivated

In the Classroom

Carol Rubino is a drafting major at a community college. In order to pay her expenses, she needs to work several hours a week. She is very organized and responsible with her school and work obligations. Most of her peers would describe Carol as motivated because she attends every class, is punctual, and works hard in both school and work. Throughout high school, Carol participated in extracurricular activities but never really enjoyed herself. She likes college but questions the connection between school and real life. As a result, Carol sometimes feels as if she is just wasting time and postponing life until graduation.

1. What strategies in this chapter can help Carol find a strong sense of purpose and motivation?

_____

_____

2. What would you recommend to Carol for creating a more resourceful and positive attitude?

_____

_____

In the Workplace

Carol is now a draftsperson for a small industrial equipment company. She has been with the company for 10 years. Carol is a valuable employee because she is competent and well liked. Carol has a supportive family, is healthy, and travels frequently. Although she enjoys her job, Carol feels bored with the mundane routine of her work. She wants to feel more motivated and excited on the job, as well as in her personal life.

3. What strategies in this chapter can help Carol become more enthusiastic about work or find new interest in her personal life?

_____

_____

4. What would you suggest to Carol to help her get motivated?

_____

_____

Applying the ABC Method of Self-Management

In the Journal Entry on page 45, you were asked to describe a time when you were angry and lost control of your emotions. Describe that event below and indicate how others reacted and what you might have done differently.

_____

_____

_____

_____

_____

Now apply the ABC method to the situation and visualize a situation under control:

A = Actual event:

B = Beliefs:

C = Challenge:

While completing this exercise, did you discover that you spend more time than you thought on negative thoughts?

PRACTICE SELF-MANAGEMENT

For more examples of learning how to manage difficult situations, see the "Self-Management Workbook" section of the Online Learning Center Web site at **www.mhhe.com/ferrett7e.**

Rewarding Myself: A Personal Reinforcement Contract

Use this example as a guide; then fill in the following contract for one or all of the courses you are taking this term.

Name *Sara Jones*

Course *General Accounting*   Date *September 2009*

If I *study for 6 hours each week in this class and attend all lectures and labs*

Then I will *reward myself with a long bike ride and picnic lunch every Saturday.*

I agree to *learn new skills, choose positive thoughts and attitudes, and try out new behaviors.*

I most want to accomplish *an "A" in this course to qualify for advanced accounting courses.*

The barriers to overcome are *my poor math skills.*

The resources I can use are *my study group and the Tutoring Center.*

I will reward myself for meeting my goals by *going out to dinner with some friends.*

The consequences for not achieving the results I want will be *to find a new major.*

REINFORCEMENT CONTRACT

Name _____

Course _____ Date _____

If I _____

Then I will _____

I agree to _____

I most want to accomplish _____

The barriers to overcome are _____

The resources I can use are _____

I will reward myself for meeting my goals by _____

The consequences for not achieving the results I want will be _____

Self-Esteem Inventory

Do this simple inventory to assess your self-esteem. Circle the number of points that reflects your true feelings.

4 = all the time

3 = most of the time

2 = some of the time

1 = none of the time

1. I like myself and I am a worthwhile person.	4	3	2	1
2. I have many positive qualities.	4	3	2	1
3. Other people generally like me and I have a sense of belonging.	4	3	2	1
4. I feel confident and know I can handle most situations.	4	3	2	1
5. I am competent and good at many things.	4	3	2	1
6. I have emotional control and I am respectful of others.	4	3	2	1
7. I am a person of integrity and character.	4	3	2	1
8. I respect the kind of person I am.	4	3	2	1
9. I am capable and willing to learn new skills.	4	3	2	1
10. Although I want to improve and grow, I am happy with myself.	4	3	2	1
11. I take responsibility for my thoughts, beliefs, and behavior.	4	3	2	1
12. I am empathetic and interested in others and the world around me.	4	3	2	1

Total points   _____ _____ _____ _____

Add up your points. A high score (36 and above) indicates high self-esteem. If you have a high sense of self-esteem, you see yourself in a positive light. If your self-esteem is low (below 24), you may have less confidence to deal with problems in college or on the job. If you scored at the lower end, list some strategies you can implement that may help boost your self-esteem:

Learning Styles and Motivation

You will feel more motivated and positive when you align your efforts with your learning and personality styles. Review your preference and style and think of the factors that help motivate you.

For example, *auditory learners* may find that they are more motivated when they listen to a tape of their favorite inspirational music and say affirmations. *Visual learners* may find that they are motivated when they surround themselves with pictures and practice visualizing themselves as motivated and positive. *Kinesthetic learners* may be more motivated when they work on activities, dance, hike, jog, and work with others. (See pages 14–17 for the complete discussion.)

Analyzers may be more motivated when they think, reflect, and organize information into sequential steps. *Supporters* may be more motivated when they work in a group and make information meaningful. *Creators* may be more motivated when they observe, make active experiments, and build models. *Directors* may be more motivated when they clearly define procedures and make practical applications. (See pages 21–27 for the complete discussion.)

List the ways you can motivate yourself that are compatible with your learning style and personality type:

1. _____

2. _____

3. _____

4. _____

5. _____

6. _____

Assessment of Personal Qualities

Category	Assessment	Yes	No
Emotional intelligence	Do I value and practice essential personal qualities?		
Character	Do I value and practice being a person of character and integrity?		
Civility	Do I treat others with respect and courtesy?		
Ethics	Do I have a code of ethics?		
Responsibility	Do I take responsibility for my thoughts and behavior?		
Self-control	Do I have self-control and know how to manage anger?		
Self-esteem	Do I have a realistic and positive sense of myself?		
Positive attitude	Do I strive to be positive and upbeat?		
Motivation	Do I create the inner drive and determination to achieve my goals?		
Self-actualization	Am I committed to growing and realizing my full potential?		
Visualization	Do I use visualization as a powerful tool for change and growth?		
Affirmation	Do I dispute and replace negative self-talk with affirmations?		
Critical thinking	Do I use critical thinking to challenge my beliefs and see new possibilities?		

The area I most want to improve is:

Strategies I will use to improve are:

3

Manage Your Time

SELF-MANAGEMENT

It's 7:30 A.M., I'm late for class, and I can't find my keys. It always seems like there's too little time and too much to do. I feel as if I have no control over my life. How can I manage my time and get organized?

Have you ever had a similar experience? Do you find yourself spending hours looking for things? Do you get angry at yourself and others because you feel frustrated and unorganized? In this chapter, you will learn how to take control of your time and your life and focus on priorities. Visualize yourself going through the day organized and centered. You have a clear vision of your goals and priorities and work steadily until tasks are finished. Feel the sense of accomplishment and completion. Visualize yourself in charge of your time and your life.

JOURNAL ENTRY In **Worksheet 3.1** on page 112, describe a time or situation when you felt overwhelmed by too much to do and too little time. What were the consequences?

THIS CHAPTER LOOKS AT TIME MANAGEMENT WITH A POSITIVE ATTITUDE. Instead of controlling, suppressing, or constricting your freedom, time management enables you to achieve the things you really want and frees up time to enjoy life. Peak performers use a systematic approach that allows them to

- Organize projects and achieve results
- Accomplish goals and priorities
- Be effective, not just efficient
- Avoid crises
- Remain calm and productive
- Feel a sense of accomplishment
- Have more free time to enjoy life

Everyone has the same amount of time—24 hours in each day. You can't save or steal time. When it's gone, it's gone. However, you can learn to invest it wisely. This chapter will help you learn how to get control of your life by managing your time wisely and by choosing to spend it on your main goals. It will also help you think about the contributions you want to make during your lifetime and the legacy you want to leave behind after you are gone. You will discover that there is always time to do the things you really want to do. Too many people waste time doing things that can be done in a few moments or doing things that should not be done at all and then ignoring their main goals.

As you go through this chapter, think about what you want to achieve and how you can use your time skillfully to perform at your peak level. This chapter will help you become effective, not just efficient. Being efficient is about doing things faster. Being effective is about doing the right things in the right way. As a wise time manager, you can avoid overwhelming feelings of losing control of tasks and falling behind in school, at work, or in your personal life. Whether you are an 18-year-old living on campus or a 45-year-old returning student juggling school, family, and work, the principles in this chapter can help you manage your time and your life.

Use Time Effectively

Time management is much more than focusing on minutes, hours, and days. Your attitude, energy level, and ability to concentrate have a great impact on how well you manage time. Clearly evaluate situations that may have spun out of control because of lack of planning or procrastination. Recall how these situations may have affected other people. You are part of the whole system. When you are late for class, miss a study group meeting, or don't do your share of a team project, it affects others.

Let's look at two important questions concerning your present use of time. The answers will help you develop a plan that will fine-tune your organizational and time-management skills—ultimately leading you to become an efficient peak performer.

1. Where does your time go? (Where are you spending your time and energy?)
2. Where should your time go?

Where Does Your Time Go?

You can divide time into three types: committed time, maintenance time, and discretionary time.

- **Committed time.** Committed time is devoted to school, labs, studying, work, commuting, and other activities involving the immediate and long-term goals you have committed to accomplishing.
- **Maintenance time.** Maintenance time is the time you spend maintaining yourself. Activities such as eating, sleeping, grooming (including showering, styling your hair, cleaning your contact lenses, getting dressed, etc.), exercising, and maintaining your home—cooking, cleaning/laundry, shopping, bill paying—use up your maintenance time.
- **Discretionary time.** The time that is yours to use as you please is discretionary time. You want to use your discretionary time for the things you value most in life. These important items include relationships with family and friends; service to the community; intellectual development; and activities that give you joy and relaxation and that contribute to your physical, mental, and spiritual well-being. These should tie in with your long-term goals of being healthy, feeling centered and peaceful, and having loving relationships.

Remember that this section asked you where your time goes and if you are using most of the day for commitments. A good place to determine your answer is with an assessment of how your time and energy are spent. Look at the sample Time Log in **Figure 3.1** on page 84 and then complete **Personal Evaluation Notebook 3.1** on page 85. The far right column asks you to indicate your energy level during the day—meaning do you feel focused and alert or are you distracted or tired? Most people find they have certain hours during the day when they are more productive.

After you have recorded your activities, review your Time Log to determine how much time you are devoting to daily tasks, such as studying, commuting, and socializing. Complete **Personal Evaluation Notebook 3.2** on page 86 and tally how much time you currently spend on various activities (and add others from your Time Log). The point of these exercises is to determine where you are currently spending your time, which will then help you determine the best way to use your time to achieve important goals. Even if you are juggling school, work, and family and feel you have no discretionary time, this will help you use what little discretionary time you do have to be most effective.

Where Should Your Time Go?

The first rule of time management is to make a commitment to what you want to accomplish—in other words, to set goals. As discussed in Chapter 2, goals are not

Figure 3.1
Sample Time Log

Knowing how you spend your time is the first step toward managing it. *Are your discretionary activities conscious choices?*

Time	Activity	Maintenance, Committed, or Discretionary	My Energy Level (High, Medium, or Low)
12:00 – 1:00 A.M.	Sleep	Maintenance	Low
1:00 – 2:00	Sleep	Maintenance	Low
2:00 – 3:00	Sleep	Maintenance	Low
3:00 – 4:00	Sleep	Maintenance	Low
4:00 – 5:00	Sleep	Maintenance	Low
5:00 – 6:00	Sleep	Maintenance	Low
6:00 – 7:00	Shower, dress	Maintenance	Medium
7:00 – 8:00	Drive kids to school	Committed	Medium
8:00 – 9:00	Make to-do list	Committed	High
9:00 – 10:00	Coffee and calls	Disc./committed	High
10:00 – 11:00	Write proposal	Committed	High
11:00 – 12:00 (noon)	Meeting	Committed	Low
12:00 – 1:00 P.M.	Lunch	Maintenance	High
1:00 – 2:00			
2:00 – 3:00			
3:00 – 4:00			
4:00 – 5:00			
5:00 – 6:00			
6:00 – 7:00			
7:00 – 8:00			
8:00 – 9:00			
9:00 – 10:00			
10:00 – 11:00			
11:00			

vague wishes or far-away dreams. They are specific, measurable, observable, and realistic. A goal is a target that motivates you and directs your efforts. Goal setting is not easy; you need to focus inward and think about your deepest values. Complete **Worksheet 3.2** on page 113 to assess your habits and level of commitment.

It's important to have a realistic picture of what your goals are and to observe and reflect constantly on how your daily activities are leading to larger goals. Written goals help clarify what you want and can give you energy, direction, and focus to put them into action. Goals can be short-term, mid-term, or long-term and are easier to identify when they flow out of a mission statement that defines what is most important to you. Placing goals within time frames can help you reach them. Complete

Personal Evaluation Notebook

Time Log

Fill in this Time Log to chart your activities throughout the day. Identify activities as maintenance, committed, or discretionary. Also determine your energy level throughout the day. (You may want to chart your activities for more than 1 day to see patterns in how you spend your time.)

Time	Activity	Maintenance, Committed, or Discretionary	My Energy Level (High, Medium, or Low)
12:00–1:00 A.M.			
1:00–2:00			
2:00–3:00			
3:00–4:00			
4:00–5:00			
5:00–6:00			
6:00–7:00			
7:00–8:00			
8:00–9:00			
9:00–10:00			
10:00–11:00			
11:00–12:00 (noon)			
12:00–1:00 P.M.			
1:00–2:00			
2:00–3:00			
3:00–4:00			
4:00–5:00			
5:00–6:00			
6:00–7:00			
7:00–8:00			
8:00–9:00			
9:00–10:00			
10:00–11:00			
11:00–12:00 (midnight)			

Personal Evaluation Notebook 3.2

How Much Time Do You Spend?

Fill in the following chart to determine how much time you spend on certain activities. Use the information you compiled in **Personal Evaluation Notebook 3.1.** Typical activities are listed. You may, of course, change or add activities to the list. Remember, the total number of hours should be 24.

Activity	Time Spent	Activity	Time Spent
Attending class		Eating	
Working		Sleeping	
Commuting		Cooking	
Studying		Shopping	
Attending meetings		Running errands	
Grooming		Socializing	
Exercising		Doing hobbies	
Doing household chores		Talking on the telephone	
Waiting in line		Watching television	
Other		Total time	

Personal Evaluation Notebook 3.3 to map out your goals. Then revisit these goals when you are completing your Career Development Portfolio.

Setting Priorities

There is always time for what is most important. Prioritizing helps you focus on activities that are most important to you at any given time. You want to make certain that your days are not just a treadmill of activities, crises, and endless tasks but that you focus on what is important as well as what is urgent.

Urgent priorities are pressing, deadline-driven projects or activities, such as dropping a class, paying your fees, or turning in papers. They directly affect your top goals and priorities and can result in spending a lot of extra time to fix the problem. For example, there is a serious consequence for missing a deadline for dropping classes, such as receiving an *F* grade. If you don't meet the deadline for adding classes, you have to pay additional fees or may not get into the class. Not paying for classes on time could result in having all your classes dropped.

Important priorities are essential activities that support your long-term goals and create the results you want—not just for today but also for future success. These activities and commitments include attending every class, creating study teams,

Personal Evaluation Notebook 3.3

Looking Ahead: Your Goals

Complete this activity to help you create major targets in your life—or long-term goals. From these goals, you can write mid-term goals (2 to 5 years), short-term goals (1 year), and then immediate (or semester) goals. Save this in your Career Development Portfolio. Use additional paper if necessary, or save it on the computer.

A. MISSION STATEMENT

You'll recall from Chapter 1 that your personal mission statement summarizes your most important lifetime goals and reflects your philosophy based on your deepest values and principles. In the blanks below, repeat (or revise) your thoughts from Chapter 1.

- Think of what you value most in life; then list those things:

  _____

- What is your life's purpose?

  _____

- What legacy do you want to leave?

  _____

MISSION STATEMENT:

_____

_____

B. LONG-TERM GOALS (ACCOMPLISH IN 10 YEARS OR SO)

Brainstorm all the specific goals that you want to accomplish during your lifetime. You should include goals for all areas of your life, such as education, career, travel, financial security, relationships, spiritual life, community, and personal growth. This list will be long, and you will want to add to it and revise it every year if goals change. Following are a few incomplete statements that might help you as you brainstorm:

- My dreams include _____
- I most want to accomplish _____
- The places I most want to visit are _____
- One thing I've always wanted to do is _____

C. MID-TERM GOALS (ACCOMPLISH IN THE NEXT 5 YEARS)

Then, what are the goals you want to accomplish in the next 5 years? Following are some examples:

- I will complete my degree.
- I will graduate with honors.
- I will buy a new sports car.
- I will take a trip to Europe.

Personal Evaluation Notebook

Looking Ahead: Your Goals *(concluded)*

D. SHORT-TERM GOALS (ACCOMPLISH THIS YEAR)

List goals that you want to accomplish in the next year. Consider your answers to these questions:

- What is the major goal for which I am striving this year?
- How does this goal relate to my life's mission or purpose?
- Is this goal in conflict with any other goal?
- What hurdles must I overcome to reach my goal?
- What resources, help, and support will I need to overcome these hurdles?
- What specific actions are necessary to complete my goal?
- What will be my reward for achieving this goal?

E. SEMESTER GOALS

List goals you want to accomplish this semester—for example,

- I will preview chapters for 10 minutes before each lecture.
- I will go to all of my classes on time.
- I will jog for 30 minutes each day.

> "Ordinary people merely think how they shall spend their time; a man of talent tries to use it."
>
> ARTHUR SCHOPENHAUER
> *German philosopher*

completing homework, forming healthy relationships, planning, and exercising regularly. People who spend time on important items on a daily basis prevent crises in their lives. For example, if you build a personal fitness routine into every day, you will increase your energy, health, and overall sense of well-being and prevent medical problems that result from inactivity and weight gain. Long-term priorities must be built into your daily activities.

Ongoing activities require continual attention and may be urgent, but they may not be important. For example, as you go through your e-mail, open mail, and answer phone calls, you will find that some must be responded to immediately or they will fall into the urgent category but they are not important for your long-term goals. These activities require continual attention and follow-up and should be managed to prevent future problems. Jot down whom you need to see or call. Follow up with deadlines and determine if these activities are worthwhile and support your top goals. For example, maybe you were pressured to join a club or community group that has been taking a lot of time. You may need to say, "This is a worthwhile project and I appreciate being inviting to attend, but I cannot participate at this time." Ask yourself if this activity meets your highest priority at this time.

Trivial activities make up all the daily stuff of life and many are major time wasters. These unimportant activities can be fun, such as talking on the phone with friends, chatting online, going to parties, blogging, gossiping, shopping, and surfing the Internet. They can also be annoying, such as dealing with junk mail—both real and virtual. The key is to stay focused on your important, top-priority items and schedule a certain amount of time for trivial activities. You want a balanced life and you need to socialize with friends, but sometimes a phone call or quick visit can turn into an hour-long gossip session. If this happens too often, you will not accomplish your important goals.

Setting priorities helps you focus on immediate goals. These essential, small steps lead you to your big goals. Your awareness of where your time goes becomes a continual habit of assessing, planning, and choosing tasks in the order of their importance, and this leads to success. After working hard on important priorities and meeting deadlines, you will want to socialize and spend time with family and friends. The key is balance.

Ask yourself the following questions: Do I have a sense of purpose and direction? Are my goals clearly defined? Are any in conflict with each other? Are they flexible enough to be modified as needed? Do I forget to write priorities and phone numbers in my planner? Do I daydream too much and have a problem with concentration? Do I invest time in high-priority tasks? Do I attend to small details that pay off in a big way? Refer to **Peak Progress 3.1** to see if the 80/20 rule applies to you.

Peak Progress (3.1)

Investing Your Time in High-Priority Items: The 80/20 Rule

Whether you are a student, an executive, or an entry-level worker, your effectiveness will increase if you focus on top-priority items. According to the 80/20 rule (the Pareto Principle), 80 percent of the results flow out of 20 percent of the activities—for example,

- Eighty percent of the interruptions come from 20 percent of the people.
- Eighty percent of the clothes you wear come from 20 percent of your wardrobe.
- Eighty percent of your phone calls come from 20 percent of the people you know.
- Eighty percent of a company's sales may come from 20 percent of their total customers.

Taking a look at your time wasters may reveal that you are spending too much time on low-priority activities and short-changing your top priorities. Wasting time on low-priority activities is unproductive and a major reason for not accomplishing major tasks.

If you want to produce results, you need to focus on what is important—for example,

- Twenty percent more effort can result in an 80 percent better paper or speech.
- Twenty percent more time being involved and prepared in classes could result in 80 percent better results.
- Twenty percent more time developing positive relationships could reduce conflicts by 80 percent.
- Twenty percent more time taking care of yourself—getting enough sleep, eating healthy, exercising, and controlling stress—can result in 80 percent more effectiveness.

The 80/20 rule is just a rule of thumb. The exact percentage may change based on the circumstance. However, the point is that you should spend your time on the activities that are really important and achieve the results you want.

Time-Management Strategies

Use the following strategies to improve your time-management skills and to help you achieve your goals in a balanced and effective way.

1. **Keep a calendar.** An inexpensive, pocket-size calendar is easy to carry with you and handy for scheduling commitments, such as classes, labs, and work for the entire semester. This helps you see the "big picture." Review your calendar each week and list top priorities, due dates, and important school, work, and family activities. Each day, review urgent priorities that must be done by a deadline, such as paying fees, dropping a class, returning a library book, paying taxes, or applying for graduating. Schedule important activities that support your goals, such as classes, exercise, study teams, and deadlines for choosing a topic. Jot down people to see or call, such as your instructor or advisor, or activities, such as meetings or social events. Remember, the shortest pencil is better than the longest memory. For example, if your advisor gives you a code for registration, put it on the date and time for your registration. Don't just write your code on your binder or toss it into your backpack. Included in the worksheets at the end of this chapter are handy calendars to help you plan your week, month, and semester.

2. **Create a daily to-do list.** Some people like to write a to-do list for the next day, taking some time at the end of a day to review briefly what they want to focus on for the next day. Others like to write their list in the morning at breakfast or when they first get to school or work. List the tasks you need to accomplish during the day and map them out on a daily calendar. You may want to circle or place a number 1 by the most important priority to make sure it gets accomplished. Make certain you build in time for family and friends. If you have children, plan special events. Bear in mind that the schedule should be flexible; you will want to allow for free time and unexpected events. Follow this schedule for 2 weeks and see how accurate it is. You can follow the format of the Time Log on page 85, or see **Worksheet 3.6** on page 118, which includes a planner for mapping out your daily to-do list.

   Once you have written your list, get going and do your urgent, top-priority items. Keep your commitments, such as attending every class, and don't do pleasant, fun activities until the most important ones are done. When you see important items checked off, you'll be inspired. It's OK if you don't get to everything on your list. If there are tasks left over, add them to your next to-do list if they are still important. Ask yourself, "What is the best use of my time right now?"

3. **Do the tough tasks first.** You will feel a sense of accomplishment as you tackle your tough tasks first. Start out with your most difficult subjects, while you're fresh and alert. For instance, if you are avoiding your statistics homework because it is difficult, get up early and do it before your classes begin. Start projects when they're assigned.

4. **Break projects down into smaller tasks.** Begin by seeing the whole project or each chapter as part of a larger system. Then break it into manageable chunks. You may get discouraged if you face a large task, whether it's writing a major

Project: Term Paper for Business Class 110

Today's date: January 23, 2009   Due date: April 23, 2009

Key Activities	Date Completed
Explore topics	**January 23**
Finalize topic	January 28
Mind map outline	February 4
Initial library research	February 8
General outline	February 22
Library research	March 5
Detailed library research	March 10
Detailed outline	March 15
First draft	March 27
Do additional research and spell-check	April 5
Proof second draft; revise	April 10
Prepare final draft and proof	April 15
Paper finished and turned in	**April 23**

Figure **3.2**

Sample Project Board

Making a project board is an effective time-management strategy. You can plan your tasks from start to end, or some people prefer to work backwards—starting with the end date. *How can you incorporate your project board into your daily planner?*

term paper or reading several chapters. Getting started is half the battle. Sometimes working for just 15 minutes before you go to bed can yield big results. For example, preview a chapter, outline or mind map the main ideas for your term paper, or write a summary at the end of a chapter. You will find inspiration in completing smaller tasks, and you will feel more in control.

Some students find using a project board helpful for long-term projects, as shown in **Figure 3.2**. Begin with today's date (or the start date), along with the due date, clearly indicated at the top. More than likely, the end date cannot change. Your start date should also be realistic—and as soon as possible. Then separate the "board" into two columns: "Key Activities" and "Date Completed." In the date column, put today's date (or start date) at the top and the project's final due date at the bottom. (Some prefer to reverse that, putting the due date at the top and working backwards. Use whichever process works best for you.) Thus, with these two dates set, begin in the activities column by listing in order the project-related tasks that need to be accomplished between the start and end dates. Go back to the date column and start plugging in optimal dates next to the tasks, working from beginning to end. You may find that the time you think you need for each task ends up with a schedule that extends beyond your due date—obviously, that's a problem. Thus, you need to revise your dates and create a new schedule that achieves your completion date. (Make certain you allow time for proofreading and potential setbacks, such as computer problems.)

5. **Consolidate similar tasks.** If you group similar tasks, you can maximize your efforts. For example, if you need to make several calls, make them all at a specific time and reduce interruptions. Set aside a block of time to shop, pay bills, and run errands. Try to answer e-mails at designated times, rather than as each one comes in. Write a list of questions for your advisor, instructor, or study team. Make certain you know expectations, so that you don't have to repeat

● **Study Anywhere and Everywhere**
Use your time between classes and while waiting for appointments to study and prepare for class. *What is something you can always carry with you, so that you are prepared for down time?*

tasks. Save your energy and use your resources by planning and combining similar activities, such as taking a walk with a friend, thus combining exercise with socializing.

6. **Study at your high-energy time.** Know your body rhythms and study your hardest subjects during your high-energy time. Review the Time Log to determine the time of day when you have the most energy. Complete **Personal Evaluation Notebook 3.4.** Guard against interruptions and don't do mindless tasks or socialize during your peak energy period. For example, if your peak time is in the morning, don't waste time by answering mail, socializing, cleaning, checking out books at the library, or doing other routine work. Use your high-energy time to do serious studying and work that requires thinking, writing, and completing projects. Use your low-energy time to do more physical work, chores, or easy reading or previewing of chapters.

7. **Study everywhere and anywhere.** Ideally, you should choose a regular study location that has few distractions, such as the library. However, you should always be prepared to study everywhere and anywhere, as you never know when you might get some unexpected down time. Carry note cards with you to review formulas, dates, definitions, facts, and important data. Bring class notes or a book with you to review during the 5 or 10 minutes of waiting between classes, for the bus, in line at the grocery store, or for appointments. Digitally record important material and lectures and listen to them while commuting, exercising, dressing, walking, or waiting for class to begin. Avoid crowded times in the library and computer labs. Even if you plan well, you will occasionally get stuck in lines, but you can make the most of this time.

8. **Study in short segments throughout the day.** Studying in short segments is much more effective than studying in marathon sessions. Your brain is much more receptive to recall when you review in short sessions at various times.

9. **Get organized.** Think of the time that you waste looking for items (and the unnecessary stress it causes). Lay out your clothes and pack your lunch the night before, put your keys on the same hook, put your backpack by the door, put your mail and assignments in the same space, and keep records of bills and important information in your file. Keep an academic file that includes your grades and transcripts. Keep a box with tests, papers, and projects. If you need to negotiate a grade, you will have the background support you will need. Make sure you save and back up any important work created on computer and can easily retrieve it (to avoid losing hours of work).

10. **Be flexible, patient, and persistent.** Don't try to make too many changes at once, and don't get discouraged if a strategy doesn't work for you. You are

Personal Evaluation Notebook 3.4

Your Daily Energy Levels

Keep track of your energy levels every day for a week or more. Revisit your Time Log on page 85 to determine your daily energy levels, so that you can become more aware of your patterns.

1. What time(s) of the day are your energy levels at their peak?

   _____

2. What time(s) of the day are your energy levels at their lowest?

   _____

3. What tasks do you want to focus on during your high-energy time?

   _____

4. What can you do to increase your energy at your low-energy time?

   _____

striving for excellence, not perfection. Change certain aspects until a strategy fits your style. If it works, do it. If not, try something new. Just make sure you've given yourself at least 30 days to develop new habits. It often feels strange and uncomfortable to do any new task or vary your schedule of daily events. For example, you might discover that you have a habit of getting a donut and coffee every morning and spending an hour or so socializing with friends before your morning classes. You might try changing this habit by doing it only once a week.

11. **Realize that you can't do it all (or at least right now).** You may feel overwhelmed by too many demands and determine that some tasks are better done by others around you. This does not mean you can offload your responsibilities onto others, but focus on your important priorities and say no to activities that don't support your goals. Consider delegating certain tasks, joining a club later in the year, or participating in a fundraiser when you are on school break. Do social activities, return phone calls, and visit with friends when you have done your top-priority tasks.

Time Management and Your Learning Style

Many time-management strategies are designed for people with left-brain dominance. Left-brain dominant people like routine, structure, and deadlines. They tend to be **convergent** thinkers because they are good at looking at several unrelated items and bringing order to them. Right-brain dominant people like variety, flexibility, creativity, and innovation. They are usually **divergent** thinkers because they branch out from one idea to many. They are good at brainstorming because one idea leads to another. They are able to focus on the whole picture. However, they can also learn to break the global view of the whole project into steps, break each of these steps into activities, and schedule and organize activities around the big goal. If you are right-brain dominant, you should

- **Focus on a few tasks.** It is very important for right-brain dominant people to focus their efforts on one or two top-priority items instead of being scattered and distracted by busywork. Imagine putting on blinders and focusing on one step until it is completed and then move on to the next step. This creates discipline.

- **Write it down.** A daily calendar is vital to making certain that your daily activities support your short- and long-term goals. Write down phone numbers, e-mail addresses, and office hours of instructors and study team members. Highlight in color any deadlines or top-priority activities. Besides a daily calendar, use a master calendar in your study area and allow for variety and change. Make certain you review both your daily calendar with to-do items and your master calendar before you go to bed at night, so that you see the big picture.

- **Use visuals.** Right-brain dominant people often like to use visuals. One creative way to brainstorm, plan, and put your vision into action is to use a mind map (see Chapter 4, page 131). Use visual cues and sticky notes. When you think of an activity that will help you meet your goal, write it down.

- **Integrate learning styles.** Visualize yourself completing a project and create a vision board of your goals and dreams. Use auditory cues by dictating ideas and planning your project on tape. Talk about the great feeling you will have when you complete this project. Make your project physical by adapting a hands-on approach and working with others to complete your project. Ask yourself, "Is there a way to simplify this task?" Planning is important, even if you are a creative person. **Peak Progress 3.2** explores the process of learning to take control of your time.

WORDS TO SUCCEED

❝You may delay, but time will not.❞

BENJAMIN FRANKLIN
Inventor, publisher, statesman

Overcome Obstacles

Stop Procrastinating

Procrastination is deliberately putting off tasks, and most of us at one time or another have been guilty of putting off doing what we know should be done. However, a continual pattern of delaying and avoiding is a major barrier to time management.

There are many reasons for procrastination. Some people prefer to do the things they like to do rather than doing what should be done. Some people are perfectionists and don't want to do something or complete steps unless they feel the outcome is the best it can be. Other people are worriers and get weighed down with details or overwhelmed by the enormity of the tasks. Some people are shy and avoid working

Peak Progress

Applying the Adult Learning Cycle to Taking Control of Your Time and Life

Applying the Adult Learning Cycle will help you establish goals and create a plan to meet them.

1. **RELATE. Why do I want to learn this?** Planning my time better and getting organized are essential for me to juggle the demands of school, work, and life. What are the areas where I need the most work?

2. **OBSERVE. How does this work?** I can learn a lot about time management by observing people who are on time, get their work done, work calmly and steadily, and seem to accomplish a lot in a short time. I'll also observe people who are unorganized, often late, miss classes, and waste a lot of time blaming, complaining, and being overly involved in other people's lives. Do their problems relate to time management and self-management? How do I manage my time?

3. **REFLECT. What does this mean?** What strategies are working for me? What are some new strategies I can try? I will explore creative ways to solve problems rather than feeling overwhelmed.

4. **DO. What can I do with this?** Each day, I'll work on one area. For example, I'll choose one place to hang my keys and consistently put them there. If I find them in my purse or on the table, I'll put them on the hook until it becomes a habit.

5. **TEACH. Whom can I share this with?** I'll share my tips and experiences with others and find out their strategies in return. I should continue to reward myself, at least mentally, for making positive changes.

Now return to Stage 1 and think about how it feels to learn this valuable new skill of managing your time and priorities.

---

with others to accomplish a task or give a speech. Others are embarrassed because they have avoided a task for too long, so they just write it off. Other people are easily distracted, blame others, or don't want to be told what to do. Some people feel they work better under extreme pressure and use it as an excuse for waiting until the last minute. Some just simply lack the discipline to sit down and complete a task. Complete **Personal Evaluation Notebook 3.5** on page 96 to determine if you procrastinate too much and, if so, why.

Self-assessment is often the key to understanding why you procrastinate and to developing strategies to help you control your life and create the results you want. Once you have identified what is holding you back, you can create positive solutions and apply them consistently until they are habits. To avoid procrastination, try the following strategies:

1. **Set daily priorities.** Begin by becoming clear on your goals and the results you want to achieve. Make certain that you allow enough time to complete your goals. Review your goals often and visualize yourself completing projects and tasks and achieving your goals. For example, see yourself walking across the stage to receive your diploma and view daily tasks as stepping stones for

Personal Evaluation Notebook

3.5

Procrastination

- What is something I should have accomplished by now but haven't?

- Why did I procrastinate?

- What are the consequences of my procrastination?

- What kind of tasks do I put off?

- When do I usually procrastinate?

- Where do I procrastinate? Am I more effective in the library or at home?

- How does my procrastination affect others in my life?

- Who supports, or enables, my procrastination?

reaching your goal. Use your to-do list to check off tasks as you complete them. This will give you a feeling of accomplishment.

2. **Break the project into small tasks.** A large project can seem overwhelming and can encourage procrastination. Do something each day that brings you closer to your goal. Use a project board or write down steps and deadlines that are necessary to achieve success. For example, as soon as a paper is assigned, start that day to choose a topic, the next day do research, and so on until each step leads to an excellent paper. Ask yourself, "What can I do in 10 minutes today that will get me started?"

96 PART ONE Building Foundation Skills

3. **Gather everything you'll need to start your project.** Clear off a space and get your notes and other material ready, such as pens, paper, and books. Reread the assignment and clarify expectations with your instructor or study team. Having everything ready creates a positive attitude and makes it easier to start the task. This strategy is effective whether you're doing a term paper, cleaning the garage, or making cookies.

4. **Focus for short spurts.** You can create a positive, "can do" attitude by focusing fully for a short amount of time: "I'm going to preview this chapter for 15 minutes with full concentration." However, telling yourself you're going to study for 2 or 3 hours creates a mind-set that says, "This is too difficult." Seeing how fully you can concentrate in a short amount of time builds confidence, yields success, and makes studying a game. You are using affirmations and creative discipline instead of guilt and willpower. Before you go to bed or when you have a few minutes during the day, use the same strategy: "I'm just going to spend 10 minutes writing a rough draft for my English paper." Ask yourself if you can do one more thing to get you started the next day. As you build on your success, you will increase your confidence, discipline, and concentration.

5. **Surround yourself with supportive people.** Ask for help from motivated friends, instructors, or your advisor, or visit the Learning Center for help and support. Sometimes talking out loud can help you clarify why you are avoiding a project. Study buddies or a study team can also help you stay on track. Sometimes just knowing that someone is counting on you to deliver is enough to keep you from procrastinating.

6. **Tackle difficult tasks during your high-energy time.** Do what is important first, while you are at your peak energy level and concentration is easiest. Once you get a difficult or unpleasant task done, you will feel more energy. Return phone calls, answer mail, visit with friends, and clean when your energy dips and you need a more physical, less mentally demanding task.

7. **Develop a positive attitude.** When you are positive and focused, you can accomplish a lot in a short time. Negative emotions are time wasters. Anger, jealousy, worry, and resentment can eat up hours of time and sap your energy. Instead, resolve to have a positive attitude and use affirmations. Think to yourself, "I get to work on my project today," instead of "I have to work on this project." Feel grateful that you have the opportunity to be in college. Resourceful and positive attitudes don't just happen; they are created. Once you get yourself into the action mode, you'll find that motivation builds. Most people don't feel like exercising every morning but, once they are out for a jog, they feel great and want to complete their run. The same strategies can be used for writing, studying, and completing any project.

8. **Reward yourself.** Look ahead and think about how you will feel when you complete this task versus how you'll feel if you don't. Focus on the sense of accomplishment you feel when you make small, steady steps and meet your deadlines. Reward yourself with a small treat or break when you complete activities and a bigger reward (such as a nice dinner or movie) when you complete a goal. Work first and play later. Do not allow yourself the reward of play until you have accomplished certain high-priority tasks and have met deadlines.

9. **Don't expect perfection.** You learn any new task by making mistakes. For example, you become a better writer or speaker with practice. Don't wait or delay because you want perfection. Your paper is not the great American novel. It is better to do your best than to do nothing. You can polish later, but avoiding writing altogether is a major trap. Do what you can today to get started on the task at hand.

Control Interruptions

Interruptions steal your time. They cause you to stop projects, disrupt your thought pattern, divert your attention, and make it difficult to build momentum again. To avoid wasting time, take control. Set everyday priorities that will help you meet your goals and reduce interruptions. Don't let endless activities, the telephone, and other people control you. For instance, if a friend calls, set a timer for 10 minutes or postpone the call until later in the day, after you have previewed an assigned chapter or outlined a speech. Set the answering machine if you are studying, or tell the caller that you will call back in an hour. When you return a call, chat for 5 or 10 minutes instead of 45 minutes. Combine socializing with exercising or eating lunch or dinner. If you watch a favorite program, turn the television off right after that show. The essence of time management is taking charge of your life and not allowing interruptions to control you. Complete **Personal Evaluation Notebook 3.6** to determine the sources of your interruptions. (Also see **Worksheet 3.3** on page 115 to identify your time wasters.)

Peak performers know how to live and work with other people and manage interruptions. Try these tips to help you reduce interruptions:

1. **Create an organized place to study.** A supportive, organized study space can help you reduce interruptions and keep you focused. Have all your study tools—a dictionary, pencils, pens, books, papers, files, notes, a calendar, a semester schedule, and study team and instructor names and phone numbers—in one place, so that you won't waste time looking for the items you need. Keep only one project on your desk at one time and file everything else away or put it on a shelf. You can increase your learning by studying in the same space and by conditioning your brain for serious studying and attention. If you have children, include a study area for them, close to yours, where they can work quietly with puzzles, crayons, or paint. This will allow study time together and create a lifelong study pattern for them.

2. **Determine your optimal time to study.** You will find that, when you are focused, you can study anywhere, anytime. However, to increase your effectiveness, do your serious studying when your energy level is at its peak. Guard against interruptions and use this time for serious studying.

3. **Create quiet time.** Discuss study needs and expectations with your roommates or family and ask for an agreement. You might establish certain study hours or agree on a signal, such as closing your door or hanging a "Quiet" sign, to let each other know when you need quiet time. Make certain that you balance study time with breaks to eat and socialize with your roommates or family.

4. **Study in the library.** If it is difficult to study at home or in the dorm, study in the library. Many students go to the library for quiet time. Once you enter, your

> ❝ Time is the coin of your life. It is the only coin you have, and only you can determine how it will be spent. Be careful lest you let other people spend it for you. ❞
>
> CARL SANDBURG
> *Author, poet*

Personal Evaluation Notebook 3.6

Interruptions!

1. Try to keep a log of interruptions for a few days. List all the interruptions you experience and their origins. Be aware of internally caused interruptions, such as procrastination, daydreaming, worry, negative thoughts, anger, and lack of concentration.

Interruptions	Frequency	Possible Solutions
Visitors		
Friends		
Family		
Telephone		
Daydreaming		
Lack of purpose		
Other		

2. Make a list of your most common time wasters. Some common time wasters are

- Socializing
- Doing what you like to do first
- Watching television
- Procrastinating
- Not setting goals and priorities
- Not keeping a calendar
- Not writing down deadlines
- Losing things and not organizing
- Failing to plan
- Having a negative attitude
- Complaining and whining
- Being overly involved with other people's problems

My common time wasters are

_____

_____

_____

_____

Possible solutions are

_____

_____

_____

_____

_____

brain can turn to a serious study mode. Sitting in a quiet place and facing the wall can reduce interruptions and distractions. You will find that you can accomplish far more in less time, and then you can enjoy your friends and family.

5. **Do first things first.** You will feel more in control if you have a list of priorities you work through every day. Having a clear purpose of what you want and need to do makes it easier to say no to distractions. Make certain that these important goals include your health. Taking time to exercise, eat right, and relax will not only save time but will also help increase your energy and focus.

6. **Just say no.** Tell your roommates or family when you have an important test or project due. If someone wants to talk or socialize when you need to study, say no. Set aside time each day to spend with your family or roommates, such as dinner, a walk, or a movie. They will understand your priorities when you include them in your plans. See **Peak Progress 3.3** for additional tips on how to say no and still maintain a positive relationship.

Juggling Family, School, and Job

Many students attending college are juggling more than coursework and school activities. Many are spouses, partners, parents, caregivers (for both children and elderly parents and relatives), and co-workers. Making the decision to attend college—or return to college—may have been very difficult because of all the other commitments and responsibilities they already have.

Having a family involves endless physical demands, including cleaning, cooking, chauffeuring to activities, helping with homework, and nonstop picking up. Anyone who lives with children knows how much time and energy they require. Children get sick, need attention, and just want you there sometimes for them.

The following strategies can help you succeed in school while juggling your many roles:

1. **Be flexible.** There are only certain kinds of studying that you can realistically expect to do around children and other kinds of studying that are hopeless even to attempt. If you expect to be interrupted a lot, use this to your advantage. Carry flash cards to use as you cook dinner or while supervising children's homework or playtime. Quiz yourself, preview chapters, skim summaries, review definitions, do a set number of problems, brainstorm ideas for a paper, outline a speech, review equations, sketch a drawing, or explain a chapter out loud. Save the work that requires deeper concentration for time alone.

2. **Communicate with your family.** Let your family know that earning a college degree is an important goal and you are going to need their support and understanding. Build in quality, fun time with those you love and give them your full attention. Use every bit of time to study before you come home. Once home, let them know when you need to study and set up a specific time. Even young children can understand that you need quiet time. Make certain that they have lots of quiet activities to keep them busy when you are working.

3. **Delegate and develop.** Clarify expectations, so that everyone contributes to the family. Even young children can learn to be team members and important contributors to making the family unit work. Preschool children can help put away

Peak Progress

How to Say No

Some people have a hard time saying no. They are afraid they will hurt someone's feelings, will send the wrong message that they aren't interested, or will miss an opportunity that may not come along again. But you just can't say yes all the time and still accomplish all you need to. Following are some tips on how to say no, limit your time, and exit situations gracefully:

- **Check your to-do list:** "It doesn't fit with my schedule." It is easy to give in to the impulse to say yes to an invitation or a request from a friend or family member. However, you need to determine what priorities and commitments must be met first. You may find you have to decline the request.

- **Answer in a timely fashion:** "I can't do this right now." If you know you can't participate, let the other person know right away. Others will be more understanding if you let them know you have other commitments rather than waiting until the last minute to give a response (or no response at all).

- **Set a later date:** "I can't right now, but can we do this later?" Find another time that works better for everyone's schedule and record it on your calendar or planner.

- **Set a time limit:** "I need to leave by_____." If phone calls or lunch dates usually turn into hours of conversation, set a time limit upfront and make it known—and then stick to it.

- **Clarify expectations:** "How much time will this involve?" It's easy to get involved in something that turns out to be much more time-consuming than originally thought. Sometimes that's unavoidable, but make sure you ask upfront as to what is expected or anticipated.

- **Ask for alternate responsibilities:** "I can't do this, but is there something else I can do?" The original request may require too much of your time (such as planning a school event), but there may be a lesser role you could take (such as lining up the speaker, contacting a caterer, or handing out flyers).

- **Sleep on it before answering:** "Let me get back to you in a day." For bigger commitments, try to take a day or two to consider if the benefits of the new opportunity outweigh the time it will take to be involved. You don't want to disappoint others by committing to a project and then not following through.

- **Don't feel guilty:** "This is the best decision for me at this time." Once you say no, don't feel guilty or have regrets. You must focus on your priorities. Be firm and polite—not defensive or overly apologetic. And definitely do not make up false excuses, which could end up causing you more stress in the long run.

toys, set the table, and feel part of the team. Preteens can be responsible for cooking a simple meal one night a week and for doing their own laundry. When your children go to college, they will know how to cook, clean, do laundry, get up on time in the morning, and take responsibility for their lives. An important goal of being a good parent is to raise independent, capable, competent, and responsible adults.

4. **Find good day care.** Explore public and private day-care centers, preschools, family day-care homes, parent cooperatives, baby-sitting pools, other family members, and nannies. Line up at least two backup sources of day care. If possible, explore renting a room in the basement or attic of your house to a child-care provider. Part of the rent can be paid with child care and light housecleaning. Trade off times with other parents.

5. **Prepare the night before.** Avoid the morning rush of getting everyone out the door by doing tasks the night before, such as taking a shower, laying out clothes, packing lunches, organizing backpacks, and checking for keys, books, any signed notes, and supplies. Good organization helps makes the rush hour a little less stressful.

6. **Use your school's resources.** Check out resources on campus through the reentry center. Set up study teams for all your classes. Make friends with other people who have children.

7. **Communicate with your employer.** Communicate your goals to your employer and point out how learning additional skills will make you a more valuable employee. Some companies offer tuition reimbursement programs or may even allow time off to take a class.

8. **Look into online options.** See if any of your classes are offered online or at alternate times, including evenings and weekends. An online class may work better with your schedule, but keep in mind it requires just as much commitment as any other class—maybe even more so. See **Peak Progress 3.4** for tips on taking online courses.

● **Balancing Your Life**
Balancing family with work sometimes requires making trade-offs to have a more fulfilling life. *What can you do to create a more balanced life?*

9. **Increase your energy—both physically and emotionally.** Focus on activities that are relaxing and help you recharge. Schedule time to relax, meditate, walk, and read for pleasure. Exercise, dance, do yoga, get enough sleep and rest, and eat healthy foods. Keep a gratitude journal and remind yourself that you are blessed with a full and rewarding life.

10. **Create positive time.** Don't buy your children toys to replace spending time with them. You can enjoy each other as you study together, garden, shop, do household chores, eat, take walks, read, play games, or watch a favorite television show. The activity is secondary to your uninterrupted presence. Spend time at bedtime sharing your day, talking about dreams, reading a story, and expressing your love and appreciation to them. Make this a positive time and avoid quarrels or harsh words. They will remember and cherish this warm and special time forever, and so will you.

11. **Model successful behavior.** Returning to school is an act that sends an important message. You are saying that learning, growing, and being able to juggle family, a job, and school are possible, worthwhile, and rewarding. It is important for children to see their parents setting personal and professional goals while knowing that the family is the center of their lives. You are modeling the importance of getting an education, setting goals, and achieving them.

Peak Progress

Online Learning

Taking classes online can be very appealing and convenient, especially if you're juggling other demands. Most of the strategies that apply to taking traditional, face-to-face courses apply to online courses; however, your time-management skills may be even more critical for success. If you are considering taking a course online, ask yourself the following questions:

- Do I like to work independently?
- Am I persistent and self-motivated?
- Am I comfortable e-mailing or phoning my instructor if I need help?
- Am I comfortable asking questions and following up if I need more clarification?
- Am I comfortable working at a computer, including opening, storing, and sending files; participating in forums; and using e-mail and basic software programs?

If you answered yes to most of these questions, taking an online course may be a good option for you. The following strategies will help you navigate online courses more successfully:

1. **Keep up on the coursework.** Think of it this way: What if your semester-long, face-to-face course was crammed into a week, including all the reading? Many people attempt to take online courses that way, waiting until the last minute to do the work. Instead, you must treat your online course as you would any other class by building it into your schedule. List due dates for assignments, tests, and projects. Build in time to read (the textbook as well as online materials) and study.

2. **Know the technology required for the course.** Make certain you have all the necessary equipment and software and work out any bugs. Do a trial run with your computer. Verify passwords and access to course Web sites, chat rooms, and so on.

3. **Communicate with the instructor.** Being in an online environment, you miss the nonverbal cues often given in a traditional course. Thus, effective communication is even more important. Clarify the expectations for the class, including reading assignments, exams, projects, and papers—as well as how to deliver finished work to the instructor. How will you know if items are received? Where will your grade be posted? Is there a set time for the class or a chat room? Find out when your instructor has office hours and the best time to respond by e-mail and phone. Ask for feedback from your instructor often and keep track of your progress. Make certain you verify your grade with your instructor before grades are submitted.

4. **Communicate with other students.** Create online study teams to share notes, ask questions, and study for tests. If this is your first time taking an online course, knowing there are other students out there to work with can make it less daunting. You may find that others have had the same questions about content and key points, technology problems, and so on that you do, and they may have answers.

5. **Check the school's tips.** Make sure to read any tips and frequently asked questions your school may have already posted about how to succeed in online courses, many of which may be specific to the needs of the institution and its instructors.

(continued)

Online Learning *(concluded)*

6. **Watch for announcements.** Know how the instructor or school will alert you to any changes that occur regarding assignments, tests, upcoming events, and so on and check for them each week.

7. **Print out essential information.** If possible, print out the syllabus, project assignments, and key content information, so that you can quickly refer to it, especially when you do not have access to your computer. Annotate the material with questions you need to follow up on, possible test questions, key points to remember, and the like.

8. **Sign in early.** If your course offers or requires participation in a chat room or message board, sign in early to make sure you are involved and can keep up on the discussion. Active participation may be a percentage of your total grade.

9. **Have a computer "Plan B."** Prepare for emergencies by checking out computer labs on campus and asking a friend, roommate, or family member if you can use his or her computer if yours crashes. Save and back up your work often. Create organized folders and back up important material, such as assignments and papers. Make sure you have enough paper and toner.

10. **Don't cheat.** All rules of ethics and academic honesty apply to online courses just as they do to traditional courses. Your work and responses must be your own.

12. **Balance your life.** Reflect on all areas of your life and the time you are presently investing in them. Decide if you are investing too much or too little time in each area. Also, look at the roles you play in each area of your life. In the family area, you may be a wife, mother, daughter, and so on. In the work area, you may be a manager, a part-time worker, or an assistant. Accompanying each role in your life are certain goals. Some goals demand greater time than others. It is OK to make a trade-off for a specific goal, but realize that you may neglect a vital area of your life. For instance, you may have a big term paper due, so you trade off a family outing to accomplish this goal. Complete **Personal Evaluation Notebook 3.7** to determine how you can achieve balance.

Personal Evaluation Notebook 3.7

Keeping your Life Goals in Balance

Several life areas are listed on this chart. Write one goal you have for each major area. Explain how you can commit a certain amount of time to meeting that goal and still maintain overall balance.

Life Areas	Goals
1. Career (job, earning a living)	_____
2. Education	_____
3. Spirituality (your inner being, peace of mind)	_____
4. Relationships (your family, friends, associates)	_____
5. Health (weight, exercise, food, stress, personal care)	_____
6. Recreation (hobbies, sports, interests)	_____
7. Finance	_____
8. Home	_____
9. Community involvement and service	_____
10. Personal growth and renewal	_____
11. Other	_____

TAKING CHARGE

Summary

In summary, in this chapter I learned to:

- **Assess where my time goes.** Knowing where I am already spending my time is essential for time management. I assess how much time I (1) commit to school, work, and other activities; (2) spend maintaining myself and home; and (3) devote to discretionary time.

- **Determine where my time should go.** I set goals to determine what I want to accomplish. I look at my values and priorities and use them to write a mission statement. I evaluate my dreams as I write my long-term goals. I break down my tasks and goals by short-term, mid-term, and long-term. I use a daily to-do list to keep me focused on top priorities. I know what I'd like to accomplish, what I should accomplish, and what is urgent and *must be accomplished*.

- **Assess my energy level.** "Doers" are organized and know how to pace themselves. They know when their energy level is high and work on top-priority goals when they are alert and focused.

- **Break down projects.** I look at a large project and then break it into manageable chunks. I make a project board, with deadlines for each assignment, and break down the assignment into realistic steps that I can do each day. I consolidate similar tasks to maximize my efforts.

- **Study everywhere and anywhere.** I make the most of waiting time, commuting time, and time between classes. I know it is more effective to study in short segments throughout the day than to study late at night in a marathon session.

- **Get organized.** I will develop a habit of putting everything in its place and getting organized. Spending a few extra minutes organizing my space and schedule pays off later.

- **Integrate learning styles.** Visualizing myself completing a project, talking to others about the project, working in groups, working alone, and using hands-on approaches whenever possible help me integrate learning styles. I look at the whole project and break it into steps, focusing on top-priority items and setting deadlines. I observe, plan, think, and do and then evaluate and do again until the project is completed.

- **Overcome procrastination and interruptions.** By setting daily priorities, breaking large projects into manageable tasks, being positive, creating an organized place to study, and being disciplined, I can accomplish what needs to be done. I've learned to just say no when necessary, and I reward myself when I complete projects and withhold rewards until I do first things first.

Performance Strategies

Following are the top 10 strategies for time management:

- Focus on goals and priorities.
- Keep a calendar and create a to-do list.
- Break down projects and consolidate similar tasks.
- Study at the right time, in the right space, and in short segments.
- Study everywhere and anywhere.
- Get organized.
- Be flexible, patient, and persistent.
- Don't procrastinate.
- Manage interruptions.
- Create balance.

Tech for Success

Take advantage of the text's Web site at **www.mhhe.com/ferrett7e** for additional study aids, useful forms, and convenient and applicable resources.

- **Semester calendar.** It's unavoidable—most of your tests and class papers will occur around the same time. Start planning your semester now by mapping out the major events and daily tasks you'll need to accomplish. A number of "planning" options are available with this text (worksheets and downloadable forms), or access planners online at a variety of Web sites, such as **www.timeanddate.com.**

- **A personal time-out.** It's easy to waste hours surfing the Internet, chatting online, and perusing the latest "find" on auction sites, such as eBay. You may need to give yourself a "time-out" or, rather, a "time's up." Set a timer as you get online and commit to turning off the computer when the timer goes off. Use your discretionary time wisely.

Study Team Notes

Career*in*focus

Deborah Page
FOOD SCIENTIST

Related Majors: Agricultural Science, Chemistry, Microbiology, Nutrition

Focus on Tasks, Not Time

Deborah Page is a food scientist for a large company in the food-processing industry. Her job is to develop new food products and ways to preserve or store foods. To do this, she engages in research and conducts tests and experiments, keeping in mind consumer demand for safety and convenience. Occasionally, she analyzes foods to determine levels of sugar, protein, vitamins, or fat.

Because her job is task-oriented, Deborah has a great deal of freedom in structuring her day. Her company allows flexible scheduling, so Deborah arrives at work at 9:30 A.M., after her children have left for school. Deborah is able to work until 6:30 P.M. because her children are involved in after-school activities and because her husband can pick them up by 5 P.M.

Deborah finds that she does her best work in late mornings and early afternoons. She plans research and testing during those times. She schedules most calls during the first hour at work, and she uses the latter part of her day to organize tasks for the next day. Good prior planning helps her manage her time well and focus on her tasks at hand.

Deborah's job includes a fair amount of reading, and she sometimes takes work home with her for the evening. That way, she can often leave work early to take her children to an appointment or to attend one of their sports activities. Giving attention to her family and personal interests helps Deborah create a balanced life.

CRITICAL THINKING Why is it important for Deborah to organize her time wisely? What are some of the prioritization strategies she uses daily to manage her time? What are some strategies to help her balance her personal and career commitments with a healthy, fulfilling lifestyle? Explore ways for Deborah to find time for herself for personal renewal.

Peak Performer

PROFILE

N. Scott Momaday

N. Scott Momaday has claimed many titles—dean of Native American authors, Pulitzer Prize winner, scholar, and Kiowa Indian.

Though born during the Great Depression in Oklahoma, Momaday grew up in a world rich with tradition. His childhood was spent on the reservations and pueblos of the Apache, Navaho, Pueblo, and Jemez Indians, where his parents taught school. The vast southwestern landscape that Momaday calls the "Indian world" was his playground. It was also his teacher and a colorful source of material for his future career. Horses, cowboy stories, and even comic books fed his imagination. As a boy, what did Momaday want to be when he grew up? A cowboy. "Comes with the territory," he explains.

Fortunately, Momaday followed in the footsteps of his mother and father, after pursuing his education at the University of New Mexico and then Stanford, where he received his doctorate. His mother, a descendent of American pioneers with Cherokee roots, was a writer and a teacher. His Kiowa father was an artist and accomplished storyteller in the Kiowa oral tradition. One reviewer described Momaday's style as using the language of his mother to tell "his story in the manner of his father's people." He later developed his innate talent as a painter and printmaker. He settled in Arizona, where he is currently a professor at the University of Arizona.

Through his novels, plays, poems, essays, folktales, artwork, and teaching, Momaday has kept the culture and beliefs of an old world alive and relevant. In his Pulitzer Prize–winning novel *House Made of Dawn*, the central character, like Momaday, faces the conflicts of straddling both the Indian and the white worlds. Momaday, however, has always known who he is: "I am an Indian and I believe I'm fortunate to have the heritage I have."

PERFORMANCE THINKING According to N. Scott Momaday, *"I simply kept my goal in mind and persisted. Perseverance is a large part of writing."* In what ways do you think Momaday has used his goals to guide his time management?

CHECK IT OUT N. Scott Momaday is dedicated to helping preserve the rich cultural heritage he enjoyed growing up. Momaday founded the Buffalo Trust, a nonprofit organization committed to "the preservation, protection, and return of their cultural heritage to Native peoples, especially children, and founded on the conviction that the loss of cultural identity—the theft of the sacred—is the most insidious and dangerous threat to the survival of Native American culture in our time." Learn more about the goals of this organization at **www.buffalotrust.org.**

Starting Today

At least one strategy I learned in this chapter that I plan to try right away is:

_____

_____

_____

What changes must I make in order for this strategy to be effective?

_____

_____

_____

Review Questions

Based on what you have learned in this chapter, write your answers to the following questions:

1. How does time management help you achieve your goals?

_____

_____

2. What is the difference between an "urgent" priority and an important priority?

_____

_____

3. Name at least five time-management strategies.

_____

_____

4. What can you do to avoid procrastination?

_____

_____

5. Why is it important to control interruptions?

_____

_____

Juggling Family and School

In the Classroom

Laura Chen is a returning part-time student. She also works full-time and takes care of her family. Her husband is verbally supportive of her goal to become a dental hygienist but is not very helpful with taking care of the children or with housework. Their children are 12 and 14 and have always depended on Laura to help them with their homework and drive them to their activities. Laura prides herself on being efficient at home, as well as being a loving mother and wife.

1. What can Laura do to get more control over her life?

_____

_____

2. What strategies in the chapter would be most helpful to Laura?

_____

_____

In the Workplace

Laura is now a dental hygienist. She has always had a busy schedule, but she expected to have more free time after she graduated. Instead, she finds herself being even busier than before. Her children are active in school, and she feels it is important for her to be involved in their activities and schoolwork. Laura is also a member of two community organizations, volunteers at the local hospital, and is active in her church. Lately, she has been late for meetings and has been rushing through her day. Because she knows her health is important, Laura has resumed her regular exercise program. Since graduation, she has had difficulty finding time for herself.

3. What strategies can help Laura gain control over her time and her life?

_____

_____

4. What areas of her life does she need to prioritize?

_____

_____

Applying the ABC Method of Self-Management

In the Journal Entry on page 81, you were asked to describe a situation when you were overwhelmed by too much to do and too little time. Describe that event below. What were the consequences?

_____

_____

_____

_____

Now apply the ABC method and visualize a more organized situation:

A = Actual event:

B = Beliefs:

C = Challenge:

While completing this exercise, did you determine ways you can become more organized and efficient?

PRACTICE SELF-MANAGEMENT

For more examples of learning how to manage difficult situations, see the "Self-Management Workbook" section of the Online Learning Center Web site at **www.mhhe.com/ferrett7e.**

My Time Management Habits

Complete the following statements with a Yes or No response.

	Yes	No
1. I do the easiest and most enjoyable task first.	✓	
2. I do my top-priority task at the time of day when my energy is the highest and I know I will perform best.	✓	
3. I use my time wisely by doing high-return activities—previewing chapters, proofreading papers.	✓	
4. Even though I find interruptions distracting, I put up with them.	✓	
5. I save trivial and mindless tasks for the time of day when my energy is low.		✓
6. I don't worry too much about making lists. I don't like planning and prefer to be spontaneous and respond as events occur.		✓
7. My work space is organized, and I have only one project on my desk at a time.		✓
8. I set goals and review them each semester and each year.	✓	
9. My workspace is open and I like to have people wander in and out.		✓
10. My study team socializes first and then we work.		
11. I have a lot of wasted waiting time, but you can't study in small blocks of time.	✓	
12. I block out a certain amount of time each week for my top-priority and hardest classes.	✓	

SCORING

1. Add the number of Yes responses to questions 2, 3, 5, 7, 8, 12.	4	
2. Add the number of No responses to questions 1, 4, 6, 9, 10, 11.	3	
3. Add the two scores together.	7	

The maximum score is 12. The higher the score, the more likely you are to be practicing good time management. Which areas do you need to improve?

|||
| ||

Time Wasters

Getting control of your time and life involves identifying time wasters and determining your peak energy level. It also involves identifying goals, setting priorities, and creating an action plan. Determining what task should be done first and overcoming procrastination are major factors in creating success. All these steps and issues involve critical thinking skills. Use critical thinking to answer the following questions.

1. What are the major activities and tasks that take up much of your time?

_____

_____

2. What activities cause you to waste time?

_____

_____

3. What activities can you eliminate or reduce?

_____

_____

4. When is your high-energy time?

_____

_____

5. When do you study?

_____

_____

6. Look at your committed time. Does this block of time reflect your values and goals?

_____

_____

7. How can you increase your discretionary time?

_____

_____

8. Do you complete top-priority tasks first?

_____

_____

(continued)

9. Look at the common reasons and excuses that some students use for not being organized and focused. Add to this list and use creative problem solving to list strategies for overcoming these barriers.

Reasons	Strategies
I ran out of time.	
I overslept.	
I'm easily distracted.	
People interrupt me.	
Instructors put too much pressure on me.	
I feel overwhelmed and panic at deadlines.	
I forgot about an assignment.	
Other	

Practice Goal Setting

Determine a personal desire or want and plan out a strategy of long-term, short-term, and daily goals that help you achieve it.

Goal-Setting Steps	Examples	Your Turn . . .
Step 1 Plainly state your *desire* or *want*.	"I want to be financially secure."	
Step 2 Develop a long-term goal that will help you fulfill your stated *desire* or *want*.	"I will earn a Bachelor of Science degree in computer technology from State University by June 2011."	
Step 3 Develop short-term goals that will help you achieve the long-term goal.	"I will enroll in all the classes recommended by my academic advisor."	
	"I will earn at least a 3.5 GPA in all my classes."	
	"I will join a small group."	
Step 4 Develop daily objectives that focus on achieving your short-term goals.	"I will set aside 2 hours of study for every 1 hour in class."	
	"I will make note cards to carry with me and review them when I'm waiting for class."	
	"I will review the day's lecture notes with my study team to make sure I didn't miss any important points."	

Map Out Your Goals

Use this illustration as a visual guide for mapping out your goals. To get started, plug in your responses from Personal Evaluation Notebook 3.3.

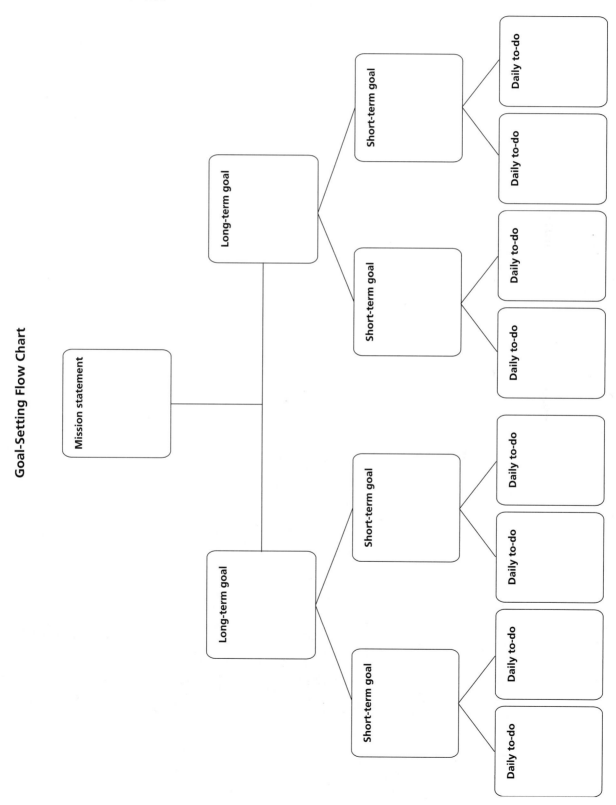

Goal-Setting Flow Chart

Daily Prioritizer and Planner: Your To-Do List

Consider the 80/20 rule on page 89 as you use this form to prioritize your tasks and schedule your daily activities. On the left side, write down the tasks you want to accomplish during the day. Then enter those tasks in the "Activity" column, focusing on urgent and important tasks first. Also make sure you include your maintenance and committed activities. Check off your tasks on the left side once they are completed. At the end of the day, see what tasks did not get accomplished and, if need be, include them on tomorrow's to-do list.

	Time	Activity
Urgent	12:00–1:00 A.M.	
	1:00–2:00	
	2:00–3:00	
	3:00–4:00	
	4:00–5:00	
Important	5:00–6:00	
	6:00–7:00	
	7:00–8:00	
	8:00–9:00	
	9:00–10:00	
	10:00–11:00	
	11:00–12:00 P.M.	
Ongoing	12:00–1:00	
	1:00–2:00	
	2:00–3:00	
	3:00–4:00	
	4:00–5:00	
	5:00–6:00	
Trivial	6:00–7:00	
	7:00–8:00	
	8:00–9:00	
	9:00–10:00	
	10:00–11:00	
	11:00–12:00	

Weekly Planner

Week of _____/_____/_____

Time	Sunday Activity	Monday Activity	Tuesday Activity	Wednesday Activity	Thursday Activity	Friday Activity	Saturday Activity
12:00–1:00 A.M.							
1:00–2:00							
2:00–3:00							
3:00–4:00							
4:00–5:00							
5:00–6:00							
6:00–7:00							
7:00–8:00							
8:00–9:00							
9:00–10:00							
10:00–11:00							
11:00–12:00 P.M.							
12:00–1:00							
1:00–2:00							
2:00–3:00							
3:00–4:00							
4:00–5:00							
5:00–6:00							
6:00–7:00							
7:00–8:00							
8:00–9:00							
9:00–10:00							
10:00–11:00							
11:00–12:00							

Urgent	Important	Ongoing

Month/Semester Calendar

Plan your projects and activities for the school term.

Date	Appointment

Date	Test

Due Date	Project

Month of _____

Demonstrating Your Time-Management Skills

List all the factors involved in time management. Indicate how you would demonstrate them to employers. Add this page to your Career Development Portfolio.

Areas	Your Demonstration
Dependability	*Haven't missed a day of work in my job*
Reliability	
Effectiveness	
Efficiency	
Responsibility	
Positive attitude	
Persistence	
Ability to plan and set goals and priorities	
Visionary	
Ability to follow through	
High energy	
Ability to handle stress	
Ability to focus	
Respect for others' time	
Ability to overcome procrastination	
Reputation as a doer and self-starter	

4

Listen and Take Effective Notes

LEARNING OBJECTIVES

In this chapter, you will learn to

4.1 Become an attentive listener

4.2 Utilize effective note-taking strategies

4.3 Take notes in alignment with your learning style

4.4 Describe the various note-taking systems

SELF-MANAGEMENT

> *I am having a problem staying focused and alert in my afternoon class. The instructor speaks in a monotone and I have a hard time following his lecture. What can I do to listen more effectively and take better notes?*

Have you ever had a similar experience? Do you find yourself daydreaming during class? Do you ever leave a class and feel frustrated because you've not been focused and your notes are unreadable? In this chapter, you will learn how to be an attentive listener and to take clear and organized notes.

JOURNAL ENTRY In **Worksheet 4.1** on page 146, describe a time when you had difficulty making sense out of a lecture and staying alert. Are there certain classes in which it is more challenging for you to be an attentive listener?

Attending lectures or meetings, listening, taking notes, and gathering information are a daily part of school and work. However, few people give much thought to the process of selecting, organizing, and recording information. Attentive listening and note taking are not just tools for school. They are essential job skills. Throughout your career, you will be processing and recording information. The volume of new information is expanding in this computer age, and the career professional who can listen, organize, and summarize information will be valuable. This chapter addresses the fine points of attentive listening and note taking.

Listening to the Message: Attentive Listening Strategies

Before you can be an effective note taker, you must become an effective listener. Most people think of themselves as good listeners. However, listening should not be confused with ordinary hearing. **Attentive listening** means that you are fully focused with the intent on understanding the speaker. It is a consuming activity that requires physical and mental attention, energy, concentration, and discipline. It requires respect, empathy, genuine interest, and the desire to understand. Researchers say that we spend about 80 percent or more of our time communicating; of that time, almost half—45 to 50 percent—is spent listening, yet few of us have been trained to listen. This helps explain why so many people are poor listeners.

Not only is listening fundamental to taking good classroom notes, but it is also directly related to how well you do in college, in your career, and in relationships. As a student, you will be expected to listen attentively to lectures, to other student presentations, and in small-group and class discussions. Career professionals attend meetings, follow directions, work with customers, take notes from professional journals and lectures, and give and receive feedback. Many organizations have been developing listening training programs to improve their employees' listening and communicating habits.

Apply the following attentive listening strategies for building effective relationships at school, at work, and in life.

Prepare to Listen

1. **Be willing to listen.** The first place to start is with your intention. You must want to be a better listener and realize that listening is an active rather than a passive process. Is your intention to learn and understand the other person? Or is your intention to prove how smart you are and how wrong the other person is? The best listening strategies in the world won't help if you are unwilling to

listen and understand another's viewpoint. Prepare mentally by creating a positive and willing attitude.

2. **Be open to new ideas.** Many people resist change, new ideas, or different beliefs. This resistance gets in the way of actively listening and learning. It is easy to misinterpret the meaning of a message if you are defensive, judgmental, bored, or emotionally upset. Be open to different points of view, different styles of lecturing, and new ideas. With practice and discipline, you can create interest in any subject.

3. **Position yourself to listen.** In the classroom, this may mean taking a chair in the front or finding a location where you feel comfortable and able to focus on the message and create a more personal relationship with the speaker.

4. **Reduce distractions.** Avoid sitting next to a friend or someone who likes to talk or is distracting. Take a sweater if it is cold in the classroom or sit by an open window if it is warm. Carry a bottle of water with you to drink when your energy starts to lag. Don't do other activities when you are listening (opening mail, doing math homework, making a to-do list, and so on). Do whatever it takes to focus and reduce distractions.

5. **Show that you are listening.** Attentive listening requires high energy. Sit up, keep your spine straight, and uncross your legs. Maintain eye contact and lean slightly forward. Participate in discussions and ask questions. Your body language is important—whether you are in a chair or engaged in a dialogue with others.

Stay Attentive

1. **Be quiet.** The fundamental rule of listening is to be quiet while the speaker is talking. Don't interrupt or talk to classmates. As a listener, your role is to understand and comprehend. The speaker's role is to make the message clear and comprehensible. Don't confuse the two roles. Listen attentively until the speaker is finished.

2. **Stay focused.** Being mentally and physically alert is vital for active listening. It's true that everyone's mind wanders during a long lecture, but being mentally preoccupied is a major barrier to effective listening. It's up to you to focus your attention, concentrate on the subject, and bring your mind back to the present. Make a determined effort to stay focused and in the present moment.

3. **Show empathy, respect, and genuine interest.** Focus on understanding the message and viewpoint of the speaker. Look for common views and ways in which you are alike.

4. **Observe the speaker.** Watch for obvious verbal and nonverbal clues about what information is important. If your instructor uses repetition, becomes more animated, or writes information on the board, it is probably important. Overhead transparencies or handouts may also include important diagrams, lists, drawings, facts, or definitions. Watch for examples and connect similar ideas. Pay attention to words and phrases that signal important information or transitions, such as "One important factor is . . ."

5. **Predict and ask questions.** Keep yourself alert by predicting and asking yourself questions. Is the story supporting the main topic? What are the main

points? How does the example clarify the readings? What test questions could be asked about the main points? Pretend that you are in a private conversation and ask your instructor to elaborate, give examples, or explain certain points. Make certain that you are paying attention in class, that you have previewed the chapter, and that you have done your homework.

6. **Integrate learning styles and use all your senses.** If you are primarily an *auditory* learner, consider taping certain lectures (be sure to ask the instructor first). Recite your book notes into a recorder and play them back several times. If you are primarily a *visual* learner, the more you see, the better you remember. Visualize what your instructor is talking about and supplement your lecture notes with drawings, illustrations, and pictures. If you are a *kinesthetic* learner, write as you listen, but also draw diagrams or pictures, rephrase what you hear in your own words, and take special note of material on the board, overhead transparencies, and handouts. Shift body position, so that you're comfortable.

7. **Postpone judgment.** Don't judge the speaker or the person's message based on clothes, reputation, voice, or teaching style. Listen with an open and curious mind and focus on the message, the course content, and your performance. Talk in private if you disagree or have an opposing viewpoint, but do not embarrass or unnecessarily challenge the person in front of others. Of course, you should use critical thinking, but be respectful and open to new ideas.

8. **Don't get caught up in drama.** Don't let another person's emotions affect your own. Stay focused on the message and be silent when silence is needed. Speak in low, quiet tones if someone is upset. Restate what you think you heard and ask questions: "I can see you are upset. How can I help?"

Review What You Have Heard

1. **Paraphrase.** Clarify the speaker's message. After a conversation, paraphrase what you think the speaker said to you—for example, "Professor Keys, it is my understanding that the paper should be four to five pages long, is due on Friday, and should include supporting documentation. Is that correct?" Show that you understand the speaker by reflecting and paraphrasing: "Jan, do I understand that you feel that you are doing more than your share of cleaning the apartment?" After a lecture, write a summary of the key points and main ideas. It is even more effective if you compare notes and summarize with your study team.

2. **Assess.** Evaluate how effective your listening skills are for recall, test taking, and studying with your study group. Reflect on conflicts, misunderstandings, and others' reactions to you. Take note of accompanying nonverbal cues. If there is a misunderstanding, assess your part. Did you jump to conclusions? Did you misunderstand nonverbal clues? Did you fail to clarify the message? Did you fail to follow up? When you feel that there is a misunderstanding or something is missing, ask simple, direct questions with the intent of understanding.

Peak Progress

Applying the Adult Learning Cycle to Becoming an Attentive Listener

Becoming an attentive listener and learning to take good notes take time and effort.

1. **RELATE. Why do I want to learn this?** How will being an attentive listener help me in school, work, and life? How would I rate my listening skills now? What areas do I need to improve?

2. **OBSERVE. How does this work?** I can learn a lot about attentive listening by watching others. I'll observe people who are good listeners and who take good notes. I'll also observe people who are not good listeners. Do their poor listening skills cause other problems for them?

3. **REFLECT. What does this mean?** I will gather information about listening and note taking and determine the better strategies for me to apply. What works and what doesn't seem to work? I'll explore creative ways to listen and take notes.

4. **DO. What can I do with this?** I will make a commitment to be a more attentive listener. I'll find opportunities to try my new listening skills. Each day, I'll focus on one area and work on it. For example, I'll choose one class in which I'm having trouble listening and experiment with new strategies.

5. **TEACH. Whom can I share this with?** I'll talk with others and share my tips and experiences. I'll demonstrate and teach the methods I've learned to others.

Now return to Stage 1 and think about how it feels to learn this valuable new skill of attentive listening.

---

3. **Practice with awareness.** It takes time to change old habits. Choose one problem you want to work on. For example, do you continue to interrupt? Think about how you feel when that happens to you and make a commitment to change. It won't happen overnight, but with consistent practice you can learn to stop annoying habits and improve your listening skills.

Peak Progress 4.1 explores how you can become a more attentive listener by applying the Adult Learning Cycle. Then, **Personal Evaluation Notebook 4.1** on page 128 asks you to think critically about your listening skills and how you can improve them.

Recording the Message

Now that you are prepared and have sharpened your listening and observation skills, let's look at how to outline your notes, so that you can organize material. **Note taking** is not a passive act of simply writing down words. It is a way to order and arrange thoughts and materials to help you remember information. You can use either a formal or an informal outline (see **Peak Progress 4.2** on page 130). The point of all note-taking systems is to distinguish between major and minor points and to add order and understanding to material. Let's start with one of the most widely used and effective note-taking systems—the Cornell System of Note Taking.

> 66 He listens well, who takes notes. 99
>
> **DANTE**
> *Author*

WORDS TO SUCCEED

Personal Evaluation Notebook 4.1

Attentive Listening

Use critical thinking to answer the following questions.

1. Do you go to class prepared and in a positive and receptive state of mind? Write down one tip that you would be willing to try to improve your listening.

   _____

   _____

   _____

2. Jot down the name of a person whom you consider to be a good listener. Consider your feelings toward this person. It is usually difficult not to like someone whom you consider to be a good listener. Attentive listening shows respect and caring and is one of the best gifts one person can give to another.

   _____

   _____

   _____

3. Write a list of daily situations in which attentive listening is required. Some situations could include talking to your child about his or her day at school, listening to your spouse's or roommate's views on politics, and meeting with a community group to plan a fundraising event. What listening strategies would increase your attention and responsiveness in the situations you've listed?

   _____

   _____

   _____

The Cornell System of Note Taking

The Cornell System of Note Taking was developed in the 1950s by Walter Pauk at Cornell University. It is effective for integrating text and lecture notes. Start with a sheet of standard loose-leaf paper and label it with the class, date, and title of the lecture. Divide your notepaper into three sections ("Notes," "Cues," and "Summary") by drawing a vertical line about 2 inches from the left-hand margin; then draw a horizontal line below that. (See **Figure 4.1**)

Notes. The right-hand side is the largest section. Record information from class lectures in whatever format works best for you. You can use a formal system

Figure 4.1
The Cornell System

This method integrates text and lecture notes and includes a summary section. *Which personality type might prefer the Cornell System?*

Seminar	Jana Rosa
Peak Performance 101	Oct. 2, 2009
Topic: Note taking	Tuesday

Cues:	Notes:
What is the	I. Purpose of Note Taking
purpose of	A. To accurately record information
note taking?	B. To become actual part of listening
	C. To enhance learning
Different	II. Note–Taking Systems
systems can	A. Formal outline
be combined	B. Cornell Systems
	C. Mind map

Summary:
Use the note-taking system that is right for you or create a combination.
Remember to date and review.

with standard Roman numerals or an informal system of indentation to distinguish between major and minor points and meaningful facts.

Cues. Then use the left side to jot down cues, main ideas, phrases, key words, or clarifications. List any pertinent examples or sample test questions from the lecture or the book. Try to pose questions that are answered by your notes. When you review, cover up the right-hand side (the "Notes" section) and try to answer the questions you have written.

Summary. On the bottom of the page, include a "Summary" section. This is a very effective way to write a summary in your own words of each class session. Fill in with details from the book and further clarify and elaborate after discussions with your study team or instructor.

The Cornell System is a great tool for reviewing and comparing notes for both lectures and books. Notes can be taken sequentially to preserve the order decided upon by the lecture. It is an effective method to review with your study team, since you can compare class notes, review summaries, and use the sample test questions on the left. One student can recite his or her notes on the right, while another uses the cues on the left for possible test questions and examples. Each can recite his or her class and chapter summaries. Many people who are left-brain dominant prefer the logical, sequential, step-by-step Cornell System.

Peak Progress

Formal (Traditional) versus Informal (Creative) Outlines

Your learning style, or whether you are a left-brain- or right-brain-dominant person, can affect what outline style works for you. Left-brain-dominant people tend to like a traditional outline that uses a logical, step-by-step, sequential pattern of thought and focuses on words and order. **Formal outlines** use Roman numerals and capital letters to outline headings, main topics, and points, and supporting points are highlighted with lowercase letters and numbers. This system requires consistency. For example, the rules require at least two headings on the same level; if you have a IA, you should also have IB. If you have a IIIA1, you must also have IIIA2.

Some students find that formal outlines are too time-consuming and restrictive for classroom lectures. However, they like using an outline because it organizes ideas and illustrates major points and supporting ideas. They prefer a free-form, or **informal, outline.** This system shows the same headings, main points, and supporting examples and associations, but it uses a system of dashes and indenting. Many students find an informal method to be easier for in-class note taking, since it allows them to focus on main ideas and supporting examples instead of worrying about rules.

Following are examples of formal (top) and informal (bottom) outlines.

Topic: Note Taking   Jana Rosa
                                                              April 9, 2009

Effective Strategies for Taking Notes

  I. The traditional outline for note taking
    A. Advantages
      1. Occupies your attention totally
      2. Organizes ideas as well as records them
    B. Disadvantages
      1. Too structured for right-brain-dominant person
      2. Time-consuming

  II. The mapping system for note taking
    A. Advantages
      1. Presents a creative and visual model
      2. Can start anywhere on the page
    B. Disadvantages
      1. Too busy for a left-brain-dominant person
      2. Too unorganized for a left-brain-dominant person

STRATEGIES

VISUALIZE

NOTE TAKING   Jana Rosa
                                                       April 9, 2009

1. Summarize
2. Organize — Traditional
      — Mind map
      — Cornell
3. Visualize and illustrate
4. Shorthand
5. Notebook
6. One side of paper
7. Write down blackboard notes
8. Review
    10 minutes
    24 hours
    Weekly

Mind Maps

A **mind map** (or a "think link") is a visual, holistic form of note taking (see **Figure 4.2** and **Figure 4.3** on page 132 for two examples of mind maps). The advantage is that you can see the big picture. You can also see connections to the main idea. Mapping starts from the main idea, placed in the center of a page, and branches out with subtopics through associations and patterns. You may find that mapping helps you increase your comprehension, creativity, and recall. Many students find mind maps useful in brainstorming ideas for speeches or papers, in serving as a framework for recalling topics, or in helping them review, but not as useful as a note-taking system during class lectures, since there is no linear or sequential order.

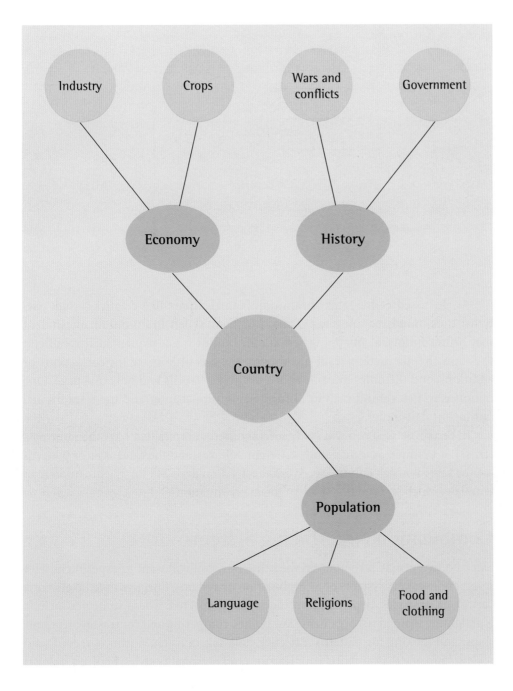

Figure 4.2
Sample Mind Map

This template can be adapted for many subjects. *In which of your courses would this format be useful for note taking?*

Figure 4.3

Another Sample Mind Map

This type of mind map uses branches to reveal concept connections and patterns. *Which mind map design do you prefer?*

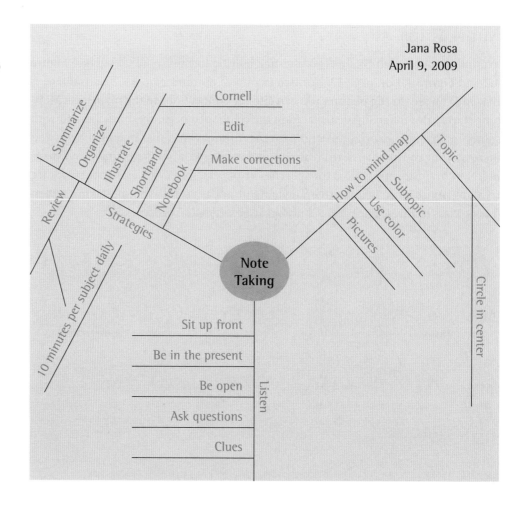

As discussed earlier, right-brain-dominant learners like creative, visual patterns; thus, mind mapping may work for them. A left-brain-dominant student may be uncomfortable mapping because the outline is not sequential; it is difficult to follow the instructor's train of thought; there is little space for corrections or additions; and the notes must be shortened to key words and only one page. One option is to use a mind map to illustrate an entire chapter and use a traditional outline for daily notes.

In certain classes, you will study several different topics that have the same patterns. For example, you may study different cultures, and the categories or patterns are the same for each culture. See **Worksheet 4.3** on page 148 for a blank mind map template, which you can use or adapt for many situations.

Combination Note-Taking Systems

Since no two people take notes in the same way, you will want to experiment with several note-taking systems or a combination of systems. Effective note takers use a variety of strategies, depending on the material covered. These strategies include highlighting main ideas, organizing key points, comparing and contrasting relationships, and looking for patterns. Effective note takers listen, organize, record, and review. Find one that supports your learning and personality styles. **Figure 4.4** shows

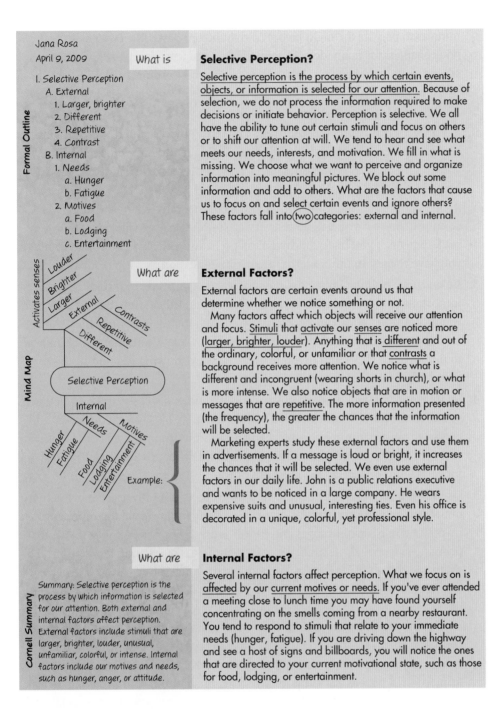

Jana Rosa
April 9, 2009

Formal Outline

What is **Selective Perception?**

I. Selective Perception
A. External
1. Larger, brighter
2. Different
3. Repetitive
4. Contrast
B. Internal
1. Needs
a. Hunger
b. Fatigue
2. Motives
a. Food
b. Lodging
c. Entertainment

Mind Map

Activates senses — Louder, Brighter, Larger — External — Contrasts, Repetitive, Different

Selective Perception

Internal — Needs (Hunger, Fatigue), Motives (Food, Lodging, Entertainment)

Example:

What are **External Factors?**

What are **Internal Factors?**

Cornell Summary

Summary: Selective perception is the process by which information is selected for our attention. Both external and internal factors affect perception. External factors include stimuli that are larger, brighter, louder, unusual, unfamiliar, colorful, or intense. Internal factors include our motives and needs, such as hunger, anger, or attitude.

Selective Perception?

Selective perception is the process by which certain events, objects, or information is selected for our attention. Because of selection, we do not process the information required to make decisions or initiate behavior. Perception is selective. We all have the ability to tune out certain stimuli and focus on others or to shift our attention at will. We tend to hear and see what meets our needs, interests, and motivation. We fill in what is missing. We choose what we want to perceive and organize information into meaningful pictures. We block out some information and add to others. What are the factors that cause us to focus on and select certain events and ignore others? These factors fall into two categories: external and internal.

External Factors?

External factors are certain events around us that determine whether we notice something or not.

Many factors affect which objects will receive our attention and focus. Stimuli that activate our senses are noticed more (larger, brighter, louder). Anything that is different and out of the ordinary, colorful, or unfamiliar or that contrasts a background receives more attention. We notice what is different and incongruent (wearing shorts in church), or what is more intense. We also notice objects that are in motion or messages that are repetitive. The more information presented (the frequency), the greater the chances that the information will be selected.

Marketing experts study these external factors and use them in advertisements. If a message is loud or bright, it increases the chances that it will be selected. We even use external factors in our daily life. John is a public relations executive and wants to be noticed in a large company. He wears expensive suits and unusual, interesting ties. Even his office is decorated in a unique, colorful, yet professional style.

Internal Factors?

Several internal factors affect perception. What we focus on is affected by our current motives or needs. If you've ever attended a meeting close to lunch time you may have found yourself concentrating on the smells coming from a nearby restaurant. You tend to respond to stimuli that relate to your immediate needs (hunger, fatigue). If you are driving down the highway and see a host of signs and billboards, you will notice the ones that are directed to your current motivational state, such as those for food, lodging, or entertainment.

Figure 4.4

Combination Note-Taking System

You can use several different note-taking systems on the left, reflecting the main text on the right. *Which note-taking system do you prefer?*

a combination note-taking system, using a formal outline, mind mapping, and the Cornell System.

Note-Taking Strategies

The following strategies will help you make the most of the note-taking system you use. Review the strategies listed at the beginning of the chapter to prepare yourself both mentally and physically for listening.

1. **Preview the material.** Can you imagine going to an important class without doing your homework; being unprepared to participate; or lacking pen, paper, and necessary material? Go to classes prepared, even if you have only a few

minutes to prepare the night before or right before class. Preview or skim textbook chapters for main ideas, general themes, and key concepts. Previewing is a simple strategy that enhances your note taking and learning. In a sense, you are priming your brain to process information efficiently and effectively. You will also want to review previous notes and connect what you have learned to new ideas.

2. **Go to every class and pay attention.** The most obvious and important part of being prepared is to attend all your classes. You cannot take effective notes if you are not there. Having someone else take notes for you is not the same as being in class. Of course, this doesn't mean "If I just show up, I should get an A." It is important to pay attention and to be mentally aware and alert. Make a commitment that you will go to every class unless you are ill. Have several backup plans if you have children. Don't schedule other appointments when you have classes. In other words, treat your education as a top priority.

3. **Be on time.** Walking in late for class indicates an attitude that class is not important to you and disrupts the instructor and other students. Set your watch 5 minutes ahead and arrive early enough to preview your notes and get settled. Punctuality also helps you prepare emotionally and mentally. You have to put forth an effort and invest in every class by showing up—on time—prepared, alert, and ready to participate.

4. **Sit up front.** You will be more physically alert, and you will see and hear better, if you sit in the front of the class. You will also be more likely to ask questions and engage the instructor in eye contact when you sit in front. You will be less likely to talk with other students, pass notes, doodle, or daydream. (See **Peak Progress 4.3** for special tips on getting the most out of your instructor's presentation.)

5. **Use all your senses.** Many people view note taking not only as a passive activity but also as an auditory activity. Actually, you will find note taking more effective if you integrate learning styles and use all your senses. For example, if you are primarily a *kinesthetic* learner, you may want to make learning more physical by writing and rephrasing material, working with your study team or partner, collecting examples, creating stories and diagrams, using note cards, and standing when taking notes from your textbook. If you are primarily a *visual* learner, develop mental pictures and use your right-brain creativity. Draw and illustrate concepts. Practice visualizing images while the speaker is talking, form mental pictures of the topic, and associate the pictures with key words. You might try using colored pencils, cartoons, or any other illustrations that make the material come alive. Supplement your lecture notes with drawings, and take special note of material on the board, overhead transparencies, and handouts. If you are primarily an *auditory* learner, listen attentively and capitalize on this style of processing information. You might want to record lectures. Explain your notes to your study group, so that you can hear the material again.

6. **Make note taking active and physical.** Physical activity gets your blood flowing throughout your body, including your brain, which is why physical activity enhances academic performance for all learning styles. Observe your body, how you hold your pen, and how your back feels against the chair. Sit up straight; slouching produces fatigue and signals the brain that this activity is not important. When you are at home taking notes and you feel your energy dip, take a walk, stretch, do deep knee bends or head rolls, or jog in

Peak Progress

Getting the Most Out of a Class Lecture

In the classroom—as well as in meetings you will attend on the job—you will come across many styles of presenters, from the very dynamic and succinct to the agonizingly vague and verbose. As discussed in Chapter 1, there are ways to adjust your learning style to your instructor's teaching style, just as you would need to adjust your work style to that of your boss. But what if your instructor's style presents specific challenges to your learning? Following are some tips if your instructor

- **Talks too softly.** If you can't hear your instructor, first ask fellow students if they are having the same problem (to make sure it's not just your hearing). Then, try a seat in the front. If it's still a problem, it's more than appropriate to approach your instructor outside of class about the issue. Your instructor may not be aware it's a problem and may be able to adjust his or her speaking level or use a microphone in subsequent classes.

- **Talks too fast.** If you find you can't keep up with your instructor as you take notes (or you are missing points), it may be that you are a little slower jotting down notes than fellow students and may have to speed it up. Focus on writing just key words. If you miss a section, leave a space in your notes with a notation (such as an asterisk or "missed") and ask another student or your study group about the missing material.

- **Is hard to understand because his or her native language is different from yours.** As our world becomes more globally connected, you will encounter instructors, colleagues, physicians, neighbors, and so on with various native languages, cultures, and experiences. No matter what language you or your instructor is most accustomed to, you are both in the room for the same reason—to teach and learn the material. Thus, it's critical for you to ask questions when you don't understand a point—and be persistent until you do understand.

- **Never allows time to ask questions.** Find out your instructor's e-mail or office hours and contact him or her directly with your questions.

- **Never addresses material from the text.** Some students get frustrated when they buy a text and then the instructor doesn't cover the same material during lecture. But it may be because the instructor is expecting you to read the text on your own and thus is using lecture time for other topics. If you are having difficulty with any of the text material, ask the instructor if you should bring that up during or outside of class.

- **Only lectures, never writes on the board or uses PowerPoint.** Listen for verbal cues (such as a louder voice) and nonverbal cues (such as hand gestures) that suggest more important points to remember. If not given, ask for examples that illustrate key points.

- **Puts a lot of content in the PowerPoint presentation.** PowerPoint presentations can be a visual way of organizing a lecture and showing key illustrations. But some get carried away and attempt to put the whole lecture in a few slides. Rather than scrambling to write every word, ask the instructor if the presentation is

(continued)

Getting the Most Out of a Class Lecture *(concluded)*

available online, and then bring it to class and take notes on it. Or look at slide headings for key words or phrases as the instructor speaks.

- **Never follows the lecture outline or PowerPoint.** Not everyone stays on course when speaking, especially if the discussion is sidetracked by questions or new topics. Remember that the PowerPoint presentation is just a blueprint, and attempt to balance your notes with the key points from it along with the instructor's discussion.

- **Seems to ramble and never gets to a point.** Some speakers are better than others. Here's where you have to be proactive and ask clarifying questions ("So what you are saying is _____, correct?") and confer with fellow classmates. Collectively, you will put the pieces together.

- **Uses too many personal anecdotes that may or may not be relevant.** Everyone loves to tell old "war stories," even though the relevance may be a stretch. However, this is an opportunity to connect personally with the instructor, and you may find you have similar experiences. Just keep an open mind and resist the urge to ask, "Will this be on the test?"

In every situation, if you still have difficulties listening and taking notes, you should promptly and politely talk with your instructor. Only with feedback does a speaker improve his or her skills, which in turn benefits listeners.

place for a few minutes. Exercise also helps relax the body, focuses the mind, and reduces stress.

7. **Link information.** Connect ideas and link similar information. Look for patterns and information that is different. Compare and contrast; find similarities and differences. Develop associations between what you are hearing for the first time and what you already know. When you link new knowledge to what you already know, you create lasting impressions. Ask yourself how this information relates to other classes or to your job.

8. **Use creative shorthand and focus on key words.** A common mistake students make is attempting to write down everything the instructor says. Notes are like blueprints, because they represent a larger subject and highlight main details. The essential element in taking effective notes is to jot down only main points and key words. Illustrations, filler statements, stories, introductions, and transitions are important for depth, interest, and understanding, but you don't have to write down every word. Devise your own system for note taking that includes abbreviations and symbols. If you frequently text message on your cell phone, you may have already developed your own "shorthand vocabulary," which may be helpful when taking notes. See **Figure 4.5** for common note-taking shortcuts.

9. **Organize your notes.** Use large, bold headlines for the main ideas and large print for key words, important points, facts, places, and other supporting data. Write your name, the topic, and the date on each sheet of paper. You

Symbol	Meaning	Abbreviation	Meaning
>	greater than; increase	i.e.	that is
<	less than; decrease	etc.	and so forth
?	question	lb.	pound
w/	with	assoc.	association
w/o	without	info	information
V or *	important ideas	e.g.	example
+	positive	p.	page
—	negative	pp.	multiple pages
X	times		
~	gaps in information		
→	leads to (e.g., motivation → success)		
^	bridge of concepts; insert		
#	number		

Figure 4.5

Note-Taking Shortcuts

This chart lists some common symbols and abbreviations you can incorporate into your own note-taking system. *What is the essential element in taking effective notes?*

may want to purchase a binder for each class to organize notes, syllabi, handouts, tests, and summaries. Leave wide margins and plenty of space to make corrections, add notes, clarify, and summarize. Don't crowd your words, or the notes will be difficult to understand. Keep all handouts you receive in class. Use a question mark if you do not understand something, so that you can ask about it later.

10. **Use note cards.** Use index cards to jot down key words, formulas, definitions, and other important information. Note cards and flash cards help you integrate all learning styles. Write down key words and main points, use them throughout the day, and review for tests.

11. **Expand on notes from others.** Many instructors lecture in conjunction with a PowerPoint presentation. Ask your instructor if the lecture outline is available as a handout, on a course Web site, or in a bookstore. Preview it before class, take a copy of the printout to class, and add notes and detail as the instructor talks. This is a handy note-taking tool that helps you follow the discussion, organize your notes, and read the text. Similarly, if you happened to miss class and borrowed notes from someone else, make sure you thoroughly review the notes, mark anything that is unclear and needs follow-up, and compare them with the textbook.

12. **Use your laptop.** Your instructor may allow you to take notes in class on a laptop computer. You may find this a convenient way to store, organize, review, and share notes after class. However, you may find it difficult to focus on discussions, nonverbal cues, and visual illustrations if you are looking at your keyboard or screen. If your power fails or you forget to save your work, you may have no back-up notes. Also, your classmates or instructor may be distracted by your typing. Consider taking lecture notes on a computer only if it makes sense and maximizes your learning.

Assess and Review Your Notes

Don't just file your notes away after class. Now it's time to reinforce your memory and understanding of the material by assessing and reviewing your notes. Research indicates that, even after only 1 hour, you will retain less than 50 percent of the lecture you just attended. (See **Figure 4.6.**) Thus, it's important to revisit your notes as soon as possible.

1. **Summarize in your own words.** When you finish taking text and lecture notes, summarize in your own words. You might want to write summaries on index cards. If you used the Cornell System, make sure you complete the summary section. Summarizing can be done quickly and can cover only main concepts. This one small action will greatly increase your comprehension and learning. It is even more effective when you read your summary out loud to others; teaching is a good way to learn.

2. **Edit and revise your notes.** Set aside a few minutes as soon as possible after the lecture to edit, revise, fill in, or copy your notes. (If possible, avoid scheduling classes back to back, so you can spend time with your notes right after class.) Underline what the instructor has indicated is important. Clean up, expand, and rewrite sections that are messy or incomplete. Compare your notes with the material in the textbook. If you are unclear on a point, leave a space and put a question mark in the margin or highlight in color. You can ask for verification from other students in class or your instructor.

3. **Create a sample test.** Ask yourself what questions might be on a test and attempt to write a few sample test questions as if you were giving the exam. Note the correct answer and any rationale why it is correct (which may prove helpful later if there is an essay or short-answer exam).

Figure 4.6
Ebbinghaus's Forgetting Curve

German philosopher Hermann Ebbinghaus determined that after only 9 hours you remember about 36 percent of what you just learned. At 31 days, that has dropped to 21 percent. Thus, constant reviewing is critical. *If you wait until midterm to review your lecture notes, how much will you remember of the first days in class?*

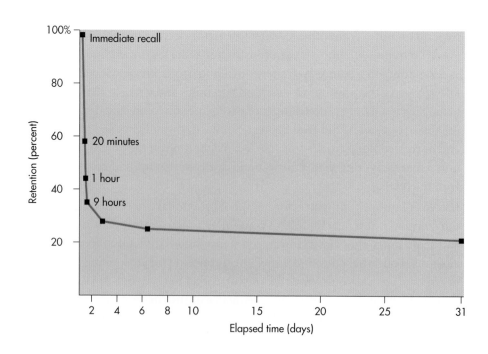

Source: Hermann Ebbinghaus, Memory: A Contribution to Experimental Psychology, 1885/1913.

4. **Use visual cues.** Consider drawing a mind map of your notes to display the main points and their connections. For math and science classes, creating flow charts may help visually reinforce processes or systems.

5. **Review your notes.** Develop a review schedule that supports continual reviewing and reflects on material you have already learned. Think of how you can review your notes within the first hour, the first day, and each week and add this to the daily planner you created in Chapter 3. There are many ways to work reviewing into your day:

   • *Arrive at class early* and spend 5 minutes reviewing your notes from the previous class. Or you can review while the instructor passes out handouts, adjusts the overhead projector, or organizes the lecture.

   • *Review right before you go to sleep,* since your mind is receptive to new information at that time.

   • *Compare notes with your study group members* to make sure you recorded and understood all the key points.

6. **Monitor and evaluate.** Periodically assess your note-taking system. Try different systems and strategies until you find the one that works best. Feedback from study group members, your instructor, and tests will help you assess how well your system is working.

● **Taking Notes on the Job**
Note taking is an essential skill in many professions. *What are some jobs or professions in which taking notes is a critical, daily task?*

Overcome Obstacles

Some students do not realize the importance of note taking and view it as a passive academic skill that they will never use once they graduate from college. As a result, their notes are often disorganized, incomplete, illegible, and of little help in preparing for tests. However, effective note taking changes the information that you hear into information that is distinctly yours. You have discarded the unessential, highlighted the essential, and organized information to give it meaning, relevance, and focus. Not only is mastering this process essential to improving your study skills, but it is a necessary job and life skill—from understanding your company's objectives and what your role will be to sitting in on a presentation about employee health benefits. If you don't listen carefully and take complete, helpful notes (or any notes at all) you have nothing to fall back on if the results aren't what you expected.

66 Obstacles are those frightful things you see when you take your eyes off your goal. 99

HENRY FORD
Founder, Ford Motor Company

WORDS TO SUCCEED

TAKING CHARGE

Summary

In summary, in this chapter I learned to:

- **Listen attentively to the message.** Developing an interest in listening and making it meaningful to me are the first steps in becoming an attentive listener. I must want to listen and am open to new information, new ideas, and different beliefs. My intent is to understand others and to focus on the message.

- **Go to every class.** I know that it is very important to make a commitment to go to every class and form a relationship with my instructor and other students. I'm on time and sit up in front, where I'm alert and aware. I sit up straight, maintain eye contact, and show that I'm listening and involved with the speaker. I reduce distractions and focus on listening, not talking. I'm in the present and concentrate on the subject.

- **Observe my instructor and watch for verbal and nonverbal clues.** I watch for examples, words, and phrases that signal important information or transitions. I take note of handouts and transparencies. I use critical thinking to postpone judgment. I focus on the message, not the presentation. I look beyond clothes, voice, teaching style, and reputation and focus on what the other person is saying. Using critical thinking helps me look for supporting information and facts and ask questions.

- **Prepare prior to class.** I preview chapters before class, so I have a general idea of the chapter, and make notes of questions to ask or concepts that I want the instructor to give examples of or elaborate on. I do homework and use index cards to jot down and memorize key words, formulas, and definitions.

- **Focus on key words.** I don't try to write down all the information but, rather, look for key words and essential information. I look for patterns, link information, and connect ideas in a way that makes sense and organizes the information. I leave space for corrections and additions and use marks, such as "?" for questions.

- **Integrate learning styles.** I not only use my preferred learning style but also integrate all styles. I make note taking active and physical. I draw pictures and make illustrations, use outlines, supplement my notes with handouts, create models, and summarize out loud.

- **Get organized.** I know that information that is not organized is not remembered. I write the date and topic on each sheet and organize notes in a folder or binder.

- **Determine the note-taking style that works best for me.** A formal outline uses my left-brain, sequential side, while an informal outline helps me see connections and the big picture. The Cornell System of note taking is organized into three sections: "Notes," "Cues," and "Summary." A mind map is more visual and includes main points that are connected to supporting points or examples. I can also combine elements of various note-taking systems to determine what works best for me.

- **Summarize in my own words when I am finished taking notes in class or from the text.** This one action greatly improves my comprehension and learning. I compare this summary with the material in my book, review it with my study team, and fill in essential information. I make notes on questions to ask my instructor or study group.

- **Review, monitor, and evaluate.** I review my notes for main ideas as soon as possible after class, but within 24 hours. This increases my memory and helps me make sense out of my notes. I edit and add to my notes. I evaluate my note-taking skills and look for ways to improve them.

Performance Strategies

Following are the top 10 strategies for attentive listening and effective note taking:

- Postpone judgment and be open to new ideas.
- Seek to understand and show respect to the speaker.
- Reduce distractions and be alert and focused.
- Maintain eye contact and look interested.
- Observe the speaker and listen for clues, examples, signal words, and phrases.
- Predict and ask questions to clarify main points.
- Look for information that is familiar to what you already know and information that is different.
- Use a note-taking system that suits your learning style.
- Summarize in your own words and review often.
- Edit and revise while information is still fresh.

Tech for Success

Take advantage of the text's Web site at **www.mhhe.com/ ferrett7e** for additional study aids, useful forms, and convenient and applicable resources.

- **Your instructor's visual presentation.** Many instructors lecture in conjunction with a PowerPoint presentation. Ask your instructor if the lecture outline is available as a handout, on a course Web site, or in a bookstore. Take a copy of the printout to class with you and add notes and detail as the instructor talks. This is a handy tool for note taking that helps you follow the discussion, organize your notes, and read the text.

- **Summarize on your computer.** Some people type faster than they can write by hand. It's very important to summarize your notes as soon as possible after class to make sure you understand the main points. If that sounds like a daunting task, take a few minutes on your computer to summarize your notes. If necessary, write incomplete sentences first and then flesh out the sentences. If you aren't sure if you really understand the main points of the lecture, consider e-mailing your recap to your instructor and ask him or her to review it. (This may also help your instructor determine if points presented in the lecture need clarification during the next class session.)

Study Team Notes

Danielle Sievert
PSYCHOLOGIST

Related Majors: Psychology, Counseling

Listening in the Workplace

Danielle Sievert provides mental health care as an industrial-organizational psychologist for a Fortune 500 company. Most industrial-organizational psychologists hold master's degrees in psychology. Psychology is the study of human behavior and the mind and its applications to mental health. When most people think of psychologists, they think of clinicians in counseling centers or hospitals, but many large companies hire psychologists to tend to the needs of staff on all levels. Danielle and other industrial-organizational psychologists use psychology to improve quality of life and productivity in the workplace.

Danielle conducts applicant screenings to select employees who will work well within the company. She provides input on marketing research. She also helps solve human relations problems that occur in various departments. Danielle occasionally conducts individual sessions with employees who face problems within or outside of the office. Danielle works a 9-to-5 schedule and is occasionally asked to work overtime. She is often interrupted to solve pressing problems.

Active listening is an important part of Danielle's job. Managers and other employees will ask for her help, she says, only when they sense that she is empathetic and desires to be of help. To hone her listening skills, Danielle asks questions to make sure she understands exactly what the person is saying. She also takes notes, either during or after a session. By using such skills, Danielle is able to fulfill her role as a psychologist in the workplace.

CRITICAL THINKING What kinds of problems might occur at the workplace that could be addressed by a firm's psychologist?

Peak Performer

PROFILE

Anna Sui

"What should I wear?" This is a question that many people ask almost daily. For international fashion designer Anna Sui (pronounced *Swee*), the answer is simple: "Dress to have fun and feel great." Her first boutique, on Greene Street in Soho, New York, illustrated her attitude with a Victorian-inspired mix of purple walls, ornate clothing racks, glass lamps, and red floors.

To the second of three children and only daughter born to Chinese immigrants, the Detroit suburbs of the early 1960s were a long way from the fashion mecca of New York City. However, even then Sui seemed to be visualizing success. Whether designing tissue-paper dresses for her neighbor's toy soldiers or making her own clothes with coordinating fabric for shoes, Sui had flair.

After graduating from high school, Sui headed for the Big Apple. She eventually opened her own business after two years of studying at Parson's School of Design and years of working in the trenches at various sportswear companies. Sui premiered her first runway show in 1991 and today has 300 stores in over 30 countries.

To create such acclaimed designs, Sui takes note of the world around her. She continues to collect her "genius files"—clippings from pages of fashion magazines—to serve as inspiration. She listens to her clients, to music, to the street, and to her own instincts. Sui is quick to say that, although her moderately priced

clothes are popular with celebrities, they are also worn by her mother. It's not about age and money, she explains, but about the "spirit of the clothing." By listening actively and staying attuned to the world around her, Sui continues to influence trends and enchant with her designs.

PERFORMANCE THINKING For the career of your choice, how would attentive listening and note taking contribute to your success?

CHECK IT OUT Look through Anna Sui's "genius files" at **www.annasuibeauty.com** (use the words *genius files* in the search box to get a complete list). Those who are profiled come from a variety of creative professions, including photographers, illustrators, filmmakers, theater and movie actors, musicians, and, of course, fashion designers and trendsetters. Consider starting your own "genius file" of people and words that inspire you.

Starting Today

At least one strategy I learned in this chapter that I plan to try right away is:

_____

_____

_____

What changes must I make in order for this strategy to be effective?

_____

_____

_____

Review Questions

Based on what you have learned in this chapter, write your answers to the following questions:

1. What is attentive listening?

_____

_____

2. Why are listening and note-taking skills critical to job success?

_____

_____

3. Name two types of note-taking systems and describe how to use them.

_____

_____

4. Why is "Go to every class" an important note-taking strategy?

_____

_____

5. What should you do with your notes after attending class?

_____

_____

Developing Attentive Listening Skills

In the Classroom

Roxanne Jackson is a fashion design student who works part-time at a retail clothing store. She has two roommates, who are also students. Roxanne is a very social person. She is outgoing, enjoys being around people, and loves to talk and tell stories. However, Roxanne is a poor listener. In class, she is often too busy talking with the person next to her to pay attention to the class assignments. She always starts off as a popular study group member, but it soon becomes clear that her assignments are always late and incorrect. Roxanne's roommates have finally confronted her. There is tension between them, because the roommates feel that Roxanne is not pulling her weight on household chores. Another major problem is that Roxanne does not seem to take accurate phone messages. She never seems to write down the correct information.

1. What strategies in this chapter can help Roxanne be a more effective listener?

   _____

   _____

2. What would you suggest she do to improve her relationship with others and to help her become better at taking down information?

   _____

   _____

In the Workplace

Roxanne is now a buyer for a large department store. She enjoys working with people. She is very talented and a responsible employee when she is actively aware and tuned in to others. People respond to her favorably and enjoy being around her. The problem with Roxanne is that she is often too busy or preoccupied to listen attentively or take correct notes. She often forgets directions, misunderstands conversations, and interrupts others in her haste and enthusiasm.

3. What would you suggest to help Roxanne become a better listener?

   _____

   _____

4. What strategies in this chapter would help her become more aware, more sensitive to others, and able to record information more effectively?

   _____

   _____

Applying the ABC Method of Self-Management

In the Journal Entry on page 123, you were asked to describe a time when you had a difficulty in making sense out of a lecture and staying alert. Are there certain classes in which it is more challenging for you to be an attentive listener?

_____

_____

_____

Now apply the ABC method to the situation and visualize yourself a more attentive listener:

A = Actual event:

B = Beliefs:

C = Challenge:

Practice deep breathing, with your eyes closed, for just 1 minute. See yourself calm, centered, and alert. See yourself enjoying your lectures, staying alert, and taking good notes.

PRACTICE SELF-MANAGEMENT

For more examples of learning how to manage difficult situations, see the "Self-Management Workbook" section of the Online Learning Center Web site at **www.mhhe.com/ferrett7e.**

Listening Self-Assessment

This simple assessment tool will give you an idea of your attentive listening skills. Read each statement. Then, check Yes or No as to whether these statements relate to you.

		Yes	No
1.	My intention is to be an attentive and effective listener.	_____	_____
2.	I concentrate on meaning, not on every word.	_____	_____
3.	I focus on the speaker and use eye contact.	_____	_____
4.	I am aware of emotions and nonverbal behavior.	_____	_____
5.	I withhold judgment until I hear the entire message.	_____	_____
6.	I am open to new information and ideas.	_____	_____
7.	I seek to understand the speaker's point of view.	_____	_____
8.	I do not interrupt, argue, or plan my response; I listen.	_____	_____
9.	I am mentally and physically alert and attentive.	_____	_____
10.	I paraphrase to clarify my understanding.	_____	_____
11.	When I'm in class, I sit in the front, so that I can hear and see better.	_____	_____
12.	I mentally ask questions and summarize main ideas.	_____	_____
13.	I increase the value of my listening by previewing the textbook before class.	_____	_____
14.	I adapt to the instructor's speaking and teaching style.	_____	_____

Total Yes Responses:

Count your Yes responses. If you marked Yes to 10 or more questions, you are well on your way to becoming an attentive and effective listener. If you did not, you have some work to do to improve those skills.

Mind Map Your Text

Make a mind map of a section or chapter of one of your textbooks using the format provided below (and edit/change as necessary). Use **Figure 4.2** on page 131 as a guide.

For example, let's say you will map out a section from Chapter 3 of this text: "Manage Your Time." In the middle circle, you might put "Time-Management Strategies." In one of the surrounding circles, you might enter "Study everywhere and anywhere." In offshoot circles from that, you might put "Carry note cards," "Listen to taped lectures," and "Avoid peak times in the library." Compare your mind maps with those drawn by other students in your class.

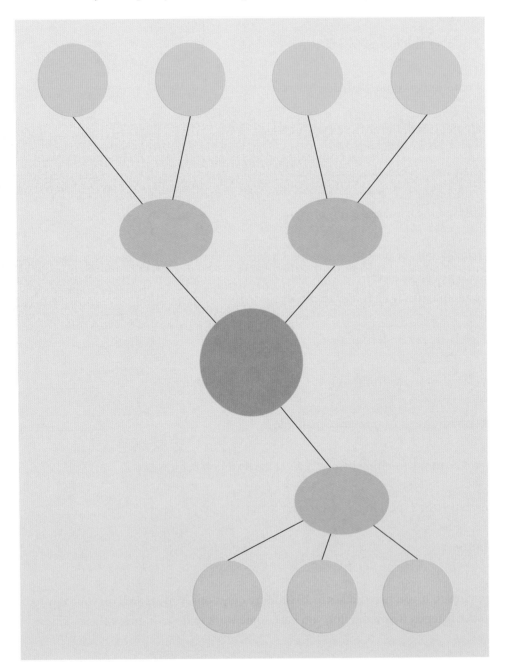

Mind Map a Lecture

Create a mind map of one of your class lectures in the space provided below (see **Figure 4.2** on page 131 and **Figure 4.3** on page 132 for examples). Compare your mind maps with those drawn by other students in your class. Are there key points that you or other students have missed? Did some include too much (or too little) detail?

Use the Cornell System of Note Taking

Take notes in one of your class lectures by using the Cornell System in the space provided below (see **Figure 4.1** on page 129 as a guide). Compare your notes with those from other students in your class. Are there key points that you or other students have missed? Did some include too much (or too little) detail? Did you summarize your notes?

Cues: Notes:

Summary:

Reviewing the Main Ideas

Review your notes and fill in this guide to create a list of the important ideas presented in a class lecture.

Class _____ Instructor _____ Date _____

Lecture topic _____

Chapters covered _____

Overall theme _____

Main ideas _____

Supporting ideas _____

Examples _____

Vocabulary terms _____

Key words _____

Important concepts and theories _____

Applications _____

How this information is similar to known information _____

How this information is different from known information _____

Listening and Note Taking in the Workplace

Write how you will demonstrate the listed listening and note-taking skills for future employers.

1. Finding meaning and interest in new information and projects

   _____

2. Showing interest and being prepared

   _____

3. Listening attentively

   _____

4. Observing and asking questions

   _____

5. Acquiring information

   _____

6. Thinking through issues

   _____

7. Organizing information and taking good notes

   _____

8. Staying alert and in the present

   _____

9. Being willing to test new strategies and learn new methods

   _____

10. Practicing attentive listening and note taking again and again

   _____

11. Teaching effective methods to others

   _____

5

Actively Read

LEARNING OBJECTIVES

In this chapter, you will learn to

5.1 List the benefits of active reading

5.2 Determine a preferred reading system, such as the Five-Part Reading System and SQ3R

5.3 Adopt active reading strategies

5.4 Build a better vocabulary

5.5 Manage language courses

5.6 Read technical material and manuals and complete forms

5.7 Address reading challenges

SELF-MANAGEMENT

"I usually love to read, but lately I feel like I'm on information overload. Sometimes I read several pages and realize that I haven't understood a word I've read. What can I do to read more effectively and actually remember what I've read?"

Do you ever close a book and feel frustrated because you don't remember what you've just read? In this chapter, you will learn how to become an active reader and how to maximize your reading. You will visualize yourself reading quickly, comprehending, and recalling information. You will see yourself discovering new information, building on facts and concepts, developing skills to retain and recall, and feeling the joy of reading.

JOURNAL ENTRY Were you read to as a child? If so, use **Worksheet 5.1** on page 180 to describe a time when you enjoyed being read to by someone, such as a teacher, parent, or librarian. Why was the experience pleasurable? What types of books did you enjoy most? Did you have a favorite book or story? If you don't like to read, why? Are there specific obstacles that keep you from devoting more time to reading?

SOME STUDENTS EXPRESS DISMAY AT THE MOUNTAIN OF READING THEY HAVE TO COMPLETE EACH WEEK. You have probably discovered that it is not just the volume of reading that is required of you in college; you are also expected to comprehend, interpret, and evaluate what you read. **Comprehension** is the ability to understand the main ideas and details as they are written. **Interpreting** what you read means developing ideas of your own and being able to summarize the material in your own words. Interpretation requires several skills, such as noting the difference between fact and opinion, recognizing cause and effect, and drawing inferences and conclusions.

Let's approach reading as a climber approaches a towering mountain. Experienced climbers are alert and aware of the terrain and weather. They are certain of their purpose, goals, and objectives and are confident of their skills. They know the importance of concentration, and they maintain a relaxed, calm, and centered focus but never allow themselves to get too comfortable or inattentive. The same sense of adventure and purpose, concentration, and attentiveness are necessary if you are going to make reading more enjoyable and effective.

Because the amount of reading required in school can be enormous and demanding, it is easy to get discouraged and put it off until it piles up. In this chapter, you will learn to create a reading system that helps you keep up with your reading assignments and increase your comprehension.

The Importance of Active Reading

When you were a child at home, you may have been told, "This is quiet time; go read a book," or "Curl up with a book and just relax." In school, your instructor may have said, "Read Chapters 1 through 5 for tomorrow's test," or "You didn't do well on the test because you didn't read the directions carefully." On the job, someone may have said to you, "I need your reactions to this report. Have them ready to discuss by this afternoon."

Whether you are reading material for enjoyment, for a test, or for a research project on the job, to be an effective reader you must become actively involved with what you are reading. If you approach reading with a lack of interest or importance, you read only what's required. Your ability to retain what you have read will be negatively influenced. **Retention** is the process by which you store information. If you think something is important, you will retain it.

Reading involves many important tasks, such as the following:

- Previewing
- Taking notes
- Outlining main points
- Digging out ideas
- Jotting down key words
- Finding definitions
- Asking and answering questions

" To read a writer is for me not merely to get an idea of what he says, but to go off with him, and travel in his company. "

ANDREW GIDE
Author

- Underlining important points
- Looking for patterns and themes
- Summarizing in your own words
- Reviewing for recall

All of these tasks can greatly improve your comprehension and your ability to interpret material. This is active reading because you, the reader, are purposeful, attentive, and physically active.

Reading Systems

Many factors affect your reading comprehension. Your skill level, vocabulary, ability to concentrate, and state of mind, as well as distractions, all affect your comprehension and ability to recall what you have read. There are a number of proven reading systems and, over the years, you may have developed a reading system that works best for you. Two reading systems that we will explore in this chapter are the Five-Part Reading System and SQ3R.

The Five-Part Reading System

The Five-Part Reading System (see **Figure 5.1**) is similar to the Adult Learning Cycle, which is explored throughout this text (see **Peak Progress 5.1** on page 156). The five parts can be remembered easily as the five **P**s and, as with many reading systems or strategies (and, in fact, many tasks that you will do in college), your first step is to prepare. Then you need to preview, predict questions, process information, and paraphrase and review.

1. **Prepare.** Prepare yourself mentally for reading by creating a positive, interested attitude. Look for ways to make the subject matter meaningful. Instead of telling yourself that the book is too hard or too boring, say, "This book looks interesting because . . . ," or "The information in this book will be helpful because . . ."

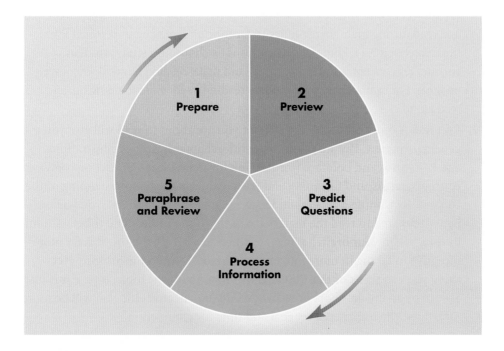

Figure **5.1**
The Five-Part Reading System

This system can be useful for increasing your reading comprehension and recall. *In what ways is this system similar to your own reading system?*

Peak Progress

Applying the Adult Learning Cycle to Becoming a Better Reader

Becoming an active reader and learning to like reading take time, effort, and practice.

1. **RELATE. Why do I want to learn this?** Being an effective reader can help me get ahead in school, work, and life. Through reading, I continually learn new things and explore new ideas. I can also escape through fiction, thus relieving the stress of the day. What do I want to improve overall about my reading?

2. **OBSERVE. How does this work?** I can learn a lot about active reading by watching, listening, and trying new things. I'll observe people who are avid readers and who remember information. Do I know someone who isn't a good or committed reader? I will try new techniques and strategies for active reading and mark my improvement.

3. **REFLECT. What does this mean?** Which techniques work and which ones don't work for me? Can I find creative ways to make reading more enjoyable and effective?

4. **DO. What can I do with this?** I will make a commitment to be a more active reader. I'll find practical applications for practicing my new reading skills. Each day, I'll work on one area. For example, I'll choose one class in which I'm having trouble reading and experiment with new strategies.

5. **TEACH. Whom can I share this with?** I'll talk with others and share my tips and experiences. I'll demonstrate and relay the methods I've learned to others. I'll read more for pleasure and read to others when possible.

Remember, the more you go through the cycle, the more interest and meaning reading will have for you.

Focus your attention on what you are about to read. Clarify your purpose and how you will use the information. Think about what you already know about the subject before you begin reading. Prepare yourself physically by being rested and read during high-energy times (refer to your Time Log in Personal Evaluation Notebook 3.1). Eliminate distractions by choosing a study area that encourages concentration. Experiment and make reading physical whenever possible. For example, take notes while reading, read while standing up, and read aloud.

2. **Preview.** A quick survey of the chapter you are about to read will give you a general overview. Pay attention to the title, chapter headings, illustrations, and key words and boldface words. Look for main ideas, connections between concepts, terms, and formulas, and try to gain a general understanding of the content. By gaining a general understanding of the assignment, you will be better prepared to read the material actively and to understand the classroom lecture. When your brain has been exposed to a subject before, it is far more receptive to taking in more information, so jot down in the margins everything you can think of that you already know about the topic, even if it is just a word or an image. Short preview sessions are effective, and you will be more motivated when there is a set goal and time for completion.

3. **Predict questions.** Next, make questions out of chapter headings, section titles, and definitions. For example, if a section is titled "Groupthink," ask the questions "What is groupthink? What conditions are required for it to occur? What is a key word or key words that define it? What are possible test questions?" Ask what, who, when, where, why, and how. The more questions you ask, the better prepared you will be to find answers. If there are sample questions at the end of the chapter, review them and tie them in with your other questions. Pretend you are talking with the author and jot down questions in the margin. Asking questions gets you interested and involved, keeps you focused, organizes information, and helps you prepare for tests. Create possible test questions on note cards and review them as you walk to classes, eat, or wait in lines. Exchange questions with your study team or partner.

4. **Process information.** Outline, underline, and highlight key words, main ideas, definitions, facts, and important concepts. Look for main ideas, supporting points, connections, and answers to the questions you have raised. This is the time to develop an outline, either a traditional outline or an informal one (such as a mind map), to help you organize the information. Integrate what you are reading into classroom lectures, notes, field trips, study group discussions, models, and graphs.

5. **Paraphrase and review.** Rewrite in your own words, summarize, and review. Write a short summary and then recite it out loud or share it in your study group. Practice reciting this summary right after class and again within 24 hours of previewing the chapter. Review several times until you understand the material and can explain it to someone else. This helps you integrate learning styles and remember the main points at the end of each major section. Review in your study teams and take turns listening to each other's summary. Remember that the best way to learn is to teach. Carry your note cards, so that you can review questions and answers and can summarize often.

● **Preview Your Reading**
You get the big picture by quickly scanning through a book, and you enhance your learning. *Besides identifying key concepts, what else should you look for when previewing?*

The SQ3R Reading System

The SQ3R Reading System is a five-step method that has helped many students improve their reading comprehension since it was first developed by Professor Francis Robinson in 1941. It breaks reading down into manageable segments, so that you understand the material before proceeding to the next step, helping you become a more effective reader.

1. **S = Survey.** Survey the material before reading it. Quickly peruse the contents, scan the main heads, look at illustrations and captions, and become familiar with the special features in each chapter. Surveying, or previewing, helps you

see how the chapter is organized and supports the main concept. You get an overview of where you're going in the material.

2. **Q = Question.** Find the main points and ask questions. Developing questions helps you determine if you really understand the material. For example, here are some questions you can ask yourself as you are reading:

- What is the main idea of this chapter?
- What is the main idea of this section?
- What are examples that support this main idea?
- Who are the main people or what key events are discussed in this chapter?
- Why are they important?
- What are possible test questions?
- What points don't I understand?

3. **R = Read.** Actively read the material and search for answers to your questions. As you read, you will be asking more questions. Even when you read a novel, you will be asking such questions as "What is the main theme of this novel? Who is this supporting character? Why did he turn up at this time in the novel? How does this character relate to the main characters? What are his motives?"

4. **R = Recite.** Recite the main ideas and key points in your words. After each section, stop and paraphrase what you have just read. Recite the answers to your questions in your own words. Reciting promotes concentration and creates understanding. It also helps raise more questions.

5. **R = Review.** Review the material carefully. Go back over your questions and make certain you have answered them. Review the chapter summary and then go back over each section. Jot down additional questions. Review and clarify questions with your study group or instructor.

The exercise in **Personal Evaluation Notebook 5.1** gives you an opportunity to try out the SQ3R Reading System.

Reading Strategies

The Five-Part and SQ3R Reading Systems include a number of strategies, such as previewing the material and reciting or paraphrasing main concepts in your own words. The following are some additional overall strategies.

1. **Determine your purpose.** Clarify your purpose and how you will use the information. Your reading assignments vary in terms of difficulty and purpose. Some are technical and others require imagination. (See **Peak Progress 5.2** on page 161 for tips on reading in different disciplines.) Ask yourself, "Why am I reading this?" Whether you are reading for pleasure, previewing information, enhancing classroom lectures, looking for background information, understanding ideas, finding facts, memorizing formulas and data, or analyzing and comprehending a difficult or complex subject, you will want to clarify your purpose.

2. **Set reading goals.** As mentioned, you may be assigned many chapters to read each week, preferably before walking into a lecture. You do not want to wait until the day before exams to open your textbook. You want to pace your reading, not only to make sure you complete it but also to give yourself time to ask

Personal Evaluation Notebook

Using the SQ3R Reading System

Look at the following table for a review of the SQ3R Reading System. Then do the activity that follows.

Letter	Meaning	Reading Activity
S	Survey	Survey the assigned reading material. Pay attention to the title, boldface terms, the introduction, and the summary.
Q	Question	Find the major heads. Try to make questions out of these heads.
3R	1. Read	Read the material section by section or part by part.
	2. Recite	After reading a section or part, try to summarize aloud what you have read. Make sure your summary answers the question you formed for the section's or part's head.
	3. Review	After reading the entire assigned reading material, review your question heads. Make sure you can recall your original questions and answers. If you cannot, then go back and reread that section or part.

Use the SQ3R Reading System for the following reading selection; then complete the questions that follow.

JOB SEARCHING

Point of departure

Before you begin to look for a job, it is important to decide what you want to do, what you like to do, and what skills and abilities you have to offer.

Self-knowledge is an understanding of your skills, strengths, capabilities, feelings, character, and motivations. It means you have done some serious reflection about what is important to you and what values you want to live your life by. It is very hard to make a career decision unless you really know yourself.

Know yourself

The more you know about yourself—your skills, values, and attitudes and the type of work you like best—the easier it will be to market your skills. Your entire job search will be faster and smoother if you

- Identify your most marketable skills
- Assess your strengths
- Review your interests
- Identify creative ways you solve problems

(continued)

Personal Evaluation Notebook

Using the SQ3R Reading System *(concluded)*

S—Survey

1. What is the title of the selection?

   _____

2. What is the reading selection about?

   _____

3. What are the major topics?

   _____

4. List any boldface terms.

   _____

Q—Question

5. Write a question for the first heading.

   _____

6. Write a question for the second heading.

   _____

3 Rs

R—Read

Read the selection section by section.

R—Recite

Briefly summarize to yourself what you read. Then share your summary with a study team member.

R—Review

7. Can you recall the questions you had for each head?   Yes _____   No _____

8. Can you answer those questions?   Yes _____   No _____

Write your answers for each section head question on the following lines.

9. Head 1

   _____

10. Head 2

   _____

Peak Progress

Reading for Different Courses

Sometimes even very successful students cringe at the thought of reading in disciplines that they are not interested in or find difficult. If you find your textbook too difficult, you might ask your instructor for supplemental reading or check out other books or sources from the library to get a different view and approach. The following are tips for different reading assignments.

Literature: Make a list of key figures and characters. Think about their personalities and motives, and see if you can predict what they will do next. Allow your imagination to expand through your senses; taste, smell, hear, and see each scene in your mind. What is the main point of the story? What are supporting points? What is the author's intent?

History: Use an outline to organize material. You may want to create a time line and place dates and events as you read. Take note of how events are related. Connect main people to key events. Relate past events to current events.

Mathematics and science: When you are reading a math book, work out each problem on paper and take notes in the margin. You will want to spend additional time reviewing graphs, tables, notations, formulas, and the visuals that are used to illustrate points and complex ideas. These are not just fillers; they are important tools for you to review and understand the concepts behind them. Ask questions when you review each visual and use note cards to write down formulas and concepts. Come up with concrete examples when you are reading about abstract and difficult concepts. (We will further explore critical thinking and problem solving in math and science in Chapter 8.)

Psychology and sociology: Jot down major theories and summarize them in your own words to gain understanding. You will be asked how these theories relate to different topics in other chapters. Use the margins to analyze research conclusions. Pay attention to how the research was conducted, such as sample size and who sponsored or funded the research. Look for biases and arguments. Was scientific evidence presented? Was the research study duplicated? Key terms and definitions are also important for building on additional information.

Anthropology: You may want to use a mind map to compare various cultures. For example, under the culture, you may look at religion, customs, food, traditions, and so on. Ask yourself if the ideas apply to all people in all cultures or in all situations. Is the author's position based on observation, research, or assumptions? Is there a different way to look at these observations? What predictions follow these arguments?

questions, make sure you understand the material, and can review it—again and again if necessary. Just as you map out the semester's exams, plan out your reading assignments in your daily planner or calendar (see Chapter 3 for many handy forms). Be realistic as to how long it takes you to read a certain number of pages, especially for courses that you find more difficult. Check off reading assignments as you complete them, and rearrange priorities if need be. Schedule blocks of time for reviewing reading assignments and preparing for exams.

3. **Concentrate.** Whether you are playing a sport, performing a dance, giving a speech, acting in a play, talking with a friend, or focusing on a difficult book, being in the present is the key to concentration. Keep your reading goals in mind and concentrate on understanding main points as you prepare to read.

Stay focused and alert by reading quickly and making it an active experience. If your mind does wander, become aware of your posture, your thoughts, and your surroundings and then gently bring your thoughts back to the task at hand. Do this consistently.

4. **Outline the main points.** Organizing information in an outline creates order and understanding. Use a traditional or an informal outline to organize the information. (See Chapter 4 for examples of outlines.) The purpose of a brief outline is to add meaning and structure to material, as well as to simplify and organize complex information. The physical process of writing and organizing material creates a foundation for committing it to memory. Use section titles and paragraph headlines to provide a guide. Continue to write questions in the margin.

5. **Identify key words and key concepts.** Underline and highlight key words, definitions, facts, and important concepts. Write them in the margins and on note cards. Draw illustrations (or embellish those in the book) to help clarify the text. Use graphics and symbols to indicate difficult material, connections, and questions that you need go over again. (Refer to Figure 4.5 on page 137 for common symbols used in note taking and reading.) You may find a highlighter useful for calling out main points and marking sections that are important to review later. Don't underline until you have previewed information. Underline just the key points and words, and think about the ideas expressed.

6. **Make connections.** Link new information with what you already know. Look for main ideas, supporting points, connections, and answers to the questions you have raised. Integrate what you are reading into classroom lectures, notes, field trips, study group discussions, models, and graphs. Asking yourself these questions may help you make associations and jog your memory:

    -   What conclusions can I make as I read the material?
    -   How can I apply this new material to other material, concepts, and examples?
    -   What information does and does not match?
    -   What have been my experiences with reading similar subjects or with reading in general?
    -   What do I know about the topic that may influence how I approach the reading?

7. **Talk with the author.** Pretend you are talking with the author and jot down points with which you agree or disagree. This exercises your critical thinking skills and helps you connect new information to what you already know or have learned. If there are points you disagree with, consider bringing them up with your instructor in class (if it's appropriate) and see if other students feel the same.

8. **Compare notes.** Compare your textbook notes with your lecture notes. Compare your notes with those of your study team members and clarify questions and answers. Ask your instructor for clarifications and how much weight the textbook has on exams. Some instructors highlight important information in class and want students to read the text for a broad overview.

9. **Take frequent breaks.** Schedule short stretching breaks about every 40 minutes. A person's brain retains information best in short study segments. Don't struggle with unclear material now. Several readings may be required to comprehend and interpret the material. Go back to the difficult areas later when you are refreshed and when the creative process is not blocked.

10. **Integrate learning styles.** Read in alignment with your learning style and integrate styles. For example, if you are a visual learner, take special note of pictures, charts, and diagrams. Visualize and develop mental pictures in your mind and actively use your imagination. Compare what you are reading with course lectures, overhead material, and notes on the board. If you are primarily an auditory learner, read out loud or into a tape recorder and then listen to the tapes.

     If you are a kinesthetic learner, read with a highlighter in hand to mark important passages and key words. Work out problems on paper and draw illustrations. Write your vocabulary, formulas, and key words on note cards. Read while standing up or recite out loud. The physical act of mouthing words and hearing your voice enhances learning. Integrate different learning styles by using all your senses. Visualize what something looks like, hear yourself repeating words, draw, and read out loud. Review your notes and summaries with your study team. This helps you integrate learning styles and increases comprehension, critical thinking, and recall.

11. **Use the entire text.** A peak performer seeks out and uses available resources. Many textbooks include a number of resources that sometimes get overlooked, such as a glossary, chapter objectives, and study questions. Make sure you read (or at least initially scan) all the elements in your textbook, as they are included to help you preview, understand, review, and apply the material. (See **Peak Progress 5.3** on page 164.) After all, you've paid for the text, so use it!

For practice on taking notes, take a look at **Figure 5.2** on page 165 and compare it with your notes for this page.

Reviewing Strategies

Reading isn't over with the turn of the last page. It's important to take the time to review what you have read to make sure you understand and retain the information.

1. **Summarize in writing.** After you finish reading, close your book and write a summary in your own words. Write down everything you can recall about the chapter and the main topics. In just four or five minutes, brainstorm main ideas and key points and summarize the material in your own words. Writing is an active process that increases comprehension and recall. Write quickly and test yourself by asking questions such as these:
     - What is the major theme?
     - What are the main points?
     - What are the connections to other concepts?

2. **Summarize out loud.** Summarizing out loud can increase learning, especially if you are an auditory or a kinesthetic reader. Some students use an empty classroom and pretend they are lecturing. If need be, recite out loud quietly to yourself, so that you don't disturb anyone, especially in the library or other populated areas. Review several times until you understand the material and can explain it to someone else. Review in your study teams and take turns listening to each other's summary. Remember that the best way to learn is to teach. You are each getting an opportunity to recite and listen to each other. You can ask questions and clarify terms and concepts.

Peak Progress

5.3

Using Your Textbook

Textbooks are developed with a number of features to help you preview, understand, review, and apply the material. As soon as you purchase your text, take a few minutes to flip through the book to see how the text is put together. Although all textbooks are designed differently, many books include the following elements:

Preface. At the beginning of the text, you will probably find a preface, and many books include two prefaces: one for the instructor who is interested in using the text in the course and the other specifically for the student. Definitely read through the student preface, as it will outline the major features of the text, explain why the information is important, describe the additional resources available with the text (such as a Web site with study tools, activities, and forms), and provide additional information to help you get off on the right foot. For example, at the beginning of this text, you will find a preface geared for the student that not only walks you through all the features and resources but also explores many issues that you may be facing the first few weeks of school (or even prior to the first day of school).

   Even if there is a student preface, it's a good idea to review the preface designed for the instructor. This preface will give you insights into the overall approach of the text, as well as new developments or research in the field. It may also describe challenges that your instructor faces when teaching the course, which can be helpful for you and your fellow students to know.

Preview features. Many texts include features that let you know what you will learn in the chapter, such as learning objectives, chapter outlines, and introductory statements or quotes. *What types of preview features can you find in this text?*

Applications. More effective texts not only provide the essential information but also give you opportunities to apply the information. This can be in the form of case studies, exercises, assessments, journal activities, Web sites, and critical thinking and discussion questions. *What are some of the features in this text that help you apply what you are learning?*

Review material. You may find a number of features that reinforce and help you understand and review the material, such as section or chapter summaries; glossaries; key tips, key points, or key words; bulleted lists of key information; comprehensive tables; and review questions. *What are some of the features in this text that are useful for reviewing the material?*

Resources beyond the text. Many texts have accompanying Web sites, workbooks, and CD-ROMs that reinforce and apply what you are learning in the text and course. Often, connections to these resources appear in the text, reminding you to use the resource for specific information. *What resources are available with this text?*

3. **Review and reflect.** You have previewed, developed questions, outlined main points, read actively, highlighted and underlined, written key words, and summarized in writing and aloud. Now it is important to review for understanding main ideas and to commit the information to long-term memory. You can increase your comprehension by reviewing the material within 24 hours of your first reading session. Reflect by bringing your own experience and knowledge to what you have learned with reading, lectures, field trips, and work with your study team. You will want to review your outline, note cards, key words, and main points. Review headings, main topics, key ideas, first and

Figure 5.2

Sample Notes

This illustration shows study notes you might take when reading page 163. Compare it with the notes you took on that page. *What are the similarities? What did you do differently? Do you have unique note-taking strategies that work for you?*

10. **Integrate learning styles.** Read in alignment with your learning style and integrate styles. For example, if you are a visual learner, take special note of pictures, charts, and diagrams. Visualize and develop mental pictures in your mind and actively use your imagination. Compare what you are reading with course lectures, overhead material, and notes on the board. If you are primarily an auditory learner, read out loud or into a tape recorder and then listen to the tapes.

Learning style—VAK

If you are a kinesthetic learner, read with a highlighter in hand to mark important passages and key words. Work out problems on paper and draw illustrations. Write your vocabulary, formulas, and key words on note cards. Read while standing up or recite out loud. The physical act of mouthing words and hearing your voice enhances learning. Integrate different learning styles by using all your senses. Visualize what something looks like, hear yourself repeating words, draw, and read out loud. Review your notes and summaries with your study team. This helps you integrate learning styles and increases comprehension, critical thinking, and recall.

Integrate

11. **Use the entire text.** As discussed in Chapter 4, a peak performer seeks out and uses available resources. Many textbooks include a number of resources that sometimes get overlooked, such as a glossary, chapter objectives, and study questions. Make sure you read (or at least initially scan) all the elements in your textbook, as they are included to help you preview, understand, review, and apply the material. (See **Peak Progress 5.3** on page 164.) After all, you've paid for the text, so use it!

Use textbook features

What's in this book?

For practice on taking notes, take a look at **Figure 5.2** on page 165 and compare it with your notes for this page.

Reviewing Strategies

Reading isn't over with the turn of the last page. It's important to take the time to review what you have read to make sure you understand and retain the information.

1. **Summarize in writing.** After you finish reading, close your book and write a summary in your own words. Write down everything you can recall about the chapter and the main topics. In just four or five minutes, brainstorm main ideas and key points and summarize the material in your own words. Writing is an active process that increases comprehension and recall. Write quickly and test yourself by asking questions such as these:

questions to ask

- What is the major theme?
- What are the main points?
- What are the connections to other concepts?

2. **Summarize out loud.** Summarizing out loud can increase learning, especially if you are an auditory or a kinesthetic reader. Some students use an empty classroom and pretend they are lecturing. If need be, recite out loud quietly to yourself, so that you don't disturb anyone, especially in the library or other populated areas. Review several times until you understand the material and can explain it to someone else. Review in your study teams and take turns listening to each other's summary. Remember that the best way to learn is to teach. You are each getting an opportunity to recite and listen to each other. You can ask questions and clarify terms and concepts.

Good for A.K

last sentences in paragraphs, and summaries. Make sure that you have answered the questions that you created as you read the material. Carry your note cards with you and review them when you have a few minutes before class. Your note cards are the most effective tool for reviewing information.

4. **Read and review often.** Reviewing often and in short sessions kicks the material into long-term memory. Review weekly and conduct a thorough review a week or so before a test. Keep a list of questions to ask your instructor and a list of possible test questions. The key is to stay on top of reading, so that it doesn't pile up, which should allow you the time you will need to review effectively.

Build Your Vocabulary

You will need a fundamental vocabulary to master any subject. Developing a good vocabulary is important for reading comprehension and success in college. To succeed in a career, you must know and understand the meaning of words that you encounter in conversations, reports, meetings, and professional reading. People often judge the intelligence of another person by the ability to communicate through words. Words are the tools of thinking and communicating. Realize the power and value of words—an effective speaker who has a command of language can influence others. Try the following methods for building your vocabulary:

1. **Observe your words and habits.** You may be unaware that you fill your conversations with annoying words, such as *you know, OK, like,* and *yeah.*

2. **Be creative and articulate.** Use precise, interesting, and expressive words.

3. **Associate with articulate people.** Surround yourself with people who have effective and extensive vocabularies.

4. **Be aware and alert.** Listen for new words. Observe how they are used and how often you hear them and see them in print.

5. **Look up words you don't know.** Keep a dictionary at your desk or study area. (See **Peak Progress 5.4,** which shows you how to navigate around a dictionary.)

6. **Write down new words.** Write new words in your journal or on note cards.

7. **Practice mentally.** Say new words again and again in your mind as you read and think of appropriate settings where you could use the words.

8. **Practice in conversation.** Use new words until you are comfortable using them.

9. **Look for contextual clues.** Try to figure out a word by the context in which it is used.

10. **Learn common word parts.** Knowing root words, prefixes, and suffixes makes it easier to understand the meaning of many new words. Also, in fields such as biology, knowing prefixes and suffixes is key to learning many new terms, such as *cardi* means "heart" (as in *cardiovascular*) and *calor* means "heat" (as in *calorie,* which is the energy content of food in the form of heat). Other examples follow:

Root	Meaning	Example
auto	self	autograph, autobiography
sub	under	submarine, submerge
circum	around	circumference, circumspect
manu	hand	manuscript, manual, manufacture

Peak Progress

Look It Up! Using the Dictionary

Here is a quick guide for using the dictionary.

Guide words: Boldface words at the top of the page indicate the first and last entries on the page.

Pronunciation: This key shows how to pronounce the word.

Part of speech: The dictionary uses nine abbreviations for the parts of speech:

n.—noun	adv.—adverb	v.t.—transitive verb
adj.—adjective	conj.—conjunction	pron.—pronoun
v.i.—intransitive verb	prep.—preposition	interj.—interjection

Etymology: This is the origin of the word, which is especially helpful if the word has a Latin or Greek root from which many other words are derived. Knowing the word's history can help you remember the word or look for similar words.

Syllabication: This shows how the word is divided into syllables.

Capital letters: The dictionary indicates if a word should be capitalized.

Definition: Dictionaries list the definition chronologically (oldest meaning first).

Restrictive labels: Three types of labels are used most often in a dictionary. Subject labels tell you that a word has a special meaning when used in certain fields (mus. for music, med. for medicine, etc.). Usage labels indicate how a word is used (slang, dial. for dialect, etc.). Geographic labels tell you the region of the country where the word is used most often.

Homographs: The dictionary indicates when a single spelling of a word has different meanings.

Variants: These are multiple correct spellings of a single word (*ax* or *axe*).

Illustrations: These are drawings or pictures used to help illustrate a word.

> 66 I was reading the dictionary. I thought it was a poem about everything. 99
>
> STEVEN WRIGHT
> *Comedian*

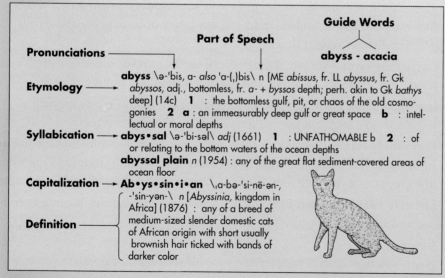

Source: By permission. From the Merriam-Webster Online Dictionary © 2008 by Merriam-Webster, Incorporated (www.Merriam-Webster.com).

Also, learn to recognize syllables. When you divide words into syllables, you learn them faster, and doing so helps with pronunciation, spelling, and memory recall.

11. **Review great speeches.** Look at how Abraham Lincoln, Benjamin Franklin, Winston Churchill, and Thomas Jefferson chose precise words. Read letters written during the Revolutionary and Civil wars. You may find that the common person at that time was more articulate and expressive than many people today.

12. **Invest in a vocabulary book.** There are a number available on the market, so you may want to ask your instructor for guidance. Also, if you have decided on your future career, you may want to see if any books are written for that field.

13. **Read.** The best way to improve your vocabulary is simply to read more.

Manage Language Courses

Building vocabulary is important if you are taking an English as a second language course or learning a foreign language. Following are a number of reading and study tips for studying languages.

1. **Do practice exercises.** As with math and science, doing practice exercises is critical in learning any language.

2. **Keep up with your reading.** You must build on previous lessons and skills. Therefore, it is important to keep up with your reading; preview chapters, so that you have a basic understanding of any new words; then complete your practice sessions several times.

3. **Carry note cards with you.** Drill yourself on the parts of speech and verb conjugation through all the tenses and practice vocabulary building.

4. **Recite out loud.** Recite new words to yourself out loud. This is especially important in a language course. Record yourself and play it back.

5. **Form study teams.** Meet with a study team and speak only the language you are studying. Recite out loud to each other, explain verb conjugation, and use words in various contexts. Recitation is an excellent strategy when studying languages.

6. **Listen to CDs and tapes.** Play practice CDs while commuting, jogging, exercising, and so on.

7. **Visualize.** During an exam, visualize yourself listening to a CD, seeing the diagrams you have drawn, and hearing yourself reciting the material.

8. **Model and tutor.** Meet with a student whose primary language is the one you are studying. Speak only his or her native language. Offer to teach the person your language in exchange for private tutoring. You can meet foreign students in classes where English as a second language is taught, usually in local schools and communities.

9. **Focus on key words.** Study the meanings, tenses, and pronunciation of key words. You can also keep these exercises on note cards. Carry them with you to review.

10. **Have fun.** Do research on the country of the language you're studying. Make the language come alive for you. Invite your study group over for an authentic meal, complete with music and costumes. Invite foreign students and your instructor. The same principles and strategies you use for reading English can be applied to reading and learning a foreign language. Your efforts will be worthwhile, especially when you are able to speak, read, and understand another language as you communicate in the real world. Remember, as you become a better reader, you will enjoy the new language more and more.

Specialized Reading

Comprehending Technical Material

Some of the subjects you are taking now or will take as your course of study progresses will include technical information. Science, math, computer science, accounting, and statistics courses tend to present their data in specialized formats. You may find yourself interpreting graphs, charts, diagrams, or tables and spreadsheets. You may be reading technical material, such as the directions for a chemistry experiment, a flow chart in a computer program, the steps for administering medication, or the statistical analysis of a financial statement. Such material can be complicated and difficult. This is why many readers may get discouraged and skip over it—which is a big mistake.

However, there are some reading strategies you can implement when you encounter graphics in your studies or on the job:

1. Identify the type of graphic you are looking at. Are you looking at a table, chart, graph, or other type of illustration? (See **Figure 5.3.**)

Figure 5.3
Illustration Examples

Both the table (left) and graph (right) include the same information but it is presented differently. *What are key elements you would look for in order to understand the material? Did you find the information easier to understand from the table or the graph? Which one might be easier to remember? What conclusions might you draw from this information regarding future statistics?*

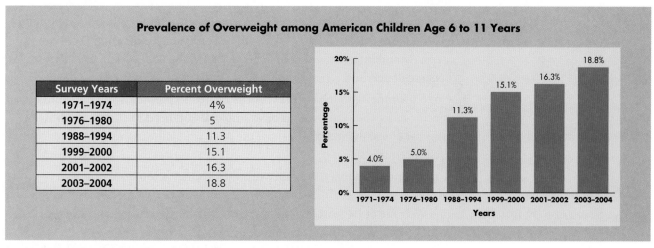

Source: JAMA: THE JOURNAL OF THE AMERICAN MEDICAL ASSOCIATION by Ogden, CL. Copyright 2006 by American Medical Association. Reproduced with permission of American Medical Association in the format Textbook via Copyright Clearance Center.

2. Read the
   - Graphic title
   - Accompanying captions
   - Column titles
   - Labels or symbols and their interpretations
   - Data (percentages, totals, figures, etc.)
3. Identify the purpose of the graphic. Is it demonstrating to the reader similarities or differences, increases or decreases, comparisons or changes?
4. See a connection between the topic of the graphic and the chapter or section topic in which it appears.
5. Explain in your own words the information depicted on the graphic.
6. Share your interpretation of the graphic with your study group members. Do they feel your interpretation is clear and on target?

Reading Manuals

Technical writing professionals spend hundreds of hours writing instructions for everything from using your new toaster, assembling a bicycle, setting up a computer system, to troubleshooting why engine lights are coming on (i.e., your car's owner's manual). However, many people strongly resist opening up the manual. We assume that, since CDs are "auto-run," shouldn't everything else be? For some, reading an instruction manual is like stopping and asking for directions: "I can figure it out on my own!" Still for others, deciphering a manual is like reading a foreign language. They have no idea where to begin.

Although not all manuals are created equal (some are better than others in providing thorough, step-by-step instructions), you should invest the time to at least scan through the manual as you get started, first reviewing the table of contents to see how the instructions are set up (such as a description or an illustration of product components, assembling or starting the product, caution or warning signs, and maintenance issues). After that, follow these time-saving tips:

1. Compare the description to what you received and make sure all the pieces are there.
2. Follow step-by-step installation or assembly instructions. Often it is helpful to read the instructions aloud to yourself or someone else as you go through the steps. Assembling something incorrectly can cause the product to fail, break, or become dangerous.
3. Go to the index and look up key words related to problems you encounter or specific tasks you want to do. For example, if you need to change the time on your car clock, the index will show the page where the manual clearly explains the procedure.
4. If the printed manual that came with the product is too brief or doesn't address a problem you are having, look online either by checking the company's Web site or by searching the product's name. You may find more detailed instructions, as well as tips from other users.
5. The manual (or Web site) may include a frequently asked questions (FAQs) section, which includes issues you may encounter using the product. Read this

even if the product appears to be working correctly, as it may warn you of potential problems or maintenance issues.

6. If the product came with access codes or other important information, record that in the manual and keep it in a place that you'll remember later.

The key to reading manuals is to be patient and not get frustrated. Approach the task as if you were solving a puzzle—eventually, you will put the pieces together.

Completing Forms

Whether you are entering school, applying for a job, filling out medical papers, or requesting a bank loan, you will probably have to complete some type of form. Although forms differ in many ways, there are many elements of information that are requested on all of them. You may need to provide your name, address, Social Security number, phone numbers, and e-mail address. Reading the form carefully and accurately can save time and prevent complications—for example, if the directions say to print your name in black or blue ink, make sure you do not use a pencil or write your name in cursive handwriting. (See Figure 5.4.) If a job application requires you to answer all the questions in your own handwriting, make sure you do not type the application. In both examples, the forms would most likely be returned to you because you had not read the directions carefully, which could result in negative consequences, such as missing a submission deadline or losing a job opportunity. Carelessness in reading forms can be avoided by using the following reading tips:

1. Scan the entire form before you begin to fill it out.

2. If you are unsure of any questions and what information is actually needed, ask or call the appropriate office or person for clarification.

3. When filling out the form, read the small print directions carefully. Often, these directions appear in parentheses below a fill-in blank.

4. Fill in all the questions that pertain to you. Pay attention when you read the directions that tell you what sections of the form or application you should fill out and what sections are to be completed by someone else.

5. Make sure you write clearly—particularly numbers.

APPLICATION FOR EMPLOYMENT
SUPERIOR MARKETS

DIRECTIONS: Please use a pen and print.
Answer all sections completely and accurately.

NAME			SOCIAL SECURITY NUMBER
LAST	FIRST	MIDDLE	
Cortez	Mark	A.	032-32-3712

HOME ADDRESS				
NUMBER	STREET	CITY	STATE	ZIP
134	North Avenue	Indianapolis	IN	46268

TELEPHONE	ALTERNATE #
(317) 555-2492	

Figure 5.4
Filling Out Forms

You can apply good reading skills when filling out forms and applications. *What could happen if you were to use cursive handwriting and a pencil to fill out this form?*

6. When reporting somewhere to fill out forms, take with you any pertinent information that may be needed. Call ahead and ask what you are expected to have with you (for example, Social Security card; proof of citizenship; and dates of employment or schooling; or names, addresses, and phone numbers of references, former employees, or teachers).

7. Reread your responses before submitting your form or application. If you are filling out a form online, check and recheck more than once before clicking "send," since you probably can't retrieve your form.

Overcome Obstacles

Reading Difficulties

Some students may have specific reading challenges to overcome. Most reading difficulties are related to decoding, comprehension, and retention, with most experts believing the root of most reading problems is decoding. **Decoding** is the process of breaking words into individual sounds. Those with decoding problems may have trouble sounding out words and recognizing words out of context, can confuse letters and the sounds they represent, and ignore punctuation while reading. Dyslexics have difficulty decoding. Experts estimate dyslexia affects as many as 15 percent of all Americans, including celebrities Jay Leno, Tom Cruise, Patrick Dempsey, and Whoopi Goldberg. Albert Einstein, Thomas Edison, George Washington, Winston Churchill, and Sir Isaac Newton were also challenged with reading difficulties.

The good news is that you can improve your reading abilities. There are many resources available, such as your school's learning center, if you are struggling with reading. Professionals there will help you understand your difficulty and provide specific tips to help you improve. Also, your instructor or physician (or even the local elementary school) can provide advice on additional resources in your community.

● **Finding Time to Read**
Investing time in reading pays off. Your reading skills improve when you read more. *How can you make time to read for pleasure?*

Create a Positive Attitude

One of the greatest barriers to effective reading is attitude. Many people are not willing to invest the time it takes to become a better reader. If the material is difficult, seems boring, or requires concentration, they may not complete the reading assignment. Many students have been raised in an era of videos and computer games. There is so much instant entertainment available that it is easy to watch a movie or television program or listen to the news instead of reading a newspaper or news magazine. Reading takes time, effort, concentration, and practice.

To create a positive attitude about reading, first pinpoint and dispel illogical thoughts, such as "I have way too much reading; I can never finish it all"; "I'm just not good at math"; or "I never will understand this material!" Many students have trouble reading certain subjects and may lack confidence in their abilities. It takes time and patience to learn to ski, ride a bike, drive a car, become proficient with computers, or become a more effective reader. Use affirmations to develop confidence: "With patience and practice, I will understand this material." Use the ABC Method of Self-Management to dispel negative thinking and create a "can do" attitude.

Some students and career professionals say that they have too much required reading and too little time for pleasure reading. Returning students have a difficult time juggling reading, lectures, homework, job, and kids. They can't even imagine having time to read for pleasure. However, it is important to read for pleasure, even if you have only a few minutes a day. (See **Peak Progress 5.5** for ways to fit in reading with children around.) Carry a book with you or keep one in your car. Although you shouldn't study in bed, many people like to read for pleasure each night before turning in and they find it relaxing.

The more you read, the more your reading skills will improve. As you become a better reader, you will find you enjoy reading more and more. You will also find that, as your attitude improves, so will your ability to keep up on assignments, build your vocabulary, understand and retain what you have read, and learn more about areas that interest you.

> 66 My alma mater was books, a good library . . . I could spend the rest of my life reading, just satisfying my curiosity. 99
>
> MALCOLM X
> *Civil rights leader*

Peak Progress   5.5

Reading with Children Around

It's true that concentrating on your reading can be challenging with children at your feet. However, it's essential that you find ways to fit reading into your daily routine (as well as theirs)—for example,

1. **Read in short segments.** Provide activities for your children and set a timer. Tell them that, when it goes off, you'll take a break from reading and will do something with them, such as have a snack or do a pleasurable activity. Then set the timer again. In 10 or 15 minutes, you can preview a chapter, outline main ideas, recite out loud, or review. Don't fall into the trap of thinking that you need 2 uninterrupted hours to tackle a chapter, or you may never get started.

2. **Read while they sleep.** Get up early and read, or consider reading at night when your kids are sleeping. Even if you're tired, read actively or outline a chapter before you turn in. Resist doing the dishes or cleaning and save those activities for when reading and concentrating would be very difficult. Do a little reading each night and notice how it pays off.

3. **Take reading with you.** If your children are in after-school activities, such as sports, music, or dance, take your reading with you and make the most of your waiting time. This is also a nice time to visit with other parents, but you may need to devote that time to keeping up with your reading.

4. **Exchange child care.** Find other parents and offer to watch each other's kids. Maybe you can take them to the park and read while they are playing.

5. **Read to your children.** Get your kids hooked on reading by reading to them and having them watch you read out loud. Have family reading time, when everyone reads a book. After you read your children a story, ask them to read by themselves or to each other or look at pictures while you read your assignments. Remember to approach reading with a positive attitude, so that they will connect reading with pleasure.

TAKING CHARGE

Summary

In summary, in this chapter I learned to:

- **Apply the Five-Part Reading System.** Very similar to the Adult Learning Cycle, this system is useful for increasing my comprehension and recall. The steps are (1) prepare, (2) preview, (3) predict questions, (4) process information, and (5) paraphrase and review. Scanning chapters gives me a quick overview of main concepts and ideas. I look for information that I already know and link it to information that is new. I look for key words, main ideas, definitions, facts, and important concepts. I make questions out of chapter headings and definitions. I go back over the chapter to find answers and jot them down in the margin or on note cards and compare my answers with those of my study team.

- **Apply the SQ3R Reading System.** A five-step process, this method can improve my reading comprehension: S = Survey; Q = Question; R = Read; R = Recite; R = Review.

- **Be an active reader.** I clarify how I will use the information and set goals. I concentrate on main points and general understanding. I read difficult material out loud or standing up. I write in the margins, draw illustrations, underline, sketch, take notes, and dig out key points and key words. I pretend that I'm talking with the author and jotting down questions.

- **Outline main points and make connections.** Organizing information in an outline creates order, meaning, and understanding and makes it easier to recall the material. It helps simplify difficult information and make connections. I link new information with what I already know and look for connections to what I don't know. I look for similarities and differences. I look for examples and read end-of-chapter summaries.

- **Review.** I increase my comprehension by reviewing my outline, note cards, key words, main points, and summaries and within 24 hours of reading and after lectures.

- **Summarize.** Summarizing in writing and out loud are powerful reading and memory strategies. I close the book at various times to write summaries and then check my brief summaries with the book. I summarize in writing after I finish a quick read of the chapter and then fill in with details.

- **Build a strong vocabulary.** A good vocabulary is critical to my success in school and my career. I can improve my vocabulary by learning and incorporating new words into my writing and conversations, using resources such as a dictionary or vocabulary book, and observing my speech habits.

- **Manage language courses.** Many of the same vocabulary-building strategies work for second language courses, such as focusing on key words, reciting out loud, carrying note cards, listening to tapes, keeping up with the reading assignments, and using practice exercises.

- **Tackle specialized reading.** Thorough and precise reading is critical when reading technical information, graphs, manuals, and forms. Tips for technical information include identifying the purpose of the material or graph, looking for connections, and explaining in my own words. Tips for manuals include reviewing the table of contents, looking up key words in the index, following step-by-step instructions, and reading aloud if necessary. Tips for forms include scanning before I begin, reading the small print, knowing what pertains to me, and asking questions when I'm unsure.

- **Address reading challenges.** I know to seek help with reading difficulties and create a positive attitude about improving my reading abilities, including reading for pleasure.

Performance Strategies

Following are the top 10 strategies for active reading:

- Find interest in the material.
- Outline the main points and identify key words.
- Gather information and predict questions.
- Stay focused by reading quickly.
- Take breaks and make reading physical.
- Reduce distractions and stay alert.
- Make connections and link information.
- Create a relationship with the author.
- Summarize in writing in your own words.
- Teach by summarizing out loud and explaining the material to others.

Tech for Success

Take advantage of the text's Web site at **www.mhhe.com/ferrett7e** for additional study aids, useful forms, and convenient and applicable resources.

- **Books online.** Many of your textbooks can be purchased online and downloaded to your computer. Most of these books are formatted to be read online, rather than printed out. Does this sound appealing, or would you rather read from a printed copy of the text? List some of the advantages and disadvantages of both options.

- **All the news that's fit to click.** What's your source for the latest news? Most major newspapers are available online and archive previous articles. Take a poll of your classmates to see who still opts for newsprint, who prefers the local and cable networks, and who relies on the Web. Discuss the pros and cons. Do your classmates' preferences match their learning styles? Which sources do the more avid readers prefer?

Study Team Notes

Career *in* focus

Brian Singer
INFORMATION TECHNOLOGY SPECIALIST

Related Majors: Computer Science, Mathematics, Information Systems

Keeping Up-to-Date

Brian Singer is an information technology specialist, or computer programmer. His job is to write instructions that computers follow to perform their functions. His programs instruct computers what to do, from updating financial records to simulating air flight as training for pilots.

When writing a program, Brian must first break the task into various instructional steps that a computer can follow. Then each step must be coded into a programming language. When finished, Brian tests the program to confirm it works accurately. Usually, he needs to make some adjustments, called debugging, before the program runs smoothly. The program must be maintained over time and updated as the need arises. Because critical problems can be intricate and time-consuming and must be fixed quickly, Brian usually finds himself working long hours, including evenings and weekends. Although his office surroundings are comfortable, Brian must be careful to avoid physical problems, such as eyestrain or back discomfort.

To stay current in his field, Brian reads about 500 pages of technical materials each week. Brian also took a class on reading technical information to improve his reading skills. Because he concentrates best when he is around people, Brian likes to read and study in a coffeehouse. When he has difficulty understanding what he reads, he gets on the Internet and asks for help from an online discussion group. To help him remember and better understand what he has read during the week, Brian tries to implement the new information in his work.

CRITICAL THINKING What strategies might help an information technology specialist when reading technical information?

Peak Performer
PROFILE

Oprah Winfrey

Accomplished actress, film producer, philanthropist, and magazine publisher, Oprah Winfrey is best known as the popular host and producer of an Emmy-award-winning talk show that aims to inspire.

Winfrey's career began when she entered Tennessee State University and soon began working in radio and television broadcasting in Nashville, Tennessee. Later, she moved to Baltimore, Maryland, where she hosted a TV talk show, which became a hit. After eight years, a Chicago TV station recruited Winfrey to host a morning show. The success of that show led her to launch the celebrated *Oprah Winfrey Show*. Today, the show is broad cast in over 134 countries, and 46 million viewers in the United States tune in weekly.

Her straightforward and winning approach has characterized Winfrey throughout her career. At 17, she was a contestant in a Nashville pageant for "Miss Fire Prevention." When asked what she would do if she had a million dollars she said, "I would be a spending fool." She won the pageant. Over three decades later, she still displays the same bravado that propelled her from rural Mississippi to *Time* magazine's list of the 100 most influential people of the twentieth century.

However, Winfrey's success doesn't rest simply on accolades but, rather, on her connection with her audience. She shares the ups and downs of her own life and the ways in which she has overcome adversity. As an abused child and runaway teenager, Winfrey found refuge with her father, a man who expected the best from her and encouraged one of her lifelong passions—reading. Her love of books inspired her to establish a book club, which opened up the world of reading to millions of people in her audience. Winfrey credits books with saving her life and making her the person she is today. She says her goal is to help make the same kind of difference in other people's lives.

PERFORMANCE THINKING Choose a favorite book you have read and explain why you like it. Do you set time aside for reading for pleasure? Have you considered joining a book club and meeting people with similar interests? How can you inspire others to become avid readers?

CHECK IT OUT According to Oprah Winfrey, "Books gave me the idea there was a life beyond my poor Mississippi home." At **www.oprah.com,** you will find not only books recommended by Oprah's Book Club but also Oprah's personal favorites and reasons they had an impact on her. (Click on "Browse Oprah.com" and then on "Oprah's Book Club.") Also included are recommended books for children of all ages. Think about books you have read, either in school or on your own, that affected you and in what ways. Consider creating your own list of personal favorites. (Note that you must register on the Web site if you want to become an active member in Oprah's Book Club. Many features and book recommendations, however, are not password protected.)

Starting Today

At least one strategy I learned in this chapter that I plan to try right away is:

_____

_____

_____

What changes must I make in order for this strategy to be effective?

_____

_____

_____

Review Questions

Based on what you have learned in this chapter, write your answers to the following questions:

1. Name and describe each part of the Five-Part Reading System.

_____

_____

2. How does outlining the main points help you improve your reading?

_____

_____

3. Name three strategies for managing language courses.

_____

_____

4. Explain how building your vocabulary can be important to your career success.

_____

_____

5. What are important elements to look for when reading graphics?

_____

_____

Effective Reading Habits

In the Classroom

Chris McDaniel has problems keeping up with her reading. She is overwhelmed by the amount of reading and the difficulty of her textbooks. She has never been much of a reader but enjoys watching television. She sometimes reads in bed or in a comfortable chair but often falls asleep. She realizes that this is not the most productive way to study, but it has become a habit. Chris has noticed that, after reading for an hour or so, she can recall almost nothing. This has caused her frustration and to self-doubt her ability to succeed in college.

1. What habits should Chris change to help her improve her reading skills?

_____

_____

_____

2. Suggest one or two specific strategies Chris could implement to become a better reader.

_____

_____

In the Workplace

Chris is now a stockbroker. She never thought that she would work in this business, but a part-time summer job led her to a career in finance, and she really likes the challenge. She is surprised, however, at the vast amount of reading involved in her job: reports, letters, magazines, and articles. She also reads several books on money management each month.

3. What strategies in this chapter would help Chris manage and organize her reading materials?

_____

_____

4. What are some specific reading strategies that apply to both school and work?

_____

_____

Applying the ABC Method of Self-Management

In the Journal Entry on page 153, you were asked to describe a time when you enjoyed being read to. Why was the experience pleasurable? What types of books did you enjoy most? Did you have a favorite book or story?

_____

_____

_____

_____

Now think about your current experiences with reading. Do you enjoy reading? If so, what are the benefits to you? Visualize either a recent positive or a recent negative reading situation. Apply the ABC steps to visualize how the situation can enhance your reading skills.

A = Actual event:

B = Beliefs:

C = Challenge:

When you are in a positive state of mind, do you see yourself reading quickly and comprehending and recalling information effortlessly? Enjoy becoming an active reader.

PRACTICE SELF-MANAGEMENT

For more examples of learning how to manage difficult situations, see the "Self-Management Workbook" section of the Online Learning Center Web site at **www.mhhe.com/ferrett7e.**

Attitudes and Reading

Read the following questions and write your answers on the lines provided.

1. What is your attitude toward reading?

_____

_____

2. What kind of books do you most like to read?

_____

_____

3. Do you read for pleasure?

_____

_____

4. Do you read the daily newspaper?   Yes _____   No _____

If yes, what sections do you read? Place a check mark.

_____ Comics   _____ Horoscope   _____ Weather

_____ Sports   _____ Classified ads   _____ World news

_____ Business   _____ Entertainment   _____ Other

5. Do you read magazines?   Yes _____   No _____

If yes, which magazines?

_____

_____

6. How would it benefit you to read faster?

_____

_____

7. What techniques can you learn to read faster and remember more?

_____

_____

_____

_____

Different Types of Reading

Find a sample of each of the following sources of reading material:
- Newspaper
- Chapter from a textbook
- Instructions for an appliance, an insurance policy, or a rental contract

Read each sample. Then answer the following questions.

1. How does the reading process differ for each type of reading?

_____

_____

_____

_____

_____

_____

_____

_____

_____

_____

2. How does knowing your purpose for reading affect how you read? Why?

_____

_____

_____

_____

_____

_____

_____

_____

_____

_____

_____

Summarize and Teach

1. Read the following paragraph on predicting questions. Underline, write in the margins, and write a summary of the paragraph. Compare your work with a study partner's work. There are many ways to highlight, so don't be concerned if yours is unique. Comparing may give you ideas on creative note taking.

Predicting Questions

Dig out key points and questions. Jot down questions either in the margin or in your reading notes as you read. Asking questions gets you interested and involved, keeps you focused, organizes information, and helps you prepare for tests. As you preview the chapter, make questions out of chapter headings, sections, titles, and definitions. If there are sample questions at the end of the chapter, review them and tie them in with your own questions. What are possible test questions? List them on note cards and review them. Exchange questions with your study team or partner.

SUMMARY

_____

_____

_____

_____

_____

_____

2. Work with a study partner in one of your classes. Read a chapter and write a summary. Compare your summary with your study partner's summary. Then summarize and teach the main concepts to your partner. Each of you can clarify and ask questions.

SUMMARY

_____

_____

_____

_____

_____

_____

_____

_____

_____

_____

_____

_____

_____

_____

Creating a Reading Outline

Outlining what you read can be a helpful study technique. Develop the habit of outlining. Use the following form as a guide. You may also develop your own form (see Chapter 4 for examples). Outline Chapter 5 on the lines below (or select another chapter in this or one of your other texts).

Course _____ Chapter _____ Date _____

I. _____

   A. _____

      1. _____

      2. _____

      3. _____

   B. _____

      1. _____

      2. _____

      3. _____

II. _____

   A. _____

      1. _____

      2. _____

      3. _____

   B. _____

      1. _____

      2. _____

      3. _____

(continued)

III. _____

   A. _____

      1. _____

      2. _____

      3. _____

   B. _____

      1. _____

      2. _____

      3. _____

IV. _____

   A. _____

      1. _____

      2. _____

      3. _____

   B. _____

      1. _____

      2. _____

      3. _____

Analyzing Chapters

As you start to read the next chapter in this book, fill in this page to prepare for reading. You may need to add additional headings. List each heading and then phrase it as a question. Then summarize as you complete your reading. Use a separate sheet of paper if needed.

Course _____ Textbook _____

Chapter _____

Heading 1 _____

Question _____

Heading 2 _____

Question _____

Heading 3 _____

Question _____

Heading 4 _____

Question _____

SUMMARY OF SECTION

_____
_____
_____
_____
_____

SUMMARY OF CHAPTER

_____
_____
_____
_____
_____

Breaking Barriers to Reading

Following is a list of the common reasons that some students use for not reading effectively. Read this list; then add to it on the lines provided. Use creative problem solving to list strategies for overcoming these barriers.

Reasons for Not Reading	Strategies for Overcoming Reading Barriers
1. My textbooks are boring.	_____
	_____
	_____
	_____
2. I can't concentrate.	_____
	_____
	_____
3. I'm easily distracted.	_____
	_____
	_____
4. I fall asleep when I read.	_____
	_____
	_____
5. I never study the right material.	_____
	_____
	_____
6. There is too much information, and I don't know what is important.	_____
	_____
	_____
7. I read for hours, but I don't understand what I have read.	_____
	_____
	_____
8. I don't like to read.	_____
	_____
	_____
	_____

Demonstrating Competencies

Follow these steps and fill in the blanks below to demonstrate your competencies. Then add this page to your Career Development Portfolio.

1. **Looking back:** Review your worksheets from other chapters to find activities from which you learned to read and concentrate.
2. **Taking stock:** Identify your strengths in reading and what you want to improve.
3. **Looking forward:** Indicate how you would demonstrate reading and comprehension skills to an employer.
4. **Documentation:** Include documentation of your reading skills.
5. **Inventory:** Make a list of the books you've read recently, including any classics. Use a separate sheet of paper.

Explain how you demonstrate these competencies:

Competencies	Your Demonstration
Active reading	_____
Critical reading	_____
Willingness to learn new words	_____
Improvement in technical vocabulary	_____
Articulation	_____
Expressiveness	_____
Ability to use a dictionary	_____
Positive attitude toward reading	_____
Technical reading	_____
Form reading	_____

6

Improve Your Memory Skills

LEARNING OBJECTIVES

In this chapter, you will learn to

6.1 Apply the five-step memory process

6.2 Describe memory strategies, including mnemonic devices

6.3 Summarize, review, and reflect for better retention and recall

SELF-MANAGEMENT

" I have been meeting so many new people. I wish I could remember their names, but I just don't have a good memory. What can I do to increase my memory skills and remember names, facts, and information more easily?"

Do you ever find yourself feeling embarrassed because you cannot remember the names of new people you've met? Do you ever get frustrated because you don't remember material for a test? In this chapter, you will learn how to increase your memory skills.

JOURNAL ENTRY In **Worksheet 6.1** on page 214, describe a situation in which you needed to learn many new names or numerous facts for a test. How did you fare? What factors helped you remember?

TECHNOLOGY HAS PROVIDED US AMPLE OPPORTU-NITIES TO STORE AND RETRIEVE INFORMATION. No longer do we memorize and recite long stories in order to pass them down to others, as was done hundreds of years ago. In fact, many people don't even know their best friend's phone number. After all, since it's programmed into their cell phone, why should they?

However, you can't whip out the latest technology gadget when sitting down to take a test. Nor can you check your personal digital assistant (PDA) when you run into a business acquaintance—and you can't remember his name. ("Is it Bob or Bill? I know it starts with a *B*."). Although you may search the Internet to access information, you still determine what the information means, how it relates to other material, and how you will use it now and in the future. For this, your brain—not your computer, cell phone, or PDA—is the most essential "device."

Do you think some people are born with better memories than others? You will discover in this chapter that memory is a complex process that involves many factors that you can control, such as your attitude, interest, intent, awareness, mental alertness, observation skills, senses, distractions, memory techniques, and willingness to practice. Most people with good memories say that the skill is mastered by learning and continually practicing the strategies for storing and recalling information. This chapter will summarize and highlight specific strategies that help you remember information.

The Memory Process

The memory process involves five main steps:

1. Intention—you are interested and have a desire to learn and remember
2. Attention—you are attentive, and you observe information and concentrate on details
3. Association—you organize and associate information to make sense of it
4. Retention—you practice and repeat until you know the information
5. Recall—you recall, teach, and share information with others

As you can see, this process is quite similar to the Adult Learning Cycle, which is explored throughout this text. (Read **Peak Progress 6.1** to see how you can use the Adult Learning Cycle to improve your memory skills.)

1. **Intention.** The first step in using memory effectively is to prepare yourself mentally. As with learning any skill, your intention, attitude, and motivation are fundamental to success. Intention means that you are interested and willing to learn. You intend to remember by finding personal meaning and interest. You must want to remember. Have you ever said, "I wish I could remember names," "I'm just not good at remembering facts for tests," or "I can't remember formulas for math"? Instead, say, "I really want to remember JoAnne's name."

Peak Progress

Applying the Adult Learning Cycle to Increasing Your Memory Skills

1. **RELATE. Why do I want to learn this?** I must become more proficient at remembering names, facts, and information. This is critical for success not only in school but also in the workplace and social situations. What strategies do I already use to remember and retain information?

2. **OBSERVE. How does this work?** Who do I know is good at remembering names and information? What tips can I pick up from him or her? Who do I know seems to struggle with remembering important information? I'll try using new techniques and strategies and observe how I'm improving.

3. **REFLECT. What does this mean?** What strategies seem to work the best for me? What strategies are ineffective? Have I eliminated negative and defeating self-talk? I continue to look for connections and associations. I use humor, songs, rhymes, and other mnemonic techniques.

4. **DO. What can I do with this?** I will practice memory skills in many different situations and make a conscious commitment to improving my skills. I'll make games out of my practice and have fun. I'll find practical applications and use my new skills in everyday life. Each day, I'll work on one area. For example, I'll choose one class in which I'm having trouble recalling information and experiment with new strategies. Or, for one person or group of people with whom I have trouble remembering names, I'll focus on improving.

5. **TEACH. Whom can I share this with?** I'll talk with others and share my tips and experiences. I'll ask if they have any strategies they find useful that I might also try.

Continue to congratulate yourself at least mentally when you have made improvements. The more you go through the cycle, the more interest and meaning recall will have for you, and the better your memory skills will become.

If you make excuses or program your mind with negative self-talk, your mind refuses to learn new information. If you think a subject is boring or unimportant, you will have difficulty remembering it. Take full responsibility for your attitude and intention. Realize that you are in control of your memory.

Develop an interest in whatever you are studying or in any task or project with which you are working. Make a conscious, active decision to remember, and state your intention with positive affirmations.

2. **Attention.** The second step in the memory process is to concentrate, observe, and be attentive to details. How many times have you physically been in one place but mentally and emotionally were thousands of miles away? **Mindfulness** is the state in which you are totally in the moment and part of the process around you. Learning occurs when your mind is relaxed, focused, receptive, and alert. Focus your attention by concentrating briefly on one thing. Visualize details by drawing mental pictures. **Personal Evaluation Notebook 6.1** helps you practice your observation skills.

Personal Evaluation Notebook 6.1

Being Observant

How observant are you? Try the following experiments to determine if you are really observing the world around you.

EXPERIMENT 1

1. Look around the room.
2. Close your eyes.
3. Mentally picture what is in the room.
4. Open your eyes.
5. Did you remember everything? If not, what didn't you remember?

_____

_____

_____

EXPERIMENT 2

1. Look at a painting, photo, or poster for one minute.
2. Without looking back, write down the details you remember.
3. Compare your list of details with the painting, photo, or poster.

   a. What details did you remember? Colors? Faces? Clothing?

   _____

   _____

   _____

   b. What details didn't you remember?

   _____

   _____

   _____

   c. Did you remember the obvious things or did you remember subtle details?

   _____

   d. Why do you think those were the details you remembered?

   _____

   _____

   _____

3. **Association.** Nothing is harder to remember than unconnected facts, dates, or theories. Ask questions about how information is interconnected: How is this information similar to other information? How is this information different?

By associating and linking new material with old material, you make it meaningful. You cannot retain or recall information unless you understand it. Understanding means that you see connections and relationships in the information you are studying and you can summarize and explain this material in your own words. Make associations by looking for similarities or differences. Create understanding by finding out why this information is important and how it relates to other information. Too often, students study just enough to get by on a quiz and forget the information immediately thereafter. It is much better to learn a subject so that it becomes interesting and part of your long-term memory. (See **Peak Progress 6.2** on page 194 on short-term versus long-term memory.)

One way to organize material to look for connections is by outlining each chapter. As discussed in Chapter 4, use the Cornell System or a mind map (or whatever outline method works for you) to organize information. (See **Personal Evaluation Notebook 6.2** on page 196 for a sample of a mind map.)

4. **Retention.** Repetition and practice help you retain information. Do it, and do it again. Repeat names or information aloud. Practice what you have learned, find new applications, and connect this information to other information you already know. Continue to ask questions and look for more examples.

5. **Recall. Memorization** is the transfer of information from short-term memory into long-term memory. Of course, the only reason to do this is so that we can retrieve it in the future for use by our short-term memory. This transfer in the other direction is known as recall. To **recall** information means you not only have retained it but also can remember it when you need to.

Share information with others; introduce a person you have just met; practice giving summaries of chapters to your study team. Teach the information, write about it, talk about it, apply it to new situations, and demonstrate that you know it. This will help you become more interested in the information, create more meaning for you, and build your confidence. Repeating this cycle will build your memory skills.

Memory Strategies

Following are a number of strategies that will help you improve your memory skills.

1. **Write it down.** Writing is physical and enhances learning. When you write down information, you are reinforcing learning by using your eyes, hand, fingers, and arm. Writing uses different parts of the brain than do speaking and listening.

   • Writing down a telephone number helps you remember it by providing a mental picture.

Peak Progress

Short-Term and Long-Term Memory

People have two basic types of memory: short-term, or active, memory and long-term, or passive, memory. Each type of memory plays its own important role in learning and the ability to respond effectively to any challenge in life.

If you own a computer, you probably have heard references to its various types of memory. Your own short-term memory is very much like the memory in your computer, which you know as random access memory (RAM) (see **Figure 6.1**).

Just as the central processing unit of your computer relies on this RAM to perform all of its processing tasks, your own short-term memory is where your mind is able to apply, create, and evaluate. Short-term memory is where all your active thinking takes place. It is a relatively limited space, yet one where tremendous potential resides.

Before short-term memory can perform its wonders, information must flow into it. This can be new information entering through your natural senses, it can be stored information that you retrieve from long-term memory, or it can be a combination of both. Using the computer analogy, you might equate your natural senses with a keyboard or mouse, while you may think of long-term memory as your hard drive or any other storage medium in which you save your work. Just as you make choices about which work you will save on your computer, you determine which information becomes stored in your long-term memory. The information you choose to save in long-term memory has great value. It can be retrieved and used as it is, or it can be retrieved and combined with other information to create something entirely new. The possibilities are endless.

When we consider the transfer of information back and forth in our memory system, think of the mind as a vast relational database. It is not enough merely to store information; for any database to be useful, the information stored in it must be organized and indexed for retrieval. This occurs naturally when we are predisposed to remember something, but what happens when we are required to memorize information we just don't care about? Not only does the information become more difficult to memorize, but also it becomes nearly impossible to recall. The good news is that we can make such information more memorable by personally relating to it. For example, we might ask ourselves questions such as "How can I use this information in my life?" Answers to such questions can create meaning, which helps our mind to naturally organize information. When it comes time to use that information, such as when we need to answer questions on an examination, it will have been naturally indexed for easier recall.

- Planning your time in a day planner and creating a to-do list can trigger accomplishing tasks later in the day when you may have become overwhelmed with distractions.
- Taking notes in class prompts you to be logical and concise and fills in memory gaps.
- Underlining important information and then copying it onto note cards reinforces information.
- Writing a summary after reading a chapter also reinforces information.
- Summarizing in your own words helps transfer information to long-term memory.

Short-Term and Long-Term Memory *(concluded)*

Figure 6.1

Short-Term and Long-Term Memory

Think of your memory as a computer. First, you input information through your natural senses (as in inputting by way of a mouse or a keyboard). Your short-term memory is like the random access memory in your computer, which is readily available for use but can be erased if the computer is shut down. Long-term memory is like information that has been stored on your hard drive, which you can retrieve (or recall) for later use. *What material from this course may be in your short-term memory? What might be in your long-term memory?*

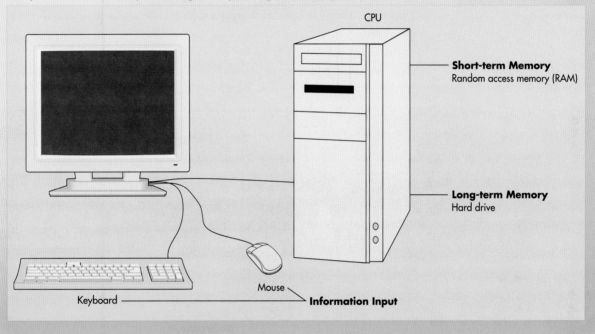

CPU

Short-term Memory
Random access memory (RAM)

Long-term Memory
Hard drive

Keyboard

Mouse

Information Input

2. **Go from the general to the specific.** Many people learn and remember best by looking at the big picture and then learning the details. Try to outline from the general (main topic) to the specific (subtopics). Previewing a chapter gives you an overview and makes the topic more meaningful. Your brain is more receptive to specific details when it has a general idea of the main topic. Read, listen, and look for general understanding, then add details.

3. **Reduce information.** You don't have to memorize certain types of information, such as deadlines, telephone messages, and assignment due dates. You just have to know where to find this information. Write deadlines and important information in your organizer or student planner or on a calendar. Write messages in a phone log, not on slips of paper, which can get lost. You can refer to any of this written information again if you need it.

4. **Eliminate distractions.** Distractions can keep you from paying attention and, consequently, from remembering what you're trying to learn. One way to avoid distractions is to study in a quiet area. Libraries and designated study rooms are good places to use for quiet study. If it is noisy in class, ask the instructor to repeat information or move closer to the front. Clarify names if you are being

Personal Evaluation Notebook

Using a Mind Map to Enhance Memory

A mind map will not only help you organize information to be memorized, but also the physical act of writing will help you commit the material to memory. Use the map figure that follows as a guide, and in the space provided create a mind map of this chapter.

- Write the main topic in the middle and draw a circle or a box around it.
- Surround the main topic with subtopics.
- Draw lines from the subtopics to the main topic.
- Under the subtopics, jot down supporting points, ideas, and illustrations.
- Be creative.
- Use different-colored ink and write main topics in block letters.
- Draw pictures for supporting points.

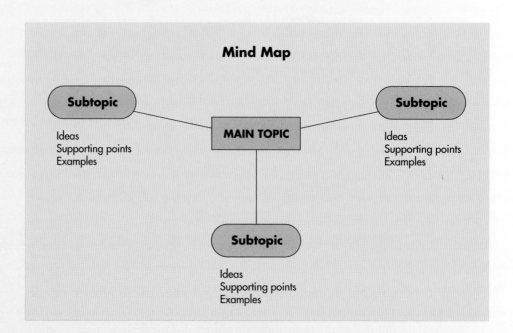

Create your own mind map.

introduced. Understand your responsibilities and avoid becoming someone else's memory support. If someone asks you to call him or her with the notes from class, ask the person to call you instead. If a study team member asks you to remind him or her about a study meeting, suggest the use of a student planner to record important dates. You have enough to remember without taking responsibility for someone else's memory. If something is bothering you, write it down and tell yourself that, as soon as your study time is over, you will address it. In this way, you can reduce distractions and focus completely on absorbing important information.

5. **Study in short sessions.** You will use the power of concentration more fully, and the brain retains information better, in short study sessions. After about 40 minutes, the brain needs a break to process information effectively. Break large goals into specific objectives and study in short sessions. For example, if you are taking a marketing course, preview a chapter in your textbook for 20 minutes and mind map the chapter for 20 minutes. Then take a 10-minute break. Stretch, drink a glass of water, or treat yourself to a small snack. Then return to complete your goal.

   Even when you are working on something complex, such as completing a term paper or studying for finals, you are more effective when you take frequent, scheduled breaks.

6. **Integrate your left brain and your right brain.** Think of both sides of your brain as members of a team that can cooperate, appreciate, and support each other. Recall the discussion about right- and left-brain dominance in Chapter 1. (See Figure 1.2 on page 13.) By using both sides of your brain, you can enhance your memory. For example, you may have a term paper assignment that constitutes 50 percent of your final grade. You want to turn in a well-researched, accurately written, neatly typed paper. The left side of your brain insists that it be error-free. Your preferred style of learning leans toward the right side, so your reaction to this assignment might be frustration, fear, and resistance. By using a computer, you can support both sides of the brain. You satisfy the structured side, which wants a flawless paper, while allowing your creative side to correct mistakes easily by using the spell-check. Strive to integrate all learning styles and use both sides of your brain to enhance memory.

7. **Use all your senses.** Memory is sensory, so using all your senses (sight, hearing, touch, smell, and taste) will give your brain a better chance of retaining information.

   • *Visualize.* Since much of what you learn and remember reaches you through sight, it is important to visualize what you want to remember. The art of retention is the art of attention. Be a keen observer of details and notice differences and similarities. Let's say that you are taking a medical terminology or vocabulary-building course. You may want to look at pictures and visualize in your mind images with the new terms or words. Look at illustrations, pictures, and information on the board.

   • *Listen.* You cannot remember a name or information in class if you are not attentive and listening. Actively listen in class, tape lectures (ask for the

● **Learning Memory**
Focusing on your preferred learning style strengthens your memory skills. *How does your learning style affect the way in which you learn memory?*

instructor's permission), and play them back later. Recite definitions and information aloud.

- *Move.* Whether you like to learn by reading or by listening, you will retain information better if you use all your senses and make learning physical. Read aloud; read while standing; jot down notes; lecture in front of the classroom to yourself or your study team; go on field trips; draw pictures, diagrams, and models; and join a study group. Practice reciting information while doing physical activity, such as showering, walking, or jogging. The more you use all your senses, the more likely you are to remember and retain information.

Complete **Personal Evaluation Notebook 6.3** to see how your senses relate to your childhood memories. Complete **Personal Evaluation Notebook 6.4** on page 200 to determine how to use your learning style and all your senses.

8. **Use mnemonic devices. Mnemonic** (neh-mon-nik) devices are memory tricks that help you remember information. However, there are problems with mnemonic devices. It can take time to develop a memory trick, and it can be hard to remember the trick if you make it too complicated. Since mnemonic devices don't help you understand the information or develop skills in critical thinking, they are best used for sheer rote memorization. Follow up by looking for associations, making connections, and writing summaries. Some mnemonic devices are

- *Rhythm and rhymes.* In elementary school, you might have learned the rhyme "In 1492 Columbus sailed the ocean blue." It helped you remember the date of Columbus's voyage. Rhythms can also be helpful. Many people have learned to spell the word *Mississippi* by accenting all the *i*s and making the word rhythmic.

- *Acronyms.* **Acronyms** are words formed from the first letters of a series of other words, such as HOMES for the Great Lakes (Huron, Ontario, Michigan, Erie, and Superior) and EPCOT (Experimental Prototype Community of Tomorrow). Consider creating your own acronyms.

- *Acrostics.* **Acrostics** are similar to acronyms, but they are made-up sentences in which the first letter stands for something, such as Every Good Boy Deserves Fun for remembering the sequence of musical notes: E, G, B, D, F. Another is My Very Easy Memory Jingle Seems Useful Now, which helps you remember the order of the planets from the sun (assuming you know that the first planet is Mercury and not Mars and that Pluto is no longer considered a planet. Can you name the rest with the help of the acrostic?) Acrostics are often used in poetry, where the first letter of every line combine to spell something, such as the poem's title. (See **Personal Evaluation Notebook 6.5** on page 201 to practice creating acronyms and acrostics.)

- *Association.* Suppose you are learning about explorer Christopher Columbus's three ships. Think of three friends whose names start with the same first letters as the ships' names: *Pinta*, *Santa Maria*, and *Nina* (e.g., Paul, Sandy, and Nancy). Vividly associate your friends' names with the three ships, and you should be able to recall the ships' names. Using associations can also be helpful in remembering numbers. For example, if your ATM identification number is 9072, you might remember it by creating associations with dates. Maybe 1990 is the year you graduated from high school, and 1972 is the year you were born.

66 No memory is ever alone; it's at the end of a trail of memories, a dozen trails that each have their own associations. **99**

LOUIS L'AMOUR
Author

Personal Evaluation Notebook

Memory Assessment

A. Sometimes your perceptions differ from reality, particularly when you are assessing your skills and personal qualities. Assess your memory and your intention. Then check Yes or No as it pertains to you.

1. Do you remember names?   Yes _____   No _____
2. Do you remember important information for tests? Yes _____   No _____
3. Did you use your senses more as a child?   Yes _____   No _____

B. Read each statement that follows and write your comments on the lines provided.

1. Write a few lines about your earliest memory.

   _____

   _____

   _____

   _____

   _____

   _____

2. Does it help your memory to look at family photos or hear about your childhood? Why?

   _____

   _____

   _____

   _____

   _____

   _____

3. What smells do you remember most from home?

   _____

   _____

   _____

   _____

   _____

   _____

Personal Evaluation Notebook 6.4

Learning Styles and Memory

Answer the following questions on the lines provided.

1. How can you use your preferred learning style to enhance your memory?

_____

_____

_____

_____

_____

_____

_____

_____

_____

_____

_____

2. What can you do to integrate both sides of your brain and to use all your senses to help you recall information?

_____

_____

_____

_____

_____

_____

_____

_____

_____

_____

_____

_____

Personal Evaluation Notebook  6.5

Acronyms and Acrostics

An *acronym* is a word formed from the first letters of a series of other words. An *acrostic* is a made-up sentence, with the first letter of each word standing for something. Create one or more acronyms and acrostics based on information you are learning right now in your courses.

Acronym example: "NATO" stands for North Atlantic Treaty Organization.

Acronym _____

Stands for _____

Acrostic example: "Old People From Texas Eat Spiders" stands for the bones of the skull (occipital, parietal, frontal, temporal, ethmoid, sphenoid).

Acrostic _____

Stands for _____

- *Chunking.* **Chunking,** or grouping, long lists of information or numbers can break up the memory task and make it easier for you. Most people can remember up to seven numbers in a row, which is why phone numbers are that long.

- *Stacking technique.* You simply visualize objects that represent points and stack them on top on each other. For example, if you were giving a speech on time management, you would start with a clock with a big pencil on it to represent how much time is saved if you write information down. On top of the clock is a big calendar, which reminds you to make the point that you must set priorities in writing. On the calendar is a time log with the name Drucker on it. This will remind you to present a quote by Peter Drucker that you must know where your time goes if you are to be effective in managing your life. You stack an object to remind you of each of the key points in the speech.

- *Method-of-place technique.* As far back as 500 B.C., the Greeks were using a method of imagery called loci—the method-of-place technique. (*Loci* is Latin for "place.") This method, which is similar to the stacking technique, is still effective today because it uses imagery and association to aid memory. Memorize a setting in detail and then place the item or information you want to remember at certain places on your memory map. Some people like to use a familiar street, their home, or their car as a map on which to place their information. The concept is the same. You memorize certain places on your street, in your home, or in your car. You memorize a specific order or path in which you visit each place. Once you have this map memorized, you can position various items to remember at different points. **Personal Evaluation Notebook 6.6** provides an opportunity to practice this technique.

Personal Evaluation Notebook 6.6

A Walk Down Memory Lane

Creating a memory map is a visual way to enhance and practice your memory skills. The key to this method is to set the items clearly in your memory and visualize them. For example, a familiar memory map involves remembering the 13 original colonies. The memory map is a garden with several distinct points. There is delicate chinaware sitting on the garden gate (Delaware); the birdbath contains a large fountain pen (Pennsylvania); in the gazebo is a new jersey calf (New Jersey); and sitting on the calf is King George (Georgia) with a cut on his finger (Connecticut). The flowerbed has a mass of flowers (Massachusetts); in the fountain, splashing, is Marilyn Monroe (Maryland); the garden sun dial is pointing south (South Carolina); a large ham is sitting on the garden bench (New Hampshire); and the gardener, named Virginia (Virginia), who is wearing an empire dress (New York), is watering the northern flowerbed (North Carolina). In the middle of the flowerbed is an island of rocks (Rhode Island) with a bottle of maple syrup. There you have the 13 original colonies in the order in which they joined the union, and it was easy to add the fourteenth state to join— Vermont.

YOUR MEMORY GARDEN

Think of your memory map as a garden rich in detail and full of flowers representing thoughts, images, and ideas. You always enter the garden through a white garden gate. You can see each distinct point in the garden: the garden gate, the birdbath, the gazebo, the fountain, the garden bench, and the flowerbed. The key is to set the items clearly in your memory and visualize them. Draw a picture of your garden in detail with these items in the space provided at the left.

Using your drawing of the garden, let's say that you want to memorize four stories that emphasize four key points for a speech you are giving in your

(continued)

Personal Evaluation Notebook  6.6

A Walk Down Memory Lane (*continued*)

Speech 101 class. The first story in your speech is about a monk, so you draw a monk at the garden gate. You want to tell a joke about a robin, so you place the robin in the birdbath. Your third point involves people of a bygone era, and you have chosen a Victorian woman as the image to represent this key point, so you place her in the gazebo. Your fourth point involves the younger generation, so you choose a little girl and place her playing in the fountain.

Follow these steps in the method-of-place technique:

1. Imagine your beautiful memory garden.

2. Imagine each distinctive detail of the location: the garden gate, birdbath, gazebo, and fountain.

3. Create a vivid image for each item you want to remember and place it at a specific location.

4. Associate each of the images representing the items with points in the garden and see the images at each location.

5. As you mentally stroll down the garden lane, create pictures in your mind of each of your items through association.

If you have additional points you want to remember, place one at the garden bench and one at the flowerbed. If you have more than six items to remember, illustrate a rainbow over your flowerbed. Flowers in various colors of the rainbow can represent each item you wish to remember.

It is easier to remember information grouped together and associated by categories. Be creative and flexible with the method-of-place technique. If a garden doesn't work for you, use a car, the mall, or your home. Just make certain that your illustration is clear and you always start in the same place. Draw it in detail and color it.

USE A CHECKLIST IN YOUR MEMORY GARDEN

A checklist provides a way to review and check off each item you want to remember. You can combine it with the method-of-place technique.

Memory Checklist

1.	Garden gate	Monk
2.	Birdbath	Bird
3.	Gazebo	Victorian woman
4.	Fountain	Little girl

Go to page 204 to see a drawn interpretation of the memory garden.

(continued)

Personal Evaluation Notebook

A Walk Down Memory Lane *(concluded)*

Source: "Memory Garden" from *The Memory Book* by Harry Lorayne, & Jerry Lucas, Stein & Day, 1996.

9. **Use note cards.** Successful students use note cards. The information is condensed and written, so the act of writing is kinesthetic and holding cards is tactile. Note cards are visual and, when the information is recited out loud or in a group, the auditory element enhances learning. A question can be on one side and the answer on the other side. Flashcards with key words, formulas, and questions can help memory. Note cards are a great way to organize information and highlight key words:

- Use index cards for recording information you want to memorize. Write brief summaries and indicate the main points of each chapter on the backs of note cards.
- Carry the cards with you and review them during waiting time, before going to sleep at night, or any other time you have a few minutes to spare.
- Organize the cards according to category, color, size, order, weight, and other areas.

10. **Recite.** Recite and repeat information, such as a name, a poem, a date, or formulas. Repeat again and again. When you say information aloud, you use your throat, voice, and lips and you hear yourself recite. You may find this recitation technique helpful when you are dealing with difficult reading material. Reading aloud and hearing the material will reinforce it for you and help move information from your short-term memory to your long-term memory. Try to use the new words in your own conversations. Write summaries in your own words and read to others. Study groups are effective because you can hear each other, clarify questions, and increase understanding as you review information.

Reciting may be helpful when preparing to give a speech. Try to practice in the place you will be speaking. Visualize the audience; practice demonstrating your visual aids; write on the board; and use gestures and pauses. Tape your speech and play it back. To remember names, when you meet someone, recite the person's name several times to yourself and out loud. **Peak Progress 6.3** on page 206 provides a number of additional tips for remembering names.

11. **Practice, practice, practice!** You must practice information that you want to remember. For example, when you first start driver training, you learn the various steps involved in driving. At first, they may seem overwhelming. You may have to stop and think through each step. After you have driven a car for awhile, however, you don't even think about all the steps required to start it and back out of the driveway. You check your mirror automatically before changing lanes, and driving safely has become a habit. The information is in your long-term memory. The more often you use information, the easier it is to recall. You could not become a good musician without hours of practice. Playing sports, speaking in public, flying an airplane, and learning to drive all require skills that need to be repeated and practiced many times.

Repetition puts information into long-term memory and allows for recall. Improve your memory by having a desire to remember, concentrating, observing and visualizing information, thinking about associations, reciting, and repeating again and again. Use the Adult Learning Cycle to practice, think positively, and reward yourself when you see improvement.

These strategies are very effective in strengthening your memory skills. Certain strategies might work better for you than others, depending on your personality and learning styles. Everyone has his or her personal strengths and abilities. You can master the use of memory strategies with effort, patience, and practice. As you build your memory skills, you will also enhance your study habits and become more disciplined and aware of your surroundings.

Peak Progress

Remembering Names

Here are some techniques that may help you remember someone's name. Many of these techniques will also help you remember material in class.

1. **Imagine the name.** Visualize the name clearly in your mind: Tom Plum. Clarify how the name is spelled: P-l-u-m.

2. **Be observant and concentrate.** Pay attention to the person's features and mannerisms.

3. **Use exaggeration.** Caricaturing the features is a fun and effective way to remember names. Single out and amplify one outstanding feature. For example, if Tom has red hair, exaggerate it to bright red and see the hair much fuller and longer than it is.

4. **Visualize the red hair and the name Tom.** See this vision clearly.

5. **Repeat Tom's name to yourself** several times as you are talking to him.

6. **Recite Tom's name aloud** during your conversation. Introduce Tom to others.

7. **Use association.** Associate the name with something you know ("Tom is the name of my cat") or make up a story using the person's name and add action and color. Tom is picking red plums that match his hair.

8. **As soon as you can, jot down the name.** Use a key word, or write or draw a description.

9. **Use rhyming to help you recall:** "Tom is not glum, nor is he dumb."

10. **Integrate learning styles.** It may help if you see the name (visual), hear it pronounced (auditory), or practice saying it and writing it several times and connecting the name with something familiar (kinesthetic).

11. **Ask people their names.** Do this if you forget or say your name first. "Hi, I'm Sam and I met you last week." If they don't offer their names, ask.

12. **Reward yourself when you remember.** Practice these techniques and reward yourself for your successes. Remember, the first requirements for improving your memory are a desire to remember and concentration.

Summarize, Review, and Reflect

Summarize a lecture or a section or a chapter of a book in your own words as soon as possible after hearing or reading it. The sooner and the more often you review information, the easier it is to recall. Ideally, your first review should be within the first hour after hearing a lecture or reading an assignment. Carry note cards with you and review them again during the first day. As discussed in Chapter 4, memory researchers suggest that, after only 48 hours, you may have forgotten 70 percent of what you have learned. However, if you review right after you hear it and again within 24 hours, your recall soars to 90 percent.

Go beyond studying for tests. Be able to connect and apply information to new situations. Uncover facts, interesting points, related materials, details, and fascinating aspects of the subject. Ask your instructor for interesting stories to enhance a point. If you have time, read a novel on the subject or look for another textbook in the library that explains the subject from a different view. You will remember information more easily if you take the time to understand and apply it.

Overcome Obstacles

A barrier to memory is disinterest. You have to want to remember. People often say, "If only I could remember names" or "I wish I had a better memory." Avoid using words such as *try, wish,* and *hope.* You can overcome the barrier of disinterest by creating a positive, curious attitude; by intending to remember; by using all your senses; and by using memory techniques. Related to disinterest is lack of attentiveness. You must be willing to concentrate by being an attentive listener and observe. Listen for overall understanding and for details. A short period of intense concentration will help you remember more than reading for hours.

Practice becoming more observant and aware. Let's say that you want to learn the students' names in all your classes. Look at each student as the instructor takes roll, copy down each name, and say each name mentally as you look around the classroom. As you go about your day, practice becoming aware of your surroundings, people, and new information.

Finally, relax. Anxiety, stress, and nervousness can make you forget. For example, let's return to remembering names again. Suppose you are with a good friend and you meet Tom. You may be so anxious to make a good impression that Tom's name is lost for a moment. Learn to relax by being totally in the moment instead of worrying about forgetting, how you look, what others may think, or your nervousness. Take a deep breath. If you still can't remember, laugh and say, "Hi, my mind just went blank. I'm Jay; please refresh my memory."

To keep your memory skills sharp, review and assess your answers to the following questions periodically. Can you answer yes to them?

- Do I want to remember?
- Do I have a positive attitude about the information?
- Have I eliminated distractions?
- Have I organized and grouped material?
- Have I reviewed the information often?
- Have I reviewed right after the lecture? Within 24 hours?
- Have I set up weekly reviews?
- Have I visualized what I want to remember?
- Have I used repetition?
- Have I summarized material in my own words?
- Have I used association and compared and contrasted new material with what I know?
- Have I used memory techniques to help me associate key words?

TAKING CHARGE

Summary

In summary, in this chapter I learned to:

- **Apply the five-step memory process.** Similar to the Adult Learning Cycle, the memory process consists of five steps: intention, attention, association, retention, and recall.

- **Intend to remember.** People who have better memories *want* to remember and make it a priority. It's important for me to increase my memory skills, and I take responsibility for my attitude and intention. I create personal interest and meaning in what I want to remember.

- **Be observant and alert.** I observe and am attentive to details. I am relaxed, focused, and receptive to new information. I reduce distractions, concentrate, and stay focused and mindful of the present. I look at the big picture, and then I look at details. Memory is increased when I pay attention.

- **Organize and associate information.** Organization makes sense out of information. I look for patterns and connections. I look for what I already know and jot down questions for areas that I don't know. I group similarities and look for what is different.

- **Retain information.** I write summaries in my own words and say them out loud. I jot down main points, key words, and important information on note cards and review them often. I study in short sessions and review often.

- **Recall.** I recall everything I know about the subject. I increase my recall by writing down information, reciting out loud, and teaching others. Practicing and reviewing information often are key to increasing recall. I reward myself for concentration, discipline, and effort.

- **Write it down.** The simple act of writing helps me create a mental picture.

- **Go from the general to the specific.** I first look at the big picture for gaining general, overall understanding and meaning. I then focus on the details and specific supporting information.

- **Reduce information and eliminate distractions.** Some information does not have to be memorized (such as e-mail addresses and phone numbers); I just need to know where to find it easily. I also need to eliminate distractions that affect my ability to concentrate on what I'm trying to learn and remember.

- **Take frequent breaks.** I study in 40- to 60-minute sessions, since I know that the brain retains information best in short study periods. I take breaks to keep up my motivation.

- **Integrate learning styles.** I incorporate various learning styles by making learning visual, auditory, and physical.

- **Use my senses.** I draw pictures and illustrations, use color, record lectures, play music, write out summaries, jot down questions, collect samples, give summaries to my study group, recite out loud, and go on field trips.

- **Try mnemonic devices.** I use various techniques, such as rhythms and rhymes, acronyms, acrostics, grouping, association, and the method-of-place technique to help me memorize and recall information.

- **Use note cards.** Using note cards is an easy and convenient way for me to review important facts, terms, and questions.

- **Find connections and recite.** I link new information with familiar material, and I summarize what I have learned, either out loud or in writing.

- **Practice!** If I want to understand and remember information, I must practice and review it again and again.

Performance Strategies

Following are the top 10 strategies for improving memory:

- Intend to remember and prepare yourself mentally.
- Be observant, be alert, and pay attention.
- Organize information to make it meaningful.
- Look for associations and connections.
- Write down information.
- Integrate learning styles.
- Study in short sessions.
- Use mnemonic devices.
- Summarize information in your own words.
- Practice, use repetition, and relax.

Tech for Success

Take advantage of the text's Web site at **www.mhhe.com/ferrett7e** for additional study aids, useful forms, and convenient and applicable resources.

- **Acrostics online.** Many disciplines (especially in the sciences) have well-known acrostics that students and professionals use to remember key information (such as human anatomy). There are a number of online sites you can access for free that have collected hundreds of useful acrostics.
- **Stored memory.** Your computer is one big memory tool, storing thousands of hours of your work and contact information. For example, if you use the "Favorites" feature in your Web browser to catalog Web sites, consider how long it would take for you to reconstruct this information if it were suddenly wiped out. Do you have back-up plans in case your hard drive becomes inaccessible, or if you lose your cell phone containing countless stored numbers? Use these many tools and features to help you organize and save time, but don't forget to write down or keep hard copies of very important documents and contact information.

Study Team Notes

Integrating Learning Styles

As a journalist, Marla Bergstrom's job is to find newsworthy local issues, collect accurate information from both sides of the story, and write an article that treats the subject fairly. As a general assignment reporter for a large newspaper, she covers stories on politics, crime, education, business, and consumer affairs.

Marla works closely with her editor when selecting a topic for an article. She often investigates leads for a story, only to realize later that she does not have enough information to make a strong story. She organizes the information she gathers, not knowing how or if it will fit into the article. Marla usually works on more than one story at a time, as some stories take weeks of research. Her hours are irregular. Marla might attend an early morning political breakfast and attend a school board meeting that evening.

Each week, Marla interviews a wide variety of people, including the mayor, the police chief, the school supervisor, and other community leaders. She always says hello to people, using their names. She prides herself on being able to remember names after only one meeting. When conducting an interview, the first thing Marla does is write down the name of the person, asking for the correct spelling. By doing this, she not only checks spelling but also sees a person's name in print. Because Marla is a visual learner, this helps her remember the name. On the way home from an interview, Marla orally reviews the names of the people she met. After an interview, Marla types her notes and memorizes pertinent information, such as the names of people, businesses, and locations. Marla knows that having good memory skills is essential for being a capable journalist.

Marla Bergstrom
JOURNALIST

Related Majors: Journalism, English, Social Studies

CRITICAL THINKING Which learning styles help Marla remember pertinent information?

Peak Performer
PROFILE

David Diaz

In first grade, David Diaz knew he wanted to be a "drawer." However, he had no idea what that meant. He knew he liked to draw. It wasn't until high school that an instructor and a sculptor became instrumental in his selection of art as his career path. The art teacher encouraged him to enter art competitions; the sculptor, Duane Hanson, demonstrated by example the life of an artist.

Diaz attended the Fort Lauderdale Art Institute before moving across the country to California to start his prolific career in graphic design and illustration. For the last 25 years, he has been illustrating for national publications, book publishers, and corporations.

Success came early in his picture-book career when he was awarded the prestigious Caldecott Medal for illustrating Eve Bunting's *Smokey Nights*, a story about a boy's point of view of the Los Angeles riots in 1992. Critics and readers continue to appreciate the honest, vibrant, painterly quality of his work.

"I'm always thinking about how to make [the book] more of an experience, not just something you read," he said. His dynamic work comes through numerous revisions of looks and feels of the characters in the stories. He keeps working over an image to get it just right.

After all this time and success, Diaz still goes back to his roots: the foundations of drawing. "All the technique in the world can't save a bad drawing. As an artist, the challenge for me is to retain the spontaneity of an initial sketch or thumbnail drawing through the creation of the final image." Here is an artist, following his instinct, education, and passion through each phase of his career.

PERFORMANCE THINKING A career in the arts is often about paying careful attention to the world around you. Unique observations and an execution of talent are two keys to garnering attention for artistic merits. How might an artist find an activity like the Memory Garden on page 202 helpful to his or her work? Why might memory be important to creating a piece of artwork?

CHECK IT OUT The largest library in the world, the Library of Congress, houses more than 130 million items and 530 miles of bookshelves. Visit the Web site **www.loc.gov** to search for various print, media, and online resources. Also available on the Web site is a section called "American Memory," which showcases historical information and resources on a number of topics, such as environment/conservation, immigration/American expansion, African American history, and women's history.

Starting Today

At least one strategy I learned in this chapter that I plan to try right away is:

_____

_____

_____

What changes must I make in order for this strategy to be effective?

_____

_____

_____

Review Questions

Based on what you have learned in this chapter, write your answers to the following questions:

1. What are the five main steps of the memory process?

_____

_____

2. Why is intending to remember so important to enhancing memory?

_____

_____

3. Why does writing down information help you remember it?

_____

_____

4. Name one mnemonic device and how it is used to help you remember. Give an example.

_____

_____

5. What is the purpose of reviewing information soon and often?

_____

_____

Overcoming Memory Loss

In the Classroom

Erin McAdams is outgoing, bright, and popular, but she also has a reputation for being forgetful. She forgets appointments, projects, and due dates. She is continually losing her keys and important papers. She is often late and forgets meetings and even social events. She always tells herself, "I'm just not good at remembering names" and "I really am going to try harder to get more organized and remember my commitments." She blames her bad memory for doing poorly on tests and wishes that people would just understand that she's doing the best she can. She insists that she's tried but just can't change.

1. What would you suggest to help Erin improve her memory skills?

   _____

   _____

2. What strategies in this chapter would be most helpful?

   _____

   _____

In the Workplace

Erin is now in hotel management. She loves the excitement, the diversity of the people she meets, and the daily challenges. She has recently been assigned to plan and coordinate special events, which include parties, meetings, and social affairs. This new job requires remembering many names, dates, and endless details.

3. How can Erin learn to develop her memory skills?

   _____

   _____

4. Suggest a program for her that would increase her memory skills.

   _____

   _____

Applying the ABC Method of Self-Management

In the Journal Entry on page 189, you were asked to describe a situation when you needed to learn many new names or numerous facts for a test. How did you fare? What factors helped you remember?

_____

_____

_____

_____

Now describe a situation in which you forgot some important information or someone's name that you really wanted to remember. Work through the ABC method and incorporate the new strategies you have learned in this chapter.

A = Actual event:

B = Beliefs:

C = Challenge:

Relax, take a deep breath, and visualize yourself recalling facts, key words, dates, and information easily.

PRACTICE SELF-MANAGEMENT

For more examples of learning how to manage difficult situations, see the "Self-Management Workbook" section of the Online Learning Center Web site at **www.mhhe.com/ferrett7e.**

Memory

A. Quickly read these lists once. Read one word at a time and in order.

1	2
the	Disney World
work	light
of	time
and	and
to	of
the	house
and	the
of	packages
light	good
of	praise
care	and
the	coffee
chair	the
and	of

B. Now cover the lists and write as many words as you can remember on the lines that follow. Then check your list against the lists in Part A.

_____   _____
_____   _____
_____   _____
_____   _____
_____   _____
_____   _____
_____   _____
_____   _____
_____   _____
_____   _____

(continued)

1. How many words did you remember from the beginning of the list? List them.

_____

_____

2. How many words did you remember from the middle of the list? List them.

_____

_____

3. How many words did you remember from the end of the list? List them.

_____

_____

4. Did you remember the term *Disney World?*   Yes _____   No _____

Most people who complete this exercise remember the first few words, the last few words, the unusual term *Disney World,* and the words that were listed more than once (*of, the,* and *and*). Did you find this to be true about yourself?   Yes _____   No _____

C. Remembering names

1. Do you have problems remembering names?   Yes _____   No _____
2. What are the benefits of remembering names now and in a career?

_____

_____

_____

D. What memory techniques work best for you?

_____

_____

_____

Mental Pictures

Use a clock or a study partner to time you as you look at the following pictures for two minutes. As you look at these pictures, create a mental picture. After the two minutes have passed, turn the page and make up a story using all these elements.

(continued)

1. Write your creative story on the following lines.

_____

_____

_____

_____

_____

_____

_____

_____

_____

_____

_____

_____

_____

_____

_____

_____

_____

_____

_____

_____

_____

_____

_____

_____

_____

_____

_____

_____

_____

_____

_____

_____

_____

_____

2. What memory strategies did you use to recall the information?

_____

_____

_____

_____

_____

_____

_____

3. What connections were you able to make among the photos?

_____

_____

_____

_____

_____

_____

_____

Applying Memory Skills

Assess your memory skills by answering the following questions. Add this page to your Career Development Portfolio.

1. **Looking back:** Review an autobiography you may have written for this or another course. Indicate the ways you applied your memory skills.

   _____

   _____

2. **Taking stock:** What are your memory strengths and what do you want to improve?

   _____

   _____

3. **Looking forward:** How would you demonstrate memory skills for employers?

   _____

   _____

4. **Documentation:** Include examples, such as poems you have memorized, literary quotes, and techniques for remembering names.

   _____

   _____

5. **Assessment and demonstration:** Critical thinking skills for memory include

   • Preparing yourself mentally and physically
   • Creating a willingness to remember
   • Determining what information is important and organizing it
   • Linking new material with known information (creating associations)
   • Integrating various learning styles
   • Asking questions
   • Reviewing and practicing
   • Evaluating your progress

   _____

   _____

   _____

   _____

   _____

   _____

7 Excel at Taking Tests

LEARNING OBJECTIVES

In this chapter, you will learn to

7.1 Prepare for tests

7.2 Describe strategies for taking tests

7.3 Use test results

7.4 Take different types of tests

7.5 Use special tips for math and science tests

7.6 Prepare for performance appraisals

7.7 Overcome test anxiety

SELF-MANAGEMENT

" I studied very hard for my last test, but my mind went blank when I tried to answer the questions. What can I do to decrease my anxiety and be more confident about taking tests? "

Have you ever had a similar experience? Do you find yourself feeling anxious and worried when you take tests? Do you suffer physical symptoms, such as sweaty palms, upset stomach, headaches, or an inability to sleep or concentrate? Everyone experiences some anxiety when faced with a situation associated with performance or evaluation. Peak performers know that the best strategy for alleviating feelings of panic is to be prepared. In this chapter, you will learn how to decrease your anxiety and learn test-taking strategies that will help you before, during, and after the test.

JOURNAL ENTRY In **Worksheet 7.1** on page 248, describe a time when you did well in a performance, sporting event, or test. What factors helped you be calm, be confident, and remember information?

ALL SUCCESSFUL ATHLETES AND PERFORMERS KNOW HOW IMPORTANT IT IS TO MONITOR AND MEASURE THEIR TECHNIQUES AND VARY THEIR TRAINING PROGRAMS TO IMPROVE RESULTS. Taking tests is part of school; performance reviews are part of a job; and tryouts and performing are part of the life of an athlete, a dancer, or an actor. In fact, there are few jobs in life that don't require you to assess skills, attitudes, and behavior. Many fields also require you to pass rigorous exams before you complete your education (such as the LSAT for law) and certification exams (as in athletic training). Thus, the goal of this chapter is to explore specific test-taking strategies that will help you both in school and in your career.

Test-Taking Strategies

Before the Test

Test taking starts long before sitting down with pencil in hand (or in front of a computer) to tackle an exam. The following tips will help you as you prepare for taking a test.

1. **Start on day one.** The best way to do well on tests is to begin by preparing on the first day of class. Prepare by attending all classes, arriving on time, and staying until the end of class. Set up a review schedule on the first day. Observe your instructors during class to see what they consider important and what points and key words they stress. As you listen to lectures or read your textbook, ask yourself what questions might be on the examination. **Peak Progress 7.1** indicates important skills that you will use as you take tests.

2. **Know expectations.** The first day of class is important because most instructors outline the course and clarify the syllabus and expectations concerning grading, test dates, and types of tests. During class or office hours, ask your instructors about test formats. Ask for sample questions, a study guide, or additional material that may be helpful for studying; also ask how much weight the textbook has on tests. Some instructors cover key material in class and assign reading for a broad overview. You are in a partnership with your instructors, and it is important in any relationship to understand expectations. A large part of fear and anxiety comes from the unknown; thus, the more you know about what is expected concerning evaluations and exams, the more at ease you will be. **Personal Evaluation Notebook 7.1** on page 224 gives you a handy guide for approaching your instructors about upcoming tests and how you are currently performing in class. (**Worksheet 7.3** on page 250 also provides a detailed guide for tracking test information.)

3. **Ask questions in class.** If you are unclear about a point, raise your hand and ask for clarification. Or ask your instructor or another student at the end of class. Don't assume all of the lecture will be covered in the textbook.

Peak Progress

Test-Taking Skills

The factors involved in taking tests and performing well on them are

1. Preparing yourself both mentally and physically
2. Determining what information is important
3. Processing information
4. Linking new material with known information
5. Creating associations
6. Creating a willingness to remember
7. Staying focused
8. Reasoning logically
9. Overcoming fear
10. Evaluating test results

---

4. **Keep up.** Manage your time and keep up with daily reading, homework, and assignments. (Use your time-management strategies from Chapter 3.) Consolidate your class notes with your reading notes. Avoid waiting until the night before to prepare for an exam. (**Worksheet 7.2** on page 249 is a handy form for keeping track of your exams.)

5. **Review early.** Start the review process by previewing chapters before classes. Take a few minutes to review your class notes immediately after class. When information is fresh, you can fill in missing pieces, make connections, and raise questions to ask later. Set up a schedule, so that you have time to review daily notes from all your classes each day. Review time can be short; 5 or 10 minutes for every class is often sufficient. A daily review should also include scanning reading notes and items that need memorization. This kind of review should continue until the final exam.

6. **Review weekly.** Spend about an hour or so for each subject to investigate and review not only the week's assignments but also what has been included thus far in the course. These review sessions can include class notes, reading notes, chapter questions, note cards, mind maps, flash cards, a checklist of items to study, and summaries written in your own words. One of the best ways to test yourself is to close your book after reading and write a summary; then, go back and fill in missing material.

7. **Do a final review.** A week or so before a test, commit to a major review. (Some instructors encourage students to allocate at least two hours per day for three days prior to the exam.) This review should include class and book notes, note cards, and summaries. You can practice test questions, compare concepts, integrate major points, and review and recite with your study team. Long-term memory depends on organizing the information. Fragmented information is difficult to remember or recall. Understanding the main ideas and connecting and relating information transfer the material into long-term memory.

Personal Evaluation Notebook 7.1

Test Taking

To help you prepare for tests, do the following activities and write your findings on the lines provided.

1. Go to each of your instructors and ask how you are doing in each class.
2. Discuss your expectations and the style of test questions you can expect on their tests.
3. Ask the instructors and make note of what you can do to earn a good grade.

Course _____

_____

_____

Course _____

_____

_____

Course _____

_____

_____

Course _____

_____

_____

Course _____

_____

_____

8. **Use memory techniques.** Determine which memory techniques will help you recall information, especially if you need to remember key dates, names, or lists. (Refer to Chapter 6 for a number of effective memory techniques.)

9. **Create sample tests.** Pretest yourself by predicting questions and creating and taking sample tests. Chapter objectives, key concepts, summaries, and end-of-chapter questions and exercises all provide examples of possible test questions. Also, many textbooks have accompanying CDs or Web sites that include sample test questions (such as what you will find at **www.mhhe.com/ferrett7e**). Review and rehearse until you have learned the material and you are confident. Save all quizzes, course materials, exercise sheets, and lab work. Ask if old tests or sample tests are available at the library.

10. **Summarize.** Pretend that the instructor said that you could take one note card to the test. Choose the most important concepts, formulas, key words, and points and condense them onto one note card. This exercise highlights important material. You will do better on a test even if you cannot use the note card during the test. The number one reason that students don't do well on tests is that they don't know the material. If you can summarize in your own words, you will understand the material versus just memorizing facts.

11. **Use your study team.** You may be tempted to skip studying one night, but you can avoid temptation if you know other people are waiting for you and depending on your contribution. Have each member of the study team provide 5 to 10 potential test questions. Share these questions and discuss possible answers. Word the questions in different formats—multiple-choice, true/false, matching, and essay. Then, simulate the test-taking experience by taking, giving, and correcting each other's timed sample tests.

12. **Use all available resources.** If your instructor offers a review before the exam, attend and take good notes and ask clarifying questions. Consider getting a tutor by checking with the learning center, academic departments, or student services. A tutor will expect that you attend all classes, keep up with reading and homework assignments, and be motivated to learn. Your tutor will not do your work for you but will review assignment expectations, explain concepts, help you summarize and understand terms and definitions, and help you study for tests.

13. **Assemble what you will need.** Pack your bag with sharpened pencils, pens, paper clips, and any other items you may need, such as a watch, calculator, or dictionary. Get a good night's sleep, eat a light breakfast, and make sure you set an alarm. You don't want to be frantic and late for a test. Arrive a few minutes early.

During the Test

The following strategies will help you as you take a test. See **Peak Progress 7.2** on page 226 for specific tips on taking online exams.

1. **Write down key information.** As soon as you get the test, write your name on it and jot down key words, facts, formulas, dates, principles, ideas, concepts, statistics, and other memory cues in pencil on the back of your paper or in the margins. If you wait until you are reading each question, you may forget important material while under pressure.

2. **Read and listen to all instructions.** Many instructors require that you use a pen and write on only one side of the paper. After clarifying the instructions, scan the entire test briefly and make sure you understand what is expected in each section. If you are unsure, ask your instructor immediately.

3. **Determine which questions are worth the most.** Look at the point value for each question and determine the importance that should be given to each section. For example, you will want to spend more time on an essay worth 25 points than on a multiple-choice section worth 5. Review subjective or essay questions to see which you can answer quickly and which will take more time. Set a plan and pace yourself based on the amount of time you have for the test. Jot down dates, key words, or related facts, which will serve as a rough outline and may stimulate your memory for another question.

Peak Progress

7.2

Taking Online Exams

Although the preparation may be similar, taking an online exam may involve more coordination on your part than a traditional pencil-and-paper exam.

- Double-check your computer's settings before you start to take a test to avoid any problems.
- Unless the test must be taken at a certain time or specific date, do not wait until the last day to take the exam. If you have technical difficulties or lose your connection, you may not have time to solve the problem.
- Shut down all other programs not needed during the exam, including e-mail.
- If your test is timed, make sure you can easily see the timer or the computer's clock.
- If allowed, have your text and any other materials nearby and easily accessible. Put key information, dates, or formulas on sticky notes next to the screen.
- Wait until the test is fully loaded before answering questions.
- Set the window size before you start. Resizing later may refresh your screen and cause the test to reload and start over.
- To avoid being accidentally kicked out of the exam, do not click outside of the test area or click the back arrow. Only use functions within the testing program to return to previous questions.
- If there is a save option, save often throughout the exam.
- If more than one question is on a page, click "Submit" or the arrow button only after all questions on that page are answered.
- Click "Submit" only once at the end of the test and confirm that the test was received.

4. **Answer objective questions.** Sometimes objective questions contain details you can use for answering essay questions. Don't panic if you don't know an answer right away. Answer the questions that are easiest for you, and mark those questions that you want go back to later.

5. **Answer essay questions.** Answer the easiest subjective or essay questions first and spend more time on the questions with the highest value. Underline or circle key words or points in the question. If you have time, do a quick outline in pencil, so that your answer is organized. Look for defining words and make sure you understand what the question is asking you. For example, are you being asked to justify, illustrate, compare and contrast, or explain? Write down main ideas and then fill in details, facts, and examples. Be complete, but avoid filler sentences that add nothing.

6. **Answer remaining questions.** Unless there is a penalty for guessing, answer all questions. Rephrase questions you find difficult. It may help you change the wording of a sentence. Draw a picture or a diagram, use a different equation, or make a mind map and write the topic and subtopics. Use association to remember items that are related.

7. **Review.** Once you have finished, reread the test carefully and check for mistakes or spelling errors. Stay the entire time, answer extra-credit and bonus questions,

and fill in details and make any necessary changes. (See **Peak Progress 7.3** for specific strategies for math and science texts.)

After the Test

The test isn't over when you hand it in. Successful test taking includes how you use the results.

1. **Reward yourself.** Reward yourself with a treat, such as a hot bath, a walk, an evening with friends, or a special dinner. Always reward yourself with a good night's sleep.

2. **Analyze and assess.** When you receive the graded test, analyze and assess the grade and your performance for many things, such as the following:

   - *Confirm your grade.* Confirm that your score was calculated or graded correctly. If you believe there has been a mistake in your grade, see your instructor immediately and ask to review it.

   - *Determine common types of mistakes.* Were your mistakes due to carelessness in reading the instructions or in a lack of preparedness on certain topics? **Peak Progress 7.4** on page 229 includes a number of common reasons for incorrect answers on tests. Do you find that there are patterns in your mistakes? If so, determine what you need to do to correct those patterns.

   - *Learn what to do differently next time.* Your test will provide valuable feedback, and you can learn from the experience. Be a detached, curious, receptive observer and view the results as feedback. Feedback is essential for improvement.

Peak Progress (7.3)

Special Strategies for Math and Science Tests

During your years of study, you will probably take math and science courses. Following are some strategies for preparing to take a math or science test.

1. **Use note cards.** Write formulas, definitions, rules, and theories on note cards and review them often. Write out examples for each theorem.

2. **Write key information.** As soon as you are given the test, jot down theorems and formulas in the margins.

3. **Survey the test.** Determine the number of questions and the worth and difficulty of each question.

4. **Answer easy to hard.** Do the easy questions first. Spend more time on questions that are worth the most points.

5. **Answer general to specific.** First, read to understand the big picture. Ask, "Why is this subject in the book? How does it connect with other topics?"

6. **Write the problem in longhand.** Translate into understandable words—for example, for $A = 1/2bh$, "For a triangle, the area is one-half the base times the height."

7. **Make an estimate.** A calculated guess will give you an approximate answer. This helps you when you double-check the answer.

(continued)

Special Strategies for Math and Science Tests *(concluded)*

8. **Illustrate the problem.** Draw a picture, diagram, or chart that will help you understand the problem—for example, "The length of a field is 6 feet more than twice its width. If the perimeter of the field is 228 feet, find the dimensions of the field."

Let l = the length of the field

Let w = the width of the field

Then $l = 2w + 6$

So $6w + 12 = 228$

$(w + 2w + 6 + w + 2w + 6)$

$6w + 12 = 228$

$6w = 216$

$w = 36$

So $l = 2w + 6 = 2(36) + 6 = 78$

Translating: The width of the field is 36 ft. and its length is 78 ft.

Checking: The perimeter is $2w + 2l = 2(36) + 2(78) = 72 + 156 = 228$

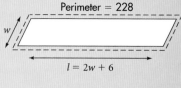

Perimeter = 228

$l = 2w + 6$

$w + 2w + 6 + w + 2w + 6 = 228$

9. **Ask yourself questions.** Ask, "What is being asked? What do I already know? What are the givens? What do I need to find out? How does this connect and relate to other concepts? What is the point of the question?" Analyze and examine the problem.

10. **Show your work.** If allowed, write down the method you used to get to the answer, which will help you retrace your steps if you get stuck. Your instructor may give you partial credit, even if the answer is incorrect. In some cases, showing your work is an expectation (and you will have points deducted for not showing complete or accurate work). Make sure you know what your instructor requires.

11. **Do a similar problem.** If you get stuck, try something similar. Which formula worked? How does this formula relate to others?

12. **State answers in the simplest terms.** For example, 4/6 instead should be answered as 2/3.

13. **Pay attention to the sign.** Note if a number is actually a negative number.

14. **Check your work.** Does your answer make sense? Is your work correct and systematic?

15. **Review.** Review your test as soon as you get it back. Where did you make your mistakes? Did you read the problems correctly? Did you use the correct formulas? What will you do differently next time?

> ❝ We learn more by looking for the answer to a question and not finding it than we do from learning the answer itself. ❞
>
> LLOYD ALEXANDER
> *Author*

Use the results of the test for self-assessment for future tests and ask yourself the following questions:

1. Did my study strategy work?
2. Did I read the test before I started?
3. What were my strengths? What did I do right?
4. What questions did I miss?

Peak Progress

Checklist for Incorrect Test Answers

Following are some of the most common reasons for incorrect answers on tests. As you review your test results, see if you seem to have recurring problems in any of the following areas. Make a point to improve and prepare yourself better the next time with these in mind.

- I did not read and/or follow the directions.
- I misread or misunderstood the question.
- I did not demonstrate reasoning ability.
- I did not demonstrate factual accuracy.
- I did not demonstrate good organization.
- My answer was incomplete.
- My answer lacked clarity.
- My handwriting was hard to read.
- I used time ineffectively.
- I did not prepare enough.
- I studied the wrong information.
- I knew the information but couldn't apply it to the questions.
- I confused facts or concepts.
- The information was not in my lecture notes.
- The information was not in the textbook.

5. Did I miss clues in the test? Did I ask the instructor for clarification?

6. How well did I know the content on which I was being tested?

7. What should I have studied more?

8. Did I anticipate the style and format of the questions?

9. What didn't I expect?

10. Did I have trouble with certain types of questions?

11. How was my recall?

12. Did I practice the right kind of thinking?

13. Did I test myself with the right questions?

14. Did I handle test anxiety well?

15. Would it have helped if I had studied with others?

16. What changes will I make in studying for the next test?

3. **Review with your instructor.** If you honestly don't know why you received the grade you did, ask your instructor to review your answers with you. Approach the meeting with a positive attitude, not a defensive one. Ask for clarification and explain your rationale for answers. Ask for advice on preparing for the next test.

4. **Review the test with your study team.** This will help you see common errors and the criteria for effective answers. Make note of how you will be able to study more effectively and answer questions better on the next test.

Remember, a test is information and feedback on how you are doing, not an evaluation of you as a person. You cannot change unless you can understand your mistakes. Learn from your mistakes and move forward. Assess what you did wrong and what you will do right the next time.

Taking Different Types of Tests

The following tips will help you as you take different types of tests.

Objective Tests

TRUE/FALSE TEST

1. **Listen and read carefully.** Read the entire question carefully before you answer it. For the question to be true, the entire question must be true. If any part of the statement is false, the entire statement is false.
2. **Pay attention to details.** Read dates, names, and places carefully. Sometimes the numbers in the dates are changed around (1494 instead of 1449) or the wording is changed slightly. Any such changes can change the meaning.
3. **Watch for qualifiers.** Watch for such words as *always, all, never,* and *every.* The question is often false because there are exceptions. If you can think of one exception, then the statement is false. Ask yourself, "Does this statement over-state or understate what I know to be true?"
4. **Watch for faulty cause and effect.** Two true statements may be connected by a word that implies cause and effect, and this word may make the statement false—for example, "Temperature is measured on the centigrade scale because water freezes at zero degrees centigrade."
5. **Always answer every question.** Unless there is a penalty for wrong answers, answer every question. You have a 50 percent chance of being right.
6. **Trust your instincts.** Often, your first impression is correct. Don't change an answer unless you are certain it is wrong. Don't spend time pondering until you have finished the entire test and have time to spare.

MULTIPLE-CHOICE TEST

1. **Read the question carefully.** Are you being asked for the correct answer or the best choice? Is there more than one answer? Preview the test to see if an answer may be included in a statement or question.
2. **Rephrase the question.** Sometimes it helps to rephrase the question in your own words, which may help trigger reading or hearing the initial discussion.
3. **Cover the potential answers.** Cover the answers (called "distractors") as you read the question and see what answer first comes to you. Then, look at the answers to see if your answer is one of the choices.
4. **Eliminate choices.** Narrow your choices by reading through all of them and eliminating those that you know are incorrect, so that you can concentrate on real choices.
5. **Go from easy to difficult.** Go through the test and complete the questions for which you know the answers. This will give you a feeling of confidence. Don't spend all your time on a few questions. With a pencil, mark the questions that

you are unsure of, but make certain that you mark your final answer clearly, so that you do not leave unclear marks.

6. **Watch for combinations.** Read the question carefully and don't just choose what appears to be the one correct answer. Some questions offer a combination of choices, such as "all of the above" or "none of the above."

7. **Look at sentence structure.** Make sure the grammatical structure of the question matches that of your choice.

8. **Use critical thinking.** Make sure you have a good reason for changing an answer. Use critical thinking and clearly know you are choosing the right answer. If not, your first impulse may be right.

MATCHING TEST

1. **Read carefully.** Read both lists quickly and watch for clues.

2. **Eliminate.** As you match the items you know, cross them out unless the directions mention that an item can be used more than once. Elimination is the key in a matching test.

3. **Look at sentence structure.** Often, verbs are matched to verbs. Read the entire sentence. Does it make sense?

FILL-IN-THE-BLANK TEST

1. **Watch for clues.** If the word before the blank is *an*, the word in the blank generally begins with a vowel. If the word before the blank is *a*, the word in the blank generally begins with a consonant.

2. **Count the number of blanks.** The number of blanks often indicates the number of words in an answer. Think of key words that were stressed in class.

3. **Watch for the length of the blank.** A longer blank may indicate a longer answer.

4. **Answer the questions you know first.** As with all tests, answer the questions you know first and then go back to those that are more difficult. Rephrase and look for key words.

5. **Answer all questions.** Try never to leave a question unanswered.

OPEN-BOOK TEST

The key to an open-book test is to prepare. Students often think that open-book tests will be easy, so they don't study. Generally, these tests go beyond basic recall and require critical thinking and analysis. Put markers in your book to indicate important areas. Write formulas, definitions, key words, sample questions, and main points on note cards. Bring along your detailed study sheet. The key is to be able to find information quickly. Use your own words to summarize. Don't copy from your textbook.

Essay Test

Being prepared is essential when taking an essay test. Make certain that you understand concepts and relationships, not just specific facts. (See **Peak Progress 7.5** on page 232 for a sample essay test.) In addition, use the following strategies to help you take an essay test.

1. **Budget your writing time.** Look over the whole test, noticing which questions are easiest. Allot a certain amount of time for each essay question and include time for review when you're finished.

2. **Read the question carefully.** Make certain you understand what is being asked in the question. Respond to key words, such as *explain, classify, define,* and *compare.* Rephrase the question into a main thesis. Always answer what is being asked directly. Don't skirt around an issue. If you are being asked to compare and contrast, do not describe, or you will not answer the question correctly. **Peak Progress 7.6** on page 234 lists a number of key words used in essay questions.

3. **Create an outline.** Organize your main points in an outline, so that you won't leave out important information. An outline will provide a framework to help

Peak Progress

7.5

Sample Essay Test

Steve Hackett
Intro to Economics Quiz
January 12, 2009

QUESTION

Describe the general circumstances under which economists argue that government intervention in a market economy enhances efficiency.

THESIS STATEMENT

Well-functioning competitive markets are efficient resource allocators, but they can fail in certain circumstances. Government intervention can generate its own inefficiencies, so economists promote the forms of government intervention that enhance efficiency under conditions of market failure.

OUTLINE

    I. Well-functioning competitive markets are efficient.

        A. Firms have an incentive to minimize costs and waste.

        B. Price approximates costs of production.

        C. Effort, quality, and successful innovation are rewarded.

        D. Shortages and surpluses are eliminated by price adjustment.

    II. Markets fail to allocate scarce resources efficiently under some circumstances.

        A. Externalities affect other people.

            1. Negative externalities, such as pollution

            2. Positive externalities and collectively consumed goods

        B. Lack of adequate information causes failure.

        C. Firms with market power subvert the competition.

  III. Government intervention can create its own inefficiencies.

        A. Rigid, bureaucratic rules can stifle innovative solutions and dilute incentives.

        B. Politically powerful groups can subvert the process.

  IV. Efficient intervention policy balances market and government inefficiencies.

(continued)

Sample Essay Test *(concluded)*

Well-functioning competitive markets allocate resources efficiently in the context of scarcity. They do so in several different ways. First, in market systems, firms are profit maximizers and thus have an incentive to minimize their private costs of production. In contrast, those who manage government agencies lack the profit motive and thus the financial incentive to minimize costs. Second, under competitive market conditions, the market price is bid down by rival firms to reflect their unit production costs. Thus, for the last unit sold, the value (price) to the consumer is equal to the cost to produce that unit, meaning that neither too much nor too little is produced. Third, firms and individuals have an incentive to work hard to produce new products and services preferred by consumers because, if successful, these innovators will gain an advantage over their rivals in the marketplace. Fourth, competitive markets react to surpluses with lower prices and to shortages with higher prices, which work to resolve these imbalances.

Markets can fail to allocate scarce resources efficiently in several different situations. First, profit-maximizing firms have an incentive to emit negative externalities (uncompensated harms generated by market activity that fall on others), such as pollution, when doing so lowers their production costs and is not prevented by law. Individual firms also have an incentive not to provide positive externalities (unpaid-for benefits) that benefit the group, such as police patrol, fire protection, public parks, and roads. A second source of market failure is incomplete information regarding product safety, quality, and workplace safety. A third type of market failure occurs when competition is subverted by a small number of firms that can manipulate prices, such as monopolies and cartels.

Government intervention can take various forms, including regulatory constraints, information provision, and direct government provision of goods and services. Government intervention may also be subject to inefficiencies. Examples include rigid regulations that stifle the incentive for innovation, onerous compliance costs imposed on firms, political subversion of the regulatory process by powerful interest groups, and lack of cost-minimizing incentives on the part of government agencies. Thus, efficient government intervention can be said to occur when markets fail in a substantial way and when the particular intervention policy generates inefficiencies that do not exceed those associated with the market failure.

you remember dates, main points, names, places, and supporting material. Use **Personal Evaluation Notebook 7.2** on page 235 to practice outlining key words and topics.

4. **Focus on main points.** Your opening sentence should state your thesis, followed by supporting information.

5. **Write concisely and correctly.** Get directly to the point and use short, clear sentences. Remember that your instructor (or even teaching assistants) may be grading a pile of other students' tests, so get to the point and avoid using filler sentences.

6. **Use key terms and phrases.** Your instructor may be looking for very specific information in your answer, including terms, phrases, events, or people. Make sure you include that in your answer (and don't just assume the instructor knows to whom or what you are referring).

Peak Progress

Important Words in Essay Questions

The following words are used frequently in essay questions. Read them and become comfortable with their meanings.

Analyze	Explain the key points, parts, or process and examine each part.
Apply	Show the concept or function in a specific context.
Compare	Show similarities between concepts, objects, or events.
Contrast	Show differences between concepts, objects, or events.
Critique	Present your view or evaluation and give supporting evidence.
Define	Give concise, clear meanings and definitions.
Demonstrate	Show function or how something works; show understanding either physically or through words.
Describe	Present major characteristics or a detailed account.
Differentiate	Distinguish between two or more concepts or characteristics.
Discuss	Give a general presentation of the issue with examples or details to support main points.
Enumerate	Present the items in a numbered list or an outline.
Evaluate	Carefully appraise the problem, citing authorities.
Explain	Make an idea or a concept clear, or give a reason for an event.
Identify	Label or explain.
Illustrate	Clarify by presenting examples.
Interpret	Explain the meaning of a concept or problem.
Justify	Give reasons for conclusions or argue in support of a position.
List	Enumerate or write a list of points, one by one.
Outline	Organize main points and subordinate supporting points in a logical arrangement.
Prove	Give factual evidence and logical reasons that something is true.
Summarize	Present core ideas in a brief review that includes conclusions.

7. **Answer completely.** Reread the question and make certain you completely answered it, including supporting documentation. Did you cover the main points thoroughly and logically?

8. **Write neatly.** Appearance and legibility are important. Use an erasable pen. Use wide margins and don't crowd your words. Write on one side of the paper only. Leave space between answers, so that you can add to an answer if time permits.

9. **Use all the available time.** Don't hurry. Pace yourself and always use all the available time for review, revisions, reflection, additions, and corrections. Proofread carefully. Answer all questions unless otherwise directed.

Last-Minute Study Tips

Cramming is not effective if you haven't studied or attended classes. You might ask yourself, however, "What is the best use of my time the night before the test?" or "What can I do right now in just a few minutes to finish preparing for a test?"

Personal Evaluation Notebook ✓ 7.2

Essay Test Preparation

Pretend you are taking an essay test on a personal topic—your life history. Your instructor has written the following essay question on the board:

> Write a brief essay on your progress through life so far, covering the highs and lows, major triumphs, and challenges.

Before you begin writing, remind yourself of the topics you want to cover in this essay. What key words, phrases, events, and dates would you jot down in the margin of your essay paper? List your thoughts on the lines provided.

_____

_____

_____

_____

_____

_____

_____

_____

_____

_____

_____

_____

_____

_____

_____

_____

_____

_____

1. **Focus on a few points.** Decide what is important. Focus on a few of the most important points or formulas, key words, definitions, and dates instead of trying to cram everything into a short study time. Preview each chapter quickly; read the chapter objectives or key concepts and the end-of-chapter summary.

2. **Intend to be positive.** Don't panic or waste precious time being negative. State your intention of being receptive and open, gaining an overview of the material, and learning a few supporting points.

3. **Review your note cards.** The physical (and visual) act of reading and flipping note cards will help you review key information.

4. **Review your notes.** Look for words or topics you have highlighted or written on the side. Reread any summaries or mind maps you created after class.

5. **Affirm your memory.** The mind is capable of learning and memorizing material in just a short time if you focus, concentrate, and apply it. Look for opportunities to connect information.

Preparing for a Performance Appraisal

Taking tests or being evaluated is part of life. If you are employed, at some time you will probably receive a performance appraisal. For many people, performance appraisals create anxiety similar to test or public speaking anxiety. A performance appraisal can be a valuable tool to let you know how your employer perceives the quality of your work, your work ethic, and your future opportunities. It also gives you the opportunity to ask similar questions of your manager or reviewer. Often, employees are asked to evaluate their own performance, which is similar to answering an essay question: Your intent is to fully address the question and provide supporting, factual evidence (and often suggest outcomes—such as new goals and challenges).

The following questions will help you focus on getting the most out of your performance appraisal. Also, complete **Personal Evaluation Notebook 7.3** to review your first performance appraisal experience.

- Review your job description, including the duties you perform. What is expected of you in your job? What additional duties do you perform that are not listed?
- How do you view your job and the working climate?
- List your goals and objectives and the results achieved.
- What documentation do you have that demonstrates your results and achievements?
- What areas do you see as opportunities for improvement?
- What are your strengths and how can you maximize them?
- What are your general concerns?
- What are your advancement possibilities?
- What additional training would be helpful for you?
- What new skills could assist in your advancement?
- How can you increase your problem-solving skills?
- How can you make more creative and sound decisions?
- What can you do to prepare yourself for stressful projects and deadlines?
- Give examples of how you have contributed to the company's profits.
- What relationships could you develop to help you achieve results?
- Do you work well with other people?
- What project would be rewarding and challenging this year?

Personal Evaluation Notebook

Performance Appraisals

Answer the following questions about your first performance appraisal.

1. Describe your first performance appraisal. Explain how you felt.

   _____

   _____

   _____

   _____

   _____

2. How did you prepare for your first performance appraisal?

   _____

   _____

   _____

   _____

   _____

3. Were you motivated by the feedback you heard? Did you become defensive after hearing criticism?

   _____

   _____

   _____

   _____

   _____

4. What would you do differently?

   _____

   _____

   _____

   _____

   _____

- What resources do you need to complete this project?
- Do you have open and effective communication with your supervisor and co-workers?
- How does your assessment of your work compare with your supervisor's assessment?

Overcome Obstacles

Some students see tests and performance assessments as huge mountains—one slip can cause them to tumble down the slope. Even capable students find that certain tests undermine their confidence. For example, even the thought of taking a math or science test causes some people to feel anxious, and it sends others into a state of panic. A peak performer learns how to manage anxiety and knows that being prepared is the road to test-taking success.

Test Anxiety

Test anxiety is a learned response to stress. The symptoms of test anxiety include nervousness, upset stomach, sweaty palms, and forgetfulness. Being prepared is the best way to reduce anxiety. You will be prepared if you have attended every class; previewed chapters; reviewed your notes; and written, summarized, and studied the material each day. Studying with others is a great way to rehearse test questions, summarize, and help each other learn through group interaction. Since exams, tests, quizzes, tryouts, presentations, interviews, and performance appraisals are all evaluations and part of life, it is worth the time to learn to overcome test anxiety.

The attitude you bring to a test has a lot to do with your performance. Approach tests with a positive attitude. Tests provide a chance to learn to face fear and transform it into positive energy. Tests are opportunities to show what you have mastered in a course. Following are more suggestions that might help:

Keeping Calm
Test anxiety can cause some people to feel overwhelmed and even panicked. *How can you reduce the feeling of anxiety before you take a test?*

1. **Dispute negative thoughts and conversations.** Some people have negative or faulty assumptions about their abilities, especially in courses such as math and science, and may think, "I just don't have a logical mind." Replace negative self-talk with affirmations, such as "I am well prepared and will do well on this test" or "I can excel in this subject." Talk to yourself in positive and encouraging ways. Practice being your own best friend! Also, avoid negative conversations that make you feel anxious—for example, if someone mentions the length of time he or she has studied.

2. **Rehearse.** Athletes, actors, musicians, and dancers practice and rehearse for hours. When performers are on stage, their anxiety is channeled into focused energy. Practice taking sample tests with your study team, and you should be more confident during the actual test.

3. **Get regular exercise.** Aerobic exercise and yoga reduce stress and tension and promote deeper and more restful sleep. Build regular exercise into your life and work out the day before a test, if possible.

4. **Eat breakfast.** Eat a light, balanced breakfast that includes protein, such as cheese or yogurt. Keep a piece of fruit or nuts and bottled water in your backpack for energy. Limit your caffeine intake, as too much can make you more nervous or agitated.

5. **Visualize success.** See yourself taking the test and doing well. Imagine being calm and focused. Before you jump out of bed, relax, breathe deeply, and visualize your day unfolding in a positive way.

6. **Stay calm.** Make your test day peaceful by laying out your clothes, books, supplies, pens, and keys the night before. Review your note cards just before you go to sleep, repeat a few affirmations, and then get a good night's rest. Set an alarm, so that you'll be awake in plenty of time. Last-minute, frantic cramming only creates a hectic climate and increases anxiety. To alleviate stress, practice relaxation techniques.

7. **Get to class early.** Get to class early enough that you are not rushed and can use the few minutes before the test to take a few deep breaths and review your note cards. Deep breathing and affirmations, along with visualization, can help you relax. While waiting for other students to arrive, the instructor will sometimes answer questions or explain material to students who are in class ahead of schedule.

8. **Focus.** When your attention wanders, bring it gently back. Stay in the present moment by focusing your attention on the task at hand. Focus on each question. Concentrate on answering the questions and you won't have room in your mind for worry.

9. **Keep a sense of perspective.** Don't exaggerate the importance of tests. Tests do not measure self-esteem, personal qualities, character, or ability to contribute to society. Even if the worse happens and you don't do well on one test, it is not the end of your college career. You can meet with the instructor to discuss options and possibly do additional work, take the test again, or take the class again, if necessary. Keep fears in proper perspective.

10. **Get help.** If you are experiencing severe anxiety that prevents you from taking tests or performing well, seek professional help from the learning center or see a counselor at your school. Services often include support groups, relaxation training, biofeedback, and other useful techniques that can help you reduce anxiety and fear.

● **Cheating Only Hurts You**
There is never an excuse to cheat. *If this student is caught cheating, what are some of the repercussions he could face?*

Reflect and use critical thinking to describe your test anxiety experiences in **Personal Evaluation Notebook 7.4** on page 241. **Peak Progress 7.7** on page 240 explores how you can apply the Adult Learning Cycle to improve your test-taking skills and reduce anxiety.

Cheating

A central theme throughout this book is that character matters. When you practice honesty during test taking, you demonstrate to your instructor, your classmates, and, most important, to yourself that you are a person of integrity and are trustworthy. Cheating is

● Looking at someone's paper during a test
● Passing answers back and forth
● Getting notes from someone who has just taken the same test
● Stealing tests from an office
● Using electronic devices (such as a calculator) when not allowed
● Having someone else complete online work for you

Even if you haven't prepared as sufficiently for an exam as you should, there is no excuse for cheating. There is a high cost to cheating, even if you don't get caught. Cheating only hurts you because it

- **Violates your integrity.** You begin to see yourself as a person without integrity; if you compromise your integrity once, you're more likely to do it again.
- **Erodes confidence.** Cheating weighs on your conscience and sends you the message that you don't have what it takes to succeed. Your confidence and self-esteem suffer.
- **Creates academic problems.** Advanced courses depend on your learning from earlier courses, and cheating only creates future academic problems. You are paying a lot of money not to learn essential information.
- **Increases stress.** You have enough stress in your life without adding the intense pressure of worrying about being caught.
- **Brings high risks.** The consequences of cheating and plagiarism can result in failing the class, being suspended for the semester, or even being expelled from school permanently. Cheating can mess up your life for a very long time. It is humiliating, stressful, and completely avoidable.

There is never a legitimate reason to cheat. Focus on being prepared, using all the resources available to help you succeed, and practicing all the strategies offered in this book to become a peak performer.

Peak Progress 7.7

Applying the Adult Learning Cycle to Improving Your Test-Taking Skills and Reducing Test Anxiety

1. **RELATE. Why do I want to learn this?** I need to reduce my test anxiety and I want to do better on tests. Knowing how to control my anxiety will help me not only when taking tests but also in other performance situations. Do I already apply specific test-taking strategies or habits? What are some of my bad habits, such as last-minute cramming, which I should work to change?

2. **OBSERVE. How does this work?** Who does well on tests, and does that person seem confident when taking tests? What strategies can I learn from that person? Who seems to be just the opposite—does poorly on tests or seems to be full of anxiety? Can I determine what that person is doing wrong? I can learn from those mistakes. I'll try using new techniques and strategies for test taking and observe how I'm improving.

3. **REFLECT. What does this mean?** What strategies are working for me? Have I broken any bad habits, and am I more confident going into tests? Has my performance improved?

4. **DO. What can I do with this?** I will map out a plan before each major test, determining what I need to accomplish in order to be prepared and confident going in. I won't wait until the last minute to prepare. Each day, I can practice reducing my anxiety in many different stressful situations.

5. **TEACH. Whom can I share this with?** I'll talk with others and share what's working for me. Talking through my effective strategies reinforces their purpose.

Now return to Stage 1 and think about how it feels to learn this valuable new skill. Remember to congratulate and reward yourself when you achieve positive results.

Personal Evaluation Notebook 7.4

Test Anxiety

Use your critical thinking skills to answer the following questions.

1. Describe your test anxiety. Describe your emotions and thoughts associated with taking all types of tests.

   _____

   _____

   _____

   _____

2. **a.** Do you have different feelings about nonacademic tests, such as a driving test or a vision test, than academic tests, such as quizzes and exams?

   _____

   _____

   _____

   _____

   b. What do you think is the source of these differences?

   _____

   _____

   _____

   _____

3. **a.** What are your memories about your best and worst test-taking experiences?

   _____

   _____

   _____

   _____

   b. What factors contributed to your ease or discomfort during these tests?

   _____

   _____

   _____

   _____

   _____

TAKING CHARGE

Summary

In summary, in this chapter I learned to:

- **Prepare for test taking.** The time before a test is critical. I must prepare early for tests, starting from the first day of class. I keep up with the daily reading and ask questions in class and while I read. I review early and often, previewing the chapter before class and reviewing the materials again after class. I save and review all tests, exercises, and notes and review them weekly. I rehearse by taking a pretest, and I predict questions by reviewing the text's chapter objectives and summaries. I summarize the chapter in my own words, either in writing or out loud, double-checking that I've covered key points. I recite my summary to my study team and listen to theirs. We compare notes and test each other.

- **Take a test effectively.** Arriving early helps me be calm and focused on doing well on the test. I get organized by reviewing key concepts and facts. I focus on neatness and getting to the point with short, clear responses. I read all the instructions, scanning the entire test briefly and writing formulas and notes in the margins. I pace myself by answering the easiest questions first, and I rephrase questions that I find difficult and look for associations to remember items. At the end, I review to make certain I've answered what was asked and check for mistakes or spelling errors. I stay the entire time that is available.

- **Follow up a test.** I should reward myself for successfully completing the test. Then I will analyze and assess how I did on the test. Did I prepare enough? Did I anticipate questions? What can I do differently for the next test? I'll use creative problem solving to explore ways to do better on future tests.

- **Be successful on different kinds of tests.** Objective tests include true/false, multiple-choice, matching, fill-in-the-blank, and open-book. I must read the question carefully, watch for clues, and look at sentence structure. Essay tests focus on my understanding of concepts and relationships. I outline my response, organize and focus on the main points, and take my time to deliver a thorough, neat, well-thought-out answer.

- **Use last-minute study tips.** I know it's not smart to wait until the last minute, but a few important things I can do include focusing on a few key points and key words, reviewing note cards, looking for connections to memorize, and not wasting time panicking—I must stay focused!

- **Prepare for a performance appraisal.** I will make the most of my performance appraisal by thinking critically about my job description and duties, as well as my goals, objectives, and results. I will focus on opportunities to advance my knowledge and skills, and I will avoid the anxiety that comes with the appraisal process.

- **Overcome test anxiety.** A positive attitude is key to alleviating anxiety before and during a test. I should prepare as much as possible and avoid last-minute cramming, practice taking a sample test, get to class early and stay calm, listen carefully to instructions, and preview the whole test and jot down notes.

- **Practice honesty and integrity when taking tests.** I know that cheating on exams hurts only me, as it lowers my self-esteem and others' opinions of me. Cheating also has long-term repercussions, including possible expulsion from school. There is never an excuse for cheating.

Performance Strategies

Following are the top 10 strategies for successful test taking:

- Prepare early.
- Clarify expectations.
- Observe and question.
- Review.
- Apply memory techniques.

- Create sample tests.
- Use your study team.
- Answer easier questions first.
- Spend more time on questions with the highest point value.
- Analyze your test results to learn how to improve.

Tech for Success

Take advantage of the text's Web site at **www.mhhe.com/ferrett7e** for additional study aids, useful forms, and convenient and applicable resources.

- **Online tutors.** A number of companies and groups provide online tutors and live tutorial services. Your school or public library may also offer access to this kind of service. Often, these are paid services, and you may find the assistance beneficial. However, you may be able to get limited assistance for free through a professional organization or related site. Ask your librarian for advice and

explain how much assistance you think you need and in what content areas.

- **Textbook accompaniments.** Many of your textbooks have accompanying Web sites that provide study materials, such as online study guides, animated flash cards, and possible essay questions. Often, this material is free when you purchase a new text. Take advantage of these resources to test your understanding of the information prior to taking the real test.

Study Team Notes

Career *in* focus

Tests in the Workplace

Carlos Fuentes
PHYSICAL THERAPIST

Related Majors: Physical Therapy, Biology

Carlos Fuentes is a physical therapist. A physical therapist works closely with physicians to help patients restore function and improve mobility after an injury or illness. Their work often relieves pain and prevents or limits physical disabilities.

When working with new patients, Carlos first asks questions and examines the patients' medical records, then performs tests to measure such items as strength, range of motion, balance and coordination, muscle performance, and motor function. After assessing a patient's abilities and needs, Carlos implements a treatment plan that may include exercise, traction, massage, electrical stimulation, and hot packs or cold compresses. As treatment continues, Carlos documents the patient's progress and modifies the treatment plan.

Carlos is self-motivated and an independent worker. He has a strong interest in physiology and sports, and he enjoys working with people. He likes a job that keeps him active and on his feet. Carlos spends much of his day helping patients become mobile. He often demonstrates an exercise for his patients while instructing them how to do it correctly. His job sometimes requires him to move heavy equipment or lift patients. Because Carlos is pursuing a master's degree in physical therapy, he works only three days a week.

Although he is not required to take tests as part of his job, Carlos does undergo an annual performance appraisal with his supervisor. After eight years of service, Carlos is familiar with the types of questions his supervisor might ask and keeps those in mind as he does his job throughout the year.

CRITICAL THINKING How might understanding test-taking skills help Carlos work more effectively with his patients? How would test-taking skills help him prepare more effectively for performance appraisals?

Peak Performer

PROFILE

Ellen Ochoa

When astronaut Ellen Ochoa was growing up in La Mesa, California, in the 1960s and early 1970s, it was an era of space exploration firsts: the first walk in space, the first man on the moon, the first space station. Even so, it would have been difficult for her to imagine that one day she would be the first Hispanic woman in space, since women were excluded from becoming astronauts.

By the time Ochoa entered graduate school in the 1980s, however, the sky was the limit. Having studied physics at San Diego State University, she attended Stanford and earned a master's of science degree and a doctorate in electrical engineering. In 1985, she and 2,000 other potential astronauts applied for admission to the National Aeronautics and Space Administration (NASA) space program. Five years later, Ochoa, 18 men, and 5 other women made the cut. The training program at the Johnson Space Center in Houston, Texas, is a rigorous mix of brain and brawn. Ochoa tackled subjects such as geology, oceanography, meteorology, astronomy, aerodynamics, and medicine. In 1991, Ochoa officially became an astronaut and was designated a mission specialist. On her first mission in 1993, Ochoa carried a pin that read "Science Is Women's Work."

From 1993 to 2002, Ochoa logged in four space shuttle missions. Her first and second missions focused on studying the sun and its impact on the earth's atmosphere. Her third mission involved the first docking of the shuttle *Discovery* on the International Space Station. Her latest flight experience was the first time crewmembers used the robotic arm to move during spacewalks.

Between shuttle flights, Ochoa enjoys talking to young people. Aware of her influence as a woman and a Hispanic, her message is that "education is what allows you to stand out"—and become a peak performer.

PERFORMANCE THINKING Ochoa had to excel in many difficult academic courses in order to realize her dream of becoming an astronaut. What are some important personal characteristics that helped her reach the top? What are some specific testing strategies she may have used to get through her coursework, as well as to prove she had the "right stuff"?

CHECK IT OUT Ochoa is among a number of space pioneers profiled by NASA at **www.nasa.gov.** This site includes a wealth of media downloads, news articles, and activities for young and old space adventurers. Also visit the "Careers@NASA" section, which describes the types of internships, cooperative programs, and positions available. According to fellow astronaut Sally Ride, the "most important steps" she followed to becoming an astronaut started with studying math and science in school.

Starting Today

At least one strategy I learned in this chapter that I plan to try right away is:

_____

_____

_____

What changes must I make in order for this strategy to be effective?

_____

_____

_____

Review Questions

Based on what you have learned in this chapter, write your answers to the following questions:

1. Describe five strategies for preparing for a test.

_____

_____

2. Why is it important to pace yourself while taking a test?

_____

_____

3. What should you do after taking a test?

_____

_____

4. Describe three strategies for taking math and science tests.

_____

_____

5. Describe three ways in which cheating hurts you.

_____

_____

Coping with Anxiety

In the Classroom

Sharon Oshinowa is a bright, hardworking student. She studies long hours, attends all her classes, and participates in class discussions. Sharon is very creative and especially enjoys her computer graphics course. When it comes to taking tests, however, she panics. She stays up late, cramming; tells herself that she might fail; and she gets headaches and stomach pains. Her mind goes blank when she takes the test, and she has trouble organizing her thoughts. Sharon could get much better grades and enjoy school more if she could reduce her stress and apply some test-taking strategies.

1. What techniques from this chapter would be most useful to Sharon?

_____

_____

_____

2. What one habit could she adopt that would empower her to be more successful?

_____

_____

_____

In the Workplace

Sharon now works as a graphic designer for a large company. She likes having control over her work and is an excellent employee. She is dedicated, competent, and willing to learn new skills. There is a great deal of pressure in her job to meet deadlines, learn new techniques, and compete with other firms. She handles most of these responsibilities well unless she is being evaluated. Despite her proficiency, Sharon panics before her performance appraisals. She feels pressure to perform perfectly and does not take criticism or even advice well.

3. What strategies in this chapter would be most helpful to Sharon?

_____

_____

_____

4. What would you suggest she do to control her performance anxiety?

_____

_____

_____

Applying the ABC Method of Self-Management

In the Journal Entry box on page 221, you were asked to describe a time when you did well in a performance, sporting event, or test. Write about that and indicate the factors that helped you be calm, confident, and focused.

_____

_____

_____

_____

Now consider a situation in which your mind went blank or you suffered anxiety. Apply the ABC method to visualize a result in which you are again calm, confident, and focused.

A = Actual event:

B = Beliefs:

C = Challenge:

Practice deep breathing with your eyes closed for just one minute. See yourself calm, centered, and relaxed as you take a test or give a performance. See yourself recalling information easily. You feel confident about yourself because you have learned to control your anxiety. You are well prepared and you know how to take tests.

PRACTICE SELF-MANAGEMENT

For more examples of learning how to manage difficult situations, see the "Self-Management Workbook" section of the Online Learning Center Web site at **www.mhhe.com/ferrett7e**.

Exam Schedule

Fill in the following chart to remind you of your exams as they occur throughout the semester or term.

Course	Date	Time	Room	Type of Exam
Student Success 101	November 7	2:15 P.M.	1012A	Essay

Preparing for Tests and Exams

Before you take a quiz, a test, or an exam, fill in this form to help you plan your study strategy. Certain items will be more applicable, depending on the type of test.

Course _____

Date of test _____ Test number (if any) _____

- Pretest(s)   Date given _____   Results _____

                           Date given _____   Results _____

                           Date given _____   Results _____

- Present grade in course _____
- Met with instructor   Yes _____   No _____   Date(s) of meeting(s) _____
- Study team members   Date(s) of meeting(s) _____

    Name _____   Phone number _____

    Name _____   Phone number _____

    Name _____   Phone number _____

    Name _____   Phone number _____

- Expected test format (circle; there can be more than one test format)

    Essay   True/false   Multiple-choice   Fill-in-the-blank

    Other _____

- Importance (circle one)

    Quiz   Midterm   Final exam   Other

- Chapters covered in the test _____

    Date for chapter review _____

- Chapter notes (use additional paper)

_____

_____

_____

- Date for review of chapter notes _____
- Note cards   Yes _____   No _____   Date note cards reviewed _____
- List of key words

Word _____ Meaning _____

Word _____ Meaning _____

Word _____ Meaning _____

Word _____ Meaning _____

(continued)

- Possible essay questions
  1. Question _____
     Thesis statement _____
     Outline _____
        I. _____
           A. _____
           B. _____
           C. _____
           D. _____
       II. _____
           A. _____
           B. _____
           C. _____
           D. _____
        - Main points

        _____

        _____

        - Examples

        _____

        _____

  2. Question _____
     Thesis statement _____
     Outline _____
        I. _____
           A. _____
           B. _____
           C. _____
           D. _____
       II. _____
           A. _____
           B. _____
           C. _____
           D. _____
        - Main points

        _____

        _____

        - Examples

        _____

        _____

Performance Appraisals

The following are qualities and competencies that are included in many performance appraisals.

Acceptance of diversity*   Safety practices

Effectiveness in working with others   Personal growth and development

Quality of work   Workplace security

Quantity of work   Technology

Positive attitude   Willingness to learn

*Diversity: Getting along with people from diverse backgrounds and cultures.

1. Using this page and a separate sheet of paper, indicate how you would demonstrate each of the listed qualities and competencies to an employer.

_____

_____

_____

_____

_____

_____

_____

_____

_____

2. Give examples of how you have used and incorporated assessment and feedback from an employer. Include sample performance appraisals in your portfolio.

_____

_____

_____

_____

_____

_____

_____

_____

_____

Assessing Your Skills and Competencies

The following are typical qualities and competencies that are included in many performance appraisals.

- Communication skills
    - Writing
    - Speaking
    - Reading
- Integrity
- Willingness to learn

- Decision-making skills
- Delegation
- Planning
- Organizational skills
- Positive attitude
- Ability to accept change

On the following lines, describe how you currently demonstrate each of the listed skills and competencies to an employer. Consider how you can improve. Add this page to your Career Development Portfolio.

1. How do you demonstrate the listed skills?

_____

_____

_____

_____

_____

_____

_____

_____

_____

_____

2. How can you improve?

_____

_____

_____

_____

_____

_____

_____

_____

_____

_____

8 Become a Critical Thinker and Creative Problem Solver

LEARNING OBJECTIVES

In this chapter, you will learn to

8.1 Define Bloom's Taxonomy

8.2 Explain the problem-solving process

8.3 Practice critical thinking and problem-solving strategies

8.4 Describe common fallacies and errors in judgment

8.5 Explain the importance of creativity in problem solving

8.6 Use problem-solving strategies for mathematics and science

8.7 Overcome math and science anxiety

SELF-MANAGEMENT

I dropped a class, thinking I could take it next semester, just to find out that it is only offered once a year and now I won't graduate when I had planned to. I just didn't realize how one decision could have such a major impact.

Have you ever made a decision without clearly thinking through all the consequences? How does your attitude affect your critical thinking and creative problem solving? In this chapter, you will learn to put your critical thinking and creative problem-solving skills into action and learn strategies to make sound decisions in all areas of your life.

JOURNAL ENTRY In **Worksheet 8.1** on page 288, think of a decision you made that has cost you a great deal in time, money, or stress. Maybe you failed to change the name of the responsible party on your electric bill when you moved out of your apartment, and now you have a bad credit rating. Maybe you were stopped for speeding and failed to go to traffic school, and now your license has been suspended. How would using critical thinking and creative problem solving have helped you make better decisions?

66 A problem is a picture with a piece missing; the answer is the missing piece. 99

JOHN HOLT
Educator, author

P
ROBLEM SOLVING—COMING UP WITH POSSIBLE SOLUTIONS—AND **DECISION MAKING**—DECIDING ON THE BEST SOLUTION—GO HAND-IN-HAND. You have to make decisions to solve a problem; conversely, some problems occur because of a decision you have made. For example, in your private life you may decide to smoke cigarettes; later, you face the problem of nicotine addiction, health problems, and a lot of your budget spent on cigarettes. In your school life, you may decide not to study mathematics and science because you consider them too difficult. Because of this decision, certain majors and careers will be closed to you. You can see that many events in your life do not just happen; they are the result of your choices and decisions. We make decisions every day and even not making a decision is making a decision. For example, if you avoid going to class, what you are saying is "I've decided that this class is not important or is not worth the time." You may have not formally dropped the class or not thought through the consequences, but the result of deciding not to go to class is an *F* grade.

In this chapter, you will learn to use critical thinking and creativity to help you solve problems and make effective and sound decisions. Mathematics and science will be discussed, as these are key areas where you can develop and improve your critical thinking and problem-solving skills. You will also learn to overcome math anxiety and develop a positive attitude toward problem solving.

Essential Critical Thinking Skills

As discussed in Chapter 1, critical thinking is a logical, rational, and systematic thought process that is necessary to understand, analyze, and evaluate information in order to solve a problem. Critical thinking is essential for school and life success. In the 1956 text *Taxonomy of Educational Objectives,* Benjamin Bloom and his colleagues outlined a hierarchy of six critical thinking skills that college requires (from lowest- to highest-order): knowledge, comprehension, application, analysis, synthesis, and evaluation. (See **Figure 8.1.**)

1. **Knowledge.** Most of your college courses will require you to memorize lists, identify facts, complete objective tests, and recognize and recall familiar terms and information.

2. **Comprehension.** You will also need to demonstrate that you comprehend ideas, and you may be asked to state ideas in your own words, outline key ideas, and translate an author's meaning.

3. **Application.** You will be asked to apply what you've learned to a new situation. You may explore case studies, solve problems, and provide examples to support your ideas. You can learn application by applying ideas to your own life. For example, how can you apply political science concepts to your community or child development ideas to your campus child-care center or to children in your life?

66 The value of a problem is not so much coming up with the answer as in the ideas and attempted ideas it forces on the would-be solver. 99

I. N. HERSTEIN
Mathematician

Evaluation ↑	Make judgments about the information
Synthesis ↑	Combine selected parts to create new information
Analysis ↑	Separate understood information into parts
Application ↑	Make practical use of the understood information
Comprehension ↑	Understand the significance of the information
Knowledge	Recall information

CRITICAL THINKING SKILLS

Figure 8.1

Bloom's Taxonomy

Actively participating in college will require you to use six core critical thinking skills. *Which skills are you using as you complete current projects or assignments?*

4. **Analysis.** You will be asked to break apart ideas and relate them to other concepts. You may be asked to write essay questions, identify assumptions, and analyze values. You may be asked to compare and contrast economic theories or two works of art.

5. **Synthesis.** You will be asked to integrate ideas, build on other skills, look for interconnections, create and defend a position, improve on an existing idea or design, and come up with creative ideas and new perspectives. You might compose a song or dance. You may be asked to find ways that a community project affects other areas of the community. Synthesis builds on other skills, so practice is important.

6. **Evaluation.** You will be asked to criticize a position or an opinion, form conclusions and judgments, list advantages and disadvantages of a project or an idea, and develop and use criteria for evaluating a decision. You can develop your evaluation skills by using helpful criteria and standards for evaluating speeches in class, evaluating group projects, and being open to suggestions from your study group and instructors.

In order to excel in school—as well as to learn how to make important decisions and sound judgments in life—you must move beyond simple knowledge and comprehension and be able to apply, analyze, synthesize, and evaluate questions and problems you are faced with. See **Peak Progress 8.1** on page 258 for an example of moving from knowledge to evaluation.

Problem-Solving Steps

You must exercise and apply your critical thinking skills when solving problems and making decisions. The problem-solving process can be broken down into four major steps: (1) Define the problem, (2) gather and interpret information, (3) develop and implement a plan of action, and (4) evaluate the plan.

Peak Progress

From Knowledge to Evaluation

If you can recall the number 8675309, but you attach no significance to the number, you have mere *knowledge*. Not tremendously useful, is it?

On the other hand, if you are familiar with a particular song performed by Tommy Tutone, you may recognize this number as the telephone number of a girl named Jenny, which the songwriter had found penned on a wall. Now you have *comprehension*. Still, you find yourself asking, "So what?"

Maybe you are intrigued. You might want to actually call the number to see whether Jenny answers. This is *application*. Unfortunately, unless you just happen to be in an area code where this telephone number exists, you will probably get a telephone company recording.

Next you break down the number into its component parts. You see that it has a 3-digit prefix and a 4-digit suffix. The prefix is 867. You have just performed a simple *analysis*.

In order to track Jenny down, you will need to combine some other bodies of information with what you already know. You know Jenny's telephone number, but there could be many identical telephone numbers throughout the country. What you need to find is a list of area codes that includes this telephone number. You have then performed *synthesis*.

Before you go any further, ask yourself just how important it is to find Jenny. How many matching telephone numbers did you turn up in the previous step? Are you going to dial each of them? How much is it going to cost you in long-distance charges? How much of your time is it going to take? Is it worth it? You have just made an *evaluation*.

Courtesy T. C. Stuwe, Salt Lake Community College, © 2002.

1. **Define the problem.** Do you understand and can you clearly state the problem? What are you trying to find out? What is known and unknown? What is the situation or context of the problem? What decision are you asked to make? Can you separate the problem into various parts? Organize the problem, or restate the decision or problem in your own words—for example, "Should I go on a study abroad exchange or do an internship?"

2. **Gather and interpret information.** What are all the possibilities? Make certain you have all the information you need to solve the problem and make a decision. How can you see the problem from different angles? Use creative problem solving and explore creative solutions. "I have visited the career center and the study abroad office. I have listed pros and cons for each choice. I have included cost and expenses." Are there other options, such as a paid internship or student teaching abroad? When deciding on a plan of action, consider all options and then narrow the list.

3. **Develop and implement a plan of action.** How would this plan work? There comes a time when you need to act on your decision and choose an appropriate strategy. Ask yourself what information would be helpful. "I have gathered information and talked to people in my chosen field. Most career professionals have suggested that I go on exchange as a way to

Personal Evaluation Notebook 8.1

Think It Through

Often we make decisions without considering the consequences. It may be because we're only thinking about the immediate result or benefit. Or maybe it's because the decision seems so "small" that the consequences are insignificant. However, a number of poor "small" decisions can result in big problems later.

Exercise your decision-making and problem-solving skills by teaming up with classmates and considering decisions you make every day. For example, let's say you've missed a couple of classes lately. One person should state the problem or issue. Then go through the problem-solving steps, ask questions, explore possibilities, and use critical thinking to make a sound decision:

1. **Define the problem.**
   - I've missed three classes in the past two weeks.

2. **Gather and interpret the information.**
   - The reasons are [such as my babysitter canceled, car broke down, alarm didn't go off, or I hate 8:00 AM classes.]
   - The consequences for missing this class are
   - If I drop the class, what would happen?
   - If I keep missing the class, what would happen?

3. **Develop and implement a plan of action.**
   - What are creative possibilities to help me get to class?
   - What is the best plan of action?

4. **Evaluate the plan.**
   - What decision is best for my goals and priorities?
   - How am I going to ensure that I make this decision successful?

Come up with other situations you may encounter daily, such as relationship issues and spending decisions, and work through them using the problem-solving steps.

---

broaden my worldview. I found out that I can apply for an internship for the following term. Since I can learn a foreign language and take valuable classes, I am going on the study abroad exchange and will do everything possible to make this a valuable experience." Your intention to make this decision successful is key.

4. **Evaluate your plan.** Why is this plan better for you than the other options? Is there one right answer? What are the likely consequences if you choose this approach? "I made valuable contacts and am learning so much from this experience. I will do an internship when I return. This was the best choice for me at this time." Observe the consequences of this decision over time and reflect on what other options may have worked better. See **Personal Evaluation Notebook 8.1** to explore the consequences of everyday decisions.

Critical Thinking and Problem-Solving Strategies

Critical thinking and problem solving will help you make day-to-day decisions about relationships, which courses to take, how to find a job, where to live, how to generate ideas for speeches and papers, and how to resolve conflicts. Making sound decisions and solving problems are important skills for school, career, and life.

There are a number of important strategies you can apply to enhance and ensure you are fully using your critical thinking and problem-solving capabilities:

1. **Have a positive attitude.** Critical thinking requires a willingness and passion to explore, probe, question, and search for answers and solutions. (See **Figure 8.2**.) Your attitude has a lot to do with how you approach and solve a problem or make a decision. Positive thinking requires a mind shift. Think of problems as puzzles to solve, rather than difficult issues or courses to avoid. Instead of avoiding, delaying, making a knee-jerk decision, or looking for the one "right answer," focus on problem-solving strategies. For example, you may have a negative attitude toward math or science, perceiving the material as too difficult or not relevant. Choose to see a problem or situation in the best possible light. Complete **Personal Evaluation Notebook 8.2** to practice turning negatives into positives.

2. **Ask questions.** It's difficult to solve a problem without knowing all the facts and opinions—or at least as many as you can find out. See **Peak Progress 8.2** on page 262 on tips for formulating effective questions.

3. **Persistence pays off.** Coming to a solution requires sustained effort. A problem may not always be solved with your first effort. Sometimes a second or third try will see the results you need or want. Analytical thinking requires time, persistence, and patience. Sometimes it pays to sleep on a decision and not make important choices under pressure. Effective problem solvers are not beaten by frustration but, rather, look for new ways to solve problems.

4. **Use creativity.** As we will explore in more detail later in this chapter, you should learn to think in new and fresh ways, look for interconnections, and brainstorm many solutions. Good problem solvers explore many alternatives and evaluate the strengths and weaknesses of different methods.

Figure **8.2**

Critical Thinking Qualities

Being able to think critically is important for understanding and solving problems. *Do you apply any of the attributes of a critical thinker when you are faced with solving a problem?*

Attributes of a Critical Thinker

- Willingness to ask pertinent questions and assess statements and arguments
- Ability to be open-minded and to seek opposing views
- Ability to suspend judgment and tolerate ambiguity
- Ability to admit a lack of information or understanding
- Curiosity and interest in seeking new solutions
- Ability to clearly define a set of criteria for analyzing ideas
- Willingness to examine beliefs, assumptions, and opinions against facts

Personal Evaluation Notebook 8.2

Using Critical Thinking to Solve Problems

Stating a problem clearly, exploring alternatives, reasoning logically, choosing the best alternative, creating an action plan, and evaluating your plan are all involved in making decisions and solving problems.

Look at the common reasons or excuses that some students use for not solving problems creatively or making sound decisions. Use creative problem solving to list strategies for overcoming these barriers.

1. I'm not a creative person.

   Strategy:

   _____

   _____

2. Facts can be misleading, I like to follow my emotions.

   Strategy:

   _____

   _____

3. I avoid conflict.

   Strategy:

   _____

   _____

4. I postpone making decisions.

   Strategy:

   _____

   _____

5. I worry that I'll make the wrong decision.

   Strategy:

   _____

   _____

5. **Pay attention to details.** Effective problem solvers show concern for accuracy. They think about what could go wrong, recheck calculations, look for errors, and pay attention to details. They are careful to gather all relevant information and proofread or ask questions. They are willing to listen to arguments, create and defend positions, and can distinguish among various forms of arguments.

Peak Progress

Asking Questions

> 66 He who asks is a fool for five minutes, but he who does not ask remains a fool forever. 99
>
> CHINESE PROVERB

"Why is the sky blue?" "Where do babies come from?" When we were children, our days were filled with endless questions, as we were excited and curious about the world around us. As adults, some of us have become reluctant and sometimes even nervous to ask for help or insightful answers. It's not that there are no questions left to ask—just the contrary. Attending college opens up the floodgates of new information to comprehend, process, apply, and question.

This reluctance can stem from possible embarrassment, as the information may have already been covered (and you were daydreaming, didn't read the assignment, didn't see the connections, etc.) and others will think you're behind for one reason or another. Or, when simply talking with friends, you may think asking questions will seem like you are prying or are "nosey," or behind on the latest trends.

Whatever your reasons, it's critical for you to work through your reluctance and learn how to formulate questions. Most careers require asking questions and the persistence it takes to get answers. A sales representative asks customers what their needs are and then attempts to fulfill those needs with his or her product. A physician not only examines physical symptoms but also queries the patient about a condition's history and progression, pain, the patient's reactions to medications, and so on.

WHO CAN BEST ANSWER YOUR QUESTION?

Before asking a question, determine whom or what you should be consulting. Could the information be found more easily or quickly by looking it up online, in the library, or another source? Is it a question more appropriate for your instructor, advisor, or financial aid officer? Is there a local "expert" in this area?

WHAT TYPE OF QUESTION SHOULD YOU ASK?

It is important to quickly and succinctly state your question and only provide background information if what you are asking isn't clear. Based on the type of response you are looking for, there are a number of ways to formulate your question:

- **Closed question.** Use this type of question when you want either a yes/no answer or specific details—for example, "Which planet is closer to the sun—Earth or Mars?"
- **Fact-finding question.** This is aimed at getting information on a particular subject and is usually asked when your core materials (such as the textbook or lecture) haven't provided the information—for example, "Which battle had the most casualties and was that considered the turning point in the war?"
- **Follow-up question.** This question clarifies a point, gathers more information, or elicits an opinion—for example, "So, what side effects might I experience from this medication?"
- **Open-ended question.** This invites discussion and a wide range of answers. Use this when you are looking for various viewpoints or others' interpretations of an issue—for example, "What do you think about the ordinance to ban smoking in local restaurants?"
- **Feedback question.** This is used when you want someone to provide you with constructive criticism—for example, "What sections of my paper supported my main points effectively, and what sections needed more back-up?"

(continued)

WHEN SHOULD YOU ASK THE QUESTION?

Ask your question as soon as possible (waiting until the speaker has completed his or her point). Most likely, your instructor has outlined parameters for class (such as "please save your questions for the last 10 minutes"). If so, immediately jot down your questions during lecture, so that you can return to them or to add answers if the content is covered in the meantime. Open-ended and feedback questions may be more appropriate for outside a typical class discussion but can often provide the most insightful answers.

6. **See all sides of the issue.** Think critically about what you read, hear, and see in newspapers and on the Internet. As you read, question sources and viewpoints. For example, when you read an article in the paper about Social Security or tax cuts, ask yourself what biases politicians or special interest groups might have in how they approach such issues. Does the argument appeal to emotion rather than to logic? Learn to question your biases, beliefs, and assumptions and try to see different viewpoints. Think of an issue you feel strongly about. Then try taking the opposite side of an argument and defend that side, using critical thinking and facts. Talk to people who have different opinions or belong to a different political party. Really listen to their views for understanding and ask them to explain their opinions and why they support certain issues.

7. **Use reasoning.** We are constantly trying to make sense of our world, so we make inferences as ways to explain and interpret events. Effective problem solvers are good at reasoning and check their inferences to see if they are sound and not based on assumptions, which often reflect their own experiences and biases. Ask yourself, "What makes me think this is true? Could I be wrong? Are there other possibilities?" Effective problem solvers do not jump to conclusions.

   Inductive reasoning is generalizing from specific concepts to broad principles. For example, you might have had a bad experience with a math class in high school and, based on that experience, might reason inductively that all math classes are hard and boring. When you get into your college math class, you may discover that your conclusion was incorrect and that you actually like mathematics. In contrast, **deductive reasoning** is drawing conclusions based on going from the general to the specific—for example, "Since all mathematics classes at this college must be taken for credit and this class is a math class, I must take it for credit." However, don't assume that the main premise is always true, as, in this example, you may discover that there are math labs, workshops, or special classes that are offered for no credit. Practice inductive versus inductive reasoning in **Personal Evaluation Notebook 8.3.** on page 264.

Common Errors in Judgment

Some thoughts and beliefs are clearly irrational, with no evidence to support them. For example, a belief that people cannot change can cause you to stay stuck in unhealthy situations and accept that there is no solution for your problems. In order to

Personal Evaluation Notebook

8.3

Inductive vs. Deductive Reasoning

Practice creating inductive and deductive statements.

INDUCTIVE EXAMPLES

- No one should even consider buying a car with a sunroof. Mine leaked every time it rained.
- Nadia ended up in the hospital with food poisoning the day after the party. I'm sure that's why Cara and Brendan said they were sick the next day, too.

_____

_____

_____

_____

DEDUCTIVE EXAMPLES

- Everyone who attended the review session for the first test received A's. If I attend the next session, I'm bound to get an A.
- All the men in our family are over 6 feet tall. I'm sure my baby son will be as well when he's an adult.

_____

_____

_____

_____

solve problems, critical thinking and frequent self-assessment of your thoughts and beliefs are necessary. You can apply the ABC Method of Self-Management you learned in this text to dispel myths and irrational and faulty thinking.

Here are some common errors in judgment or faulty thinking that interfere with effective critical thinking:

- *Stereotypes* are judgments held by a person or a group about the members of another group—for example, "All instructors are absentminded intellectuals." Learn to see individual differences between people.

- *All-or-nothing thinking* means you see events or people in black or white. You may turn a single negative event into a pattern of defeat—for example, "If I don't get an A in this class, I'm a total failure." Be careful about using the terms *always* and *never*.

- *Snap judgments* are decisions made before all the necessary information or facts have been gathered. For example, you may conclude that someone doesn't like you because of one comment or because of a comment made by someone else. Instead, find out the reason for the comment, as you may have misinterpreted the meaning.

- *Unwarranted assumptions* are beliefs and ideas that you assume are true in different situations. For example, your business instructor allows papers to be turned in late, so you assume that your real estate instructor will allow the same.

- *Projection* is the tendency to attribute to others some of your own traits in an attempt to justify your own faulty judgments or actions—for example, "It's OK if I cheat because everyone else is cheating."

- *Sweeping generalizations* are based on one experience and are generalized to a whole group or issue. For example, if research has been conducted using college students as subjects, you cannot generalize the results to the overall work population.

- The *halo effect* is the tendency to label a person good at many things based on one or two qualities or actions. For example, Serena sits in the front row, attends every class, and gets good grades on papers. Based on this observation, you decide that she is smart, organized, and nice and is a great student in all her classes. First impressions are important in the halo effect and are difficult to change. However, you can make this work for you. For example, say you start out the semester by giving it your all; you go to every class, establish a relationship with the instructor, are involved in class, and work hard. Later in the semester, you may need to miss a class or ask to take an exam early. Your instructor has already formed an opinion of you as a good student and may be more willing to give you extra help or understand your situation, since you have created a positive impression.

- *Negative labeling* is focusing on and identifying with shortcomings, either yours or others. Instead of saying, "I made a mistake when I quit going to my math study group," you tell yourself, "I'm a loser." You may also pick a single negative trait or detail and focus on it exclusively. You discount positive qualities or accomplishments. "I've lost my keys again. I am so disorganized. Yes, I did organize a successful club fundraiser, but that doesn't count."

Creative Problem Solving

Creativity is thinking of something different and using new approaches to solve problems. Many inventions have involved a break from traditional thinking and resulted in an "ah-ha!" experience. For example, Albert Einstein used many unusual approaches and "riddles" that revolutionized scientific thought. (On the Internet, you will find a number of sites that include "Einstein's Riddle." Locate one and test yourself to see if you can answer "who owns the fish?")

> 66 Imagination will often carry us to worlds that never were. But without it we go nowhere. 99
>
> CARL SAGAN
> *Astronomer, author*

WORDS TO SUCCEED

Use creativity at each step to explore alternatives, look for relationships among different items, and develop imaginative ideas and solutions. Use critical thinking skills to raise questions, separate facts from opinions, develop reasonable solutions, and make logical decisions. Try the following strategies to unlock your mind's natural creativity:

1. **Expect to be creative.** Everyone can be creative. To be a creative person, try to see yourself as a creative person. Use affirmations that reinforce your innate creativity:

   - I am a creative and resourceful person.
   - I have many imaginative and unusual ideas.
   - Creative ideas flow to me many times a day.
   - I act on many of these ideas.
   - I act responsibly, use critical thinking, check details carefully, and take calculated risks.

2. **Challenge the rules.** Habit often restricts you from trying new approaches to problem solving. Often, there is more than one solution. List many alternatives, choices, and solutions and imagine the likely consequences of each. Empty your mind of the "right" way of looking at problems and strive to see situations in a fresh, new way. How many times have you told yourself that you must follow certain rules and perform tasks a certain way? If you want to be creative, try new approaches, look at things in a new order, break the pattern, and challenge the rules. Practice a different approach by completing the Nine-Dot Exercise in **Personal Evaluation Notebook 8.4**.

3. **Use games, puzzles, and humor.** Turn problems into puzzles to be solved. Rethinking an assignment as a puzzle, a challenge, or a game instead of a difficult problem allows an open frame of mind and encourages your creative side to operate. Creative people often get fresh ideas when they are having fun and are involved in an unrelated activity. When your defenses are down, your brain is relaxed and your subconscious is alive; creative thoughts can flow.

4. **Brainstorm.** Brainstorming is a common creativity strategy that frees the imagination. You can brainstorm alone or with a group, which may be more effective in generating as many ideas as possible. Brainstorming encourages the mind to explore new approaches without judging the merit of these ideas. In fact, even silly and irrelevant ideas can lead to truly inventive ideas. While brainstorming ideas for a speech, one study group started making jokes about the topic, and new ideas came from all directions. Humor can generate ideas, put you in a creative state of mind, and make work fun. Top executives, scientists, doctors, and artists know that they can extend the boundaries of their knowledge by allowing themselves to extend their limits. They ask, "What if?" Complete the brainstorming exercise in **Personal Evaluation Notebook 8.5** on page 268.

5. **Work to change mind-sets.** It is difficult to see another frame of reference once your mind is set. The exercise in **Personal Evaluation Notebook 8.6** on page 269 is an "ah-ha" exercise. It is exciting to watch people really see the other picture. There is enormous power in shifting your perception and gaining new ways of seeing things, events, and people. Perceptual exercises of this kind clearly demonstrate that you see what you focus on and when you reframe. You are conditioned to see certain things, depending on your beliefs and attitudes. Rather than seeing facts, you may see your interpretation of reality. Perceptual distortion can influence how you solve problems and make decisions. For example, John was told

Personal Evaluation Notebook

Nine-Dot Exercise

Connect the following nine dots by drawing only four (or fewer) straight lines without lifting the pencil from the paper. Do not retrace any lines. You can see the solution at the end of this chapter on page 282.

that his math instructor was aloof, not student-oriented, and boring. John had a mind-set as he attended the first class and, as a result, sat in the back of class and did not ask questions or get involved. He later found out that his friend was referring to another instructor. John immediately changed his opinion and could see that his mind-set was influencing how he first viewed his instructor. He reframed his impression and developed a positive relationship with the instructor.

6. **Change your routine.** Try a different route to work or school. Read different kinds of books. Become totally involved in a project. Spend time with people who are different from you. In other words, occasionally break away from your daily routine and take time every day to relax, daydream, and renew your energy. Look at unexpected events as an opportunity to retreat from constant activity and hurried thoughts. Perhaps this is a good time to brainstorm ideas for a speech assignment or outline an assigned paper. Creative ideas need an incubation period in which to develop.

7. **Use both sides of the brain.** You use the logical, analytical side of your brain for certain activities and your imaginative and multidimensional side for others. When you develop and integrate both the left and the right sides of your brain, you become more imaginative, creative, and productive. Learn to be attentive to details and to trust your intuition.

8. **Keep a journal.** Keep a journal of creative ideas, dreams, and thoughts and make a commitment to complete journal entries daily. Collect stories of creative people. Write in your journal about the risks you take and your imaginative and different ideas.

9. **Evaluate.** Go through each step and examine your work. Look at what you know and don't know and examine your hypotheses. Can you prove that each step is correct? Examine the solution carefully. Can you obtain the solution differently? Investigate the connections of the problem. What formulas did you

Personal Evaluation Notebook

Brainstorming Notes

Creating an idea is not always enough to solve a problem; it also involves convincing others that your idea is the best solution. Read the following brainstorming notes. Then, on the lines that follow, write your own brainstorming notes about how Basil can sell his ideas to his staff.

Basil's Pizza   Sept. 29, 2009

Brainstorming Notes

Problem: Should I hire temporary employees or increase overtime of my regular employees to meet new production schedule?

Ideas	Evaluation	Plus + or Minus –	Solution
hire temp. employees	may lack training	–	1. hire temps
	additional benefits	–	
work regular employees overtime	may result in fatigue	–	2. work overtime explore further
	extra $ for employee	+	
	higher morale	+	
	possible advancement	+	
	cross training	+	
	save on overhead and benefits	+	
turn down contract	not possible	–	
reduce hours store is open	not feasible	–	
reduce product line	not acceptable	–	

_____

_____

_____

_____

_____

_____

_____

Personal Evaluation Notebook  8.6

Mind-Sets

Look at the following figure. Do you see an attractive young woman or an old woman with a hooked nose?

I see a(n) _____

If you saw the young woman first, it is very hard to see the old woman. If you saw the old woman first, it is just as hard to see the young woman.

use? Can you use the same method for other problems? Work with your study team to talk problems out and to see if there are other ways to solve a problem. Practice your decision-making skills by working through the case scenarios in **Personal Evaluation Notebook 8.7** and **8.8** on the following pages.

10. **Support, acknowledge, and reward creativity.** If you honor new ideas, they will grow. Get excited about new ideas and approaches, and acknowledge and reward yourself and others for creative ideas. Give yourself many opportunities to get involved with projects that encourage you to explore and be creative. Monitor your daily life as well. How often do you put your creative ideas into action? Is there anything you want to change but keep putting it off? What new hobby or skill have you wanted to try? If you find yourself getting

(continued on page 274)

Personal Evaluation Notebook 8.7

Decision-Making Application

Use critical thinking and creative problem-solving skills as you consider the following case scenario:

I am currently attending a career school and will soon earn my associate's degree in computer-aided design. Once I obtain my degree, should I continue my education or look for a full-time job? My long-term goal is to be an architect. My wife and I have been married for three years and we want to start a family soon.

- **Define the problem.** "Should I continue my education or get a job?"
- **Gather information and ask questions.** "What are the advantages and disadvantages? Whom should I talk with, such as my advisor, instructors at my current school and potential schools, family members, and career professionals?"
- **List pros and cons for each choice.** "What are the factors I should consider, such as cost, opportunities, and time?"

Consider the following pros and cons for each decision and list additional reasons that you think should be considered.

Decision: *Continue education at a local state university*

Pros	Cons
I'll get a better job with a four-year degree.	I'll have to take out more student loans.
I'm enjoying school and the learning process.	I want to put my skills into practice in the job.
I'll meet new, diverse friends and contacts.	A lot of my time at home will be devoted to studying.

Decision: *Get a job*

Pros	Cons
I can make more money than I am now and start paying off debts.	The opportunities would be better with a four-year degree.
We can start a family.	It will take longer to become an architect.
I get to put my skills to work.	Once I start working full-time, it may be hard to go back to school.

(continued)

Personal Evaluation Notebook

Decision-Making Application (*concluded*)

- **Choose what you believe is the best solution.** "I have decided to get a job."

- **Review and assess.** "My choice is reasonable and makes sense for me now in my situation. I won't have to work such long hours and juggle both school and work, and I can pay back loans and save money. We can start our family. I can review my long-term goal and determine an alternate way to achieve it."

Would you arrive at the same decision? What would be your decision and your main reasons?

_____

_____

Now set up a problem or decision that you are facing and follow the same steps.

- Problem

  _____

  _____

- Where can I get help or information?

  _____

  _____

POSSIBLE SOLUTIONS AND PROS AND CONS

Solution #1: _____

_____

Pros	Cons
1. _____	_____
2. _____	_____
3. _____	_____

Solution #2: _____

_____

Pros	Cons
1. _____	_____
2. _____	_____
3. _____	_____

SOLUTION CHOSEN AND WHY

_____

_____

Personal Evaluation Notebook 8.8

Solving Problems and Making Choices

Every day you solve problems and make choices. Some problems are easy to solve: *What's for dinner?* Some problems are harder: *Can I afford to buy a car?* Some problems change a life forever: *Should I get married?*

You will face problems and choices. You might make good or poor choices. You don't know how a choice will turn out. However, you can follow some steps to help you review your options. They may help you see changes, show you risks, and point out other choices.

Step 1 Know what the problem really is. Is it a daily problem? Is it a once-in-a-lifetime problem?

Step 2 List the things you know about the problem. List the things you don't know. Ask questions. Seek help and advice.

Step 3 Explore alternate choices.

Step 4 Think about the pros and cons for the other choices. Rank them from best to worst choice.

Step 5 Pick the choice you feel good about.

Step 6 After choosing, study what happens. Are you happy about the choice? Would you make it again?

Read the following story and apply the steps in the following exercise.

JOSÉ'S CHOICE

José is 50 years old. He has a wife and three kids. He has worked as a bookkeeper for 20 years for the same company. The company is relocating. Only a few people will move with the company. Many workers will be losing their jobs.

José's boss says he can keep his job, but he has to move. If he doesn't, he won't have a job. The family has always lived in this town. José's daughter is a senior in high school and wants to go to the local college next year. His twin boys are looking forward to playing next year for the ninth-grade football team. José's wife works part-time in a bakery. She has many friends and all of her family live nearby.

The family talked about the move. His wife is afraid. His daughter doesn't want to move. The twins will miss their friends. The family has to decide about the move. What is their problem? What are the choices? Can you help them?

Step 1 The problem is _____

_____

_____

(continued)

Personal Evaluation Notebook ✓ 8.8

Solving Problems and Making Choices *(concluded)*

Is it a daily problem? _____

_____

_____

Is it a once-in-a-lifetime problem? _____

_____

_____

Step 2 You know _____

_____

_____

You don't know _____

_____

_____

Step 3 The other choices are _____

_____

_____

Step 4 Rank the choices. _____

_____

_____

Step 5 Pick a choice the family might feel good about. _____

_____

_____

Step 6 What might happen? _____

_____

_____

lazy, set a firm deadline to complete a specific project. If you find yourself running frantically, then take an hour or so to review your life's goals and to set new priorities. If you are feeling shy and inhibited, clear some time to socialize and risk meeting new people. Reward your creativity and risk taking by acknowledging them.

11. **Allow failure.** Remember that, if you don't fail occasionally, you are not risking anything. Mistakes are stepping-stones to growth and creativity. Fear of failure undermines the creative process by forcing us to play it safe. Eliminate the fear and shame of failure experienced in earlier years and learn to admit mistakes. Ask yourself, "What did I learn from this mistake? How can I handle the same type of situation the next time? How can I prepare for a situation like this the next time?" Creative people aren't afraid to look foolish at times, to generate unusual ideas, and to be nonconformists. They tend not to take themselves too seriously. Being creative takes courage to explore new ways of thinking and to risk looking different, foolish, impractical, and even wrong.

12. **Practice and be persistent.** Problem solving requires discipline and focused effort. It takes time, practice, and patience to learn any new skill. Stay with the problem and concentrate. **Peak Progress 8.3** provides a handy checklist to help you think of new ways to find solutions.

Math and Science Applications

Critical thinking and creative problem solving are essential for success in mathematics, science, and computer science courses. A critical and creative approach is not only important in all academic classes but also vital for job and life success. For example, using logic and the analytical process can help you write papers, prepare for tests, compare historical events, and learn different theories in philosophy. By studying mathematics and science, you will learn such everyday skills as understanding interest rates on credit cards, calculating your tuition, managing your personal finances, computing your GPA, and understanding how your body and the world around you works. Basic arithmetic can help you figure out a tip at a restaurant, algebra can help you compute the interest on a loan, basic probability can help you determine the chance that a given event will occur, and statistics can help you with the collection, analysis, and interpretation of data.

Problem-Solving Strategies for Math and Science

The basic problem-solving strategies discussed earlier in this chapter, starting on page 260, also apply to math and science. There are a number of additional strategies you can use, many of them designed to get you physically involved. The following strategies integrate all learning styles and make learning physical and personal. Included are sample problems to help you practice these strategies.

1. **Make a model or diagram.** Physical models, objects, diagrams, and drawings can help organize information and can help you visualize problem situations.

Peak Progress

Creative Ideas Checklist

Use this checklist of questions to challenge your usual thought patterns. When exploring alternative approaches to problem solving, you can put each category on a separate card. Here are some examples you might find helpful:

- What other idea does this situation suggest?
- How can I modify?
- What can I subtract? Can I take it apart?
- What can I streamline?
- What can I rearrange?
- Can I transfer?
- Can I combine or blend?
- What are other uses if modified?
- Have I written it out?
- Can I use another approach?
- Can I interchange components?
- Are there any opposites?
- What are the positives and negatives?
- Have I used a mind map, model, diagram, list, or chart?
- Have I used a drawing or picture?
- Have I acted it out?
- Have I talked it out?
- Have I tried it out?
- Should I sleep on it?
- List some of your own suggestions for creative problem solving:

  _____

  _____

  _____

  _____

Use objects, cut up a model, measure lengths, and create concrete situations— for example,

Problem: What is the length of a pendulum that makes one complete swing in one second?

Strategy: Make a model (see page 276). With a 50 cm string and some small weights, make a pendulum that is tied to a pencil taped to a desk. To determine the length of the pendulum, measure the distance from the pencil to the center of the weight.

Solution: Since it is difficult to measure the time period accurately, time 10 swings and use the average. The correct answer is approximately 25 cm.

Evaluation: If the length is fixed, the amount of weight does not affect the time period. The amount of deflection does affect the period when large deflections are used, but it is not a factor for small amounts of 5 cm or less. The length of the pendulum always affects the time period.

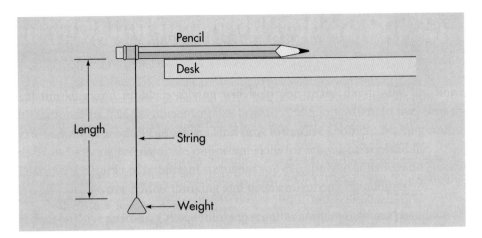

2. **Draw, illustrate, and make tables, charts, or lists.** This is a way to organize data presented in a problem, and it helps you look for patterns. For example, a fruit punch dispenser mixes 4 ml of orange juice with 6 ml of pineapple juice. How many milliliters of orange juice does it mix with 240 ml of pineapple juice?

			Answer
Orange juice ml	4	16	160
Pineapple juice ml	6	24	240

3. **Look for patterns and connections.** A pattern is a regular, systematic repetition that helps you predict what will come next. Field trips and laboratory work can help you find patterns and categorize information, and so can creating tables. For example, an empty commuter train is picking up passengers at the following rate: One passenger got on at the first stop, three got on at the second stop, and five got on at the third stop. How many passengers got on the train at the sixth stop?

						Answer
Stops	1	2	3	4	5	6
Number of passengers	1	3	5	7	9	11

4. **Act out the problem.** Sometimes it is helpful to physically act out the problem. For example, there are 5 people in your study group and each person initiates a handshake with every member one time. How many total handshakes will there be? There will be 20 handshakes total, because each person shakes hands 4 times (since you cannot shake your own hand). Thus, 5 people times 4 handshakes

equals 20 total handshakes. You multiply the total number of people times one number fewer for the handshakes.

5. **Simplify.** Sometimes the best way to simplify a problem is first to solve easier cases of the same problem. For example, consider the study group handshakes and simplify by solving it for 2 people instead of 5. When each person initiates a handshake, 2 people shake hands a total of 2 times. Using the formula determined in number 4, you see that the equation is $2 \times 1 = 2$. Fill in the rest of the table:

Number of People	Each Person Initiates Handshake × Times	Total Number Handshakes
2	1	2
3	2	
4		
5	4	20
6		

Along the same lines, when working on homework, studying in your group, or taking a test, always do the easiest problems first. When you feel confident about your ability to solve one kind of problem, you gain enthusiasm to tackle more difficult questions or problems. Also, an easier problem may be similar to a more difficult problem.

6. **Translate words into equations.** Highlight visual and verbal learning by showing connections between words and numbers. Write an equation that models that problem. For example, Sarah has a total of $82.00, consisting of an equal number of pennies, nickels, dimes, and quarters. How many coins does she have in all? You know how much all of Sarah's coins are worth and you know how much each coin is worth. (In the following equation, p = pennies, n = nickels, d = dimes, and q = quarters.)

$$p + 5n + 10d + 25q = 8,200$$

We know that she has an equal number of each coin; thus, $p = n = d = q$. Therefore, we can substitute p for all the other variables:

$$1p + 5p + 10p + 25p = 41p = 8,200, \text{ so } p = 200$$

Sarah has 200 pennies, 200 nickels, 200 dimes, and 200 quarters. Therefore, she has 800 coins.

7. **Estimate, make a reasonable guess, check the guess, and revise.** Using the example in number 6, if you were told that Sarah had a large number of coins that added up to $82.00, you could at least say that the total would be no more than 8,200 (the number of coins if they were all pennies) and no less than 328 (the number of coins if they were all quarters).

8. **Work backwards and eliminate.** For example, what is the largest 2-digit number that is divisible by 3 whose digits differ by 2? First, working backwards from 99, list numbers that are divisible by 3:

99, 96, 93, 90, 87, 84, 81, 78, 75, 72, 69, 66, 63, 60, . . .

Now cross out all numbers whose digits do not differ by 2. The largest number remaining is 75.

9. **Summarize in a group.** Working in a group is the best way to integrate all learning styles, keep motivation and interest active, and generate lots of ideas and support. Summarize the problem in your own words and talk through the problem out loud. Explain the problem to your group and why you arrived at the answer. Talking out loud, summarizing chapters, and listening to others clarifies thinking and is a great way to learn.

10. **Take a quiet break.** If you still can't find a solution to the problem as a group, take a break. Sometimes it helps to find a quiet spot and reflect. Sometimes working on another problem or relaxing for a few minutes while listening to music helps you return to the problem refreshed.

Overcome Math and Science Anxiety

Many people suffer from some math and science anxiety—having a preconceived notion that the material is difficult to learn, "over" their heads, or too precise (i.e., there is only one correct answer). As with the fear many experience with public speaking, the first step in learning any subject is to use critical thinking and creative problem solving to manage and overcome these anxieties. (See **Personal Evaluation Notebook 8.9** to evaluate your comfort level.)

Anxiety is a learned emotional response—you were not born with it. And, since it is learned, it can be unlearned. We explored strategies for overcoming speech anxiety, and many apply to math and science as well. Additional strategies include

● **Anxiety about Math and Science**
Some students are nervous about taking courses in math and science, even though the basic principles have many everyday applications. *What are some of the tasks you do daily that involve a working knowledge of basic math and science?*

1. **Do your prep work.** Don't take a math or science class if you haven't taken the proper prerequisites. It is better to spend the summer or an additional semester to gain the necessary skills, so that you don't feel overwhelmed and discouraged.

2. **Keep up and review often.** If you prepare early and often, you will be less anxious. The night before your test should be used for reviewing, not learning new material.

3. **Discipline yourself.** Focus your attention away from your fears and concentrate on the task at hand. You can overcome your math anxiety by jotting down ideas and formulas, drawing pictures, and writing out the problem. You keep your energy high when you stay active and involved. Reduce interruptions and concentrate fully for 45 minutes. Discipline your mind to concentrate for short periods. Time yourself on problems to increase speed and make the most of short study sessions.

4. **Study in groups.** Learning does not take place in isolation but, rather, in a supportive environment where anxiety is reduced and each person feels safe to use trial-and-error methods. Creativity, interaction, and multiple solutions are proposed when you study in groups. You will build confidence as you learn to

Personal Evaluation Notebook

The History of Your Anxiety

If you've experienced anxiety with math or science, it may be helpful to retrace the history of your anxiety. Write your responses to the following questions and exercises.

1. Try to recall your earliest experiences with math and science. Were those experiences positive or negative? Explain what made them negative or positive.

_____

_____

_____

_____

2. If you struggled with math or science, did you get help? What support did you tap into?

_____

_____

_____

_____

3. Summarize your feelings about math.

_____

_____

_____

_____

4. List all the reasons you want to succeed at math.

_____

_____

_____

_____

think out loud, brainstorm creative solutions, and solve problems. See **Peak Progress 8.4** on page 280 for a comprehensive checklist of questions to use as you problem solve.

5. **Have a positive attitude.** As mentioned earlier, having a positive attitude is key to learning any subject. Do you get sidetracked by negative self-talk that questions your abilities or the reason for learning math skills? Choose to focus on the positive feelings you have when you are confident and in control. Replace negative

> " Faith is taking the first step even when you don't see the whole staircase. "
>
> MARTIN LUTHER KING, JR.
> *Civil rights leader*

WORDS TO SUCCEED

Peak Progress

> 66 Man's mind,
> once stretched by
> a new idea, never
> regains its original
> dimensions. 99

OLIVER WENDALL HOLMES
Author

Problem-Solving Checklist

When you enroll in any course, including a math or science course, consider these questions:

- Have you approached the class with a positive attitude?
- Have you built confidence by getting involved in problems?
- Have you clearly defined the problems?
- What do you want to know and what are you being asked to find out?
- Have you separated essential information from the unessential?
- Have you separated the known from the unknown?
- Have you asked a series of questions: How? When? Where? What? If?
- Have you devised a plan for solving the problem?
- Have you gone from the general to the specific?
- Have you explored formulas, theories, and so on?
- Have you made an estimate?
- Have you illustrated or organized the problem?
- Have you made a table or a diagram, drawn a picture, or summarized data?
- Have you written the problem?
- Have you discovered a pattern to the problem?
- Have you alternated intense concentration with frequent breaks?
- Have you tried working backwards, completing similar problems, and solving small parts?
- Have you determined if you made careless errors or do not understand the concepts?
- Do you think, apply, reflect, and practice?
- Have you asked for help early?
- Have you been willing to put in the time required to solve problems?
- Have you analyzed the problem? Was your guess close? Did your plan work? How else can you approach the problem?
- Have you brainstormed ideas on your own?
- Have you brainstormed ideas in a group setting?
- Have you rewarded yourself for facing your fears, overcoming anxiety, and learning valuable skills that will increase your success in school, in your job, and in life?

and defeating self-talk with positive "I can" affirmations. Much of math anxiety, like stage fright and other fears, is compounded by this negative thinking and self-talk. Approach math and science with a positive "can do," inquisitive attitude.

6. **Dispute the myths.** Many times, fears are caused by myths, such as "Men are better than women at math and science" or "Creative people are not good at math and science." There is no basis for the belief that gender has anything to do with math ability, nor is it unfeminine to be good at math and science. Success in math and science requires creative thinking. As mathematician Augustus De Morgan said, "The moving power of mathematics is not reasoning, but imagination." Use critical thinking to overcome myths.

7. **Ask for help.** Don't wait until you are in trouble or frustrated. Talk with the instructor, visit the learning center, get a tutor, and join a study group. If you continue to have anxiety or feel lost, go to the counseling center. Try enrolling in a summer refresher course. You'll be prepared and confident when you take the required course later.

See **Peak Progress 8.5** to apply the Adult Learning Cycle to overcoming anxiety.

Peak Progress 8.5

Applying the Adult Learning Cycle to Overcoming Math and Science Anxiety

1. **RELATE. Why do I want to learn this?** I want to be confident in math and science. Avoiding math and science closes doors and limits opportunities. More than 75 percent of all careers use math and science, and these are often higher-status and better-paying jobs. This is essential knowledge I'll use in all facts of life.

2. **OBSERVE. How does this work?** I can learn a lot about applying critical thinking and creative problem solving to mathematics and science by watching, listening, and trying new things. I'll observe people who are good at math and science. What do they do? I'll also observe people who experience anxiety and don't do well and learn from their mistakes, I'll try using new critical thinking techniques for dealing with fear and observe how I'm improving.

3. **REFLECT. What does this mean?** I'll apply critical thinking to mathematics and science. What works and doesn't work? I'll think about and test new ways of reducing anxiety and break old patterns and negative self-talk that are self-defeating I'll look for connections and associations with other types of anxiety and apply what I learn.

4. **DO. What can I do with this?** I will practice reducing my anxiety. I'll find practical applications for connecting critical thinking and creative problem solving to math and science. Each day I'll work on one area. For example, I'll maintain a positive attitude as I approach math and science classes.

5. **TEACH. Whom can I share this with?** I'll form and work with a study group and share my tips and experiences. I'll demonstrate and teach the methods I've learned to others. I'll reward myself when I do well.

Remember, attitude is everything. If you keep an open mind, apply strategies you have learned in this chapter, and practice your critical thinking skills, you will become more confident in your problem-solving abilities.

TAKING CHARGE

Summary

In summary, in this chapter I learned to:

- **Appreciate the importance of critical thinking.** Critical thinking is fundamental for understanding and solving problems in coursework, in my job, and in all areas of my life. I have learned to examine beliefs, assumptions, and opinions against facts, to ask pertinent questions, and to analyze data.

- **Apply essential critical thinking skills.** Bloom's Taxonomy outlines the six critical thinking skills that college requires (from lowest- to highest-order): knowledge, comprehension, application, analysis, synthesis, and evaluation.

- **Use the problem-solving process.** When I problem solve, I will (1) state and understand the problem; (2) gather and interpret information; (3) develop and implement a plan of action; and (4) evaluate the plan or solution.

- **Incorporate problem-solving strategies.** My attitude has a lot to do with how I approach problem solving. I have developed a positive, inquisitive attitude and a willingness to explore, probe, question, and search for answers and solutions. I will replace negative self-talk with affirmations. I will use my critical thinking skills and be persistent in solving problems. I will participate in a supportive, group environment, such as a study group.

- **Avoid errors in judgment.** I will avoid using stereotypes, all-or-nothing thinking, snap judgments, unwarranted assumptions, projection, sweeping generalizations, the halo effect, and negative labeling. I will not project my habits onto others in order to justify my behavior or decisions.

- **Use creative problem solving.** I will use creative problem solving to approach the problem from a different direction and explore new options. What problems are similar? Is there a pattern to the problem? I will brainstorm various strategies. I will act out the problem, move it around, picture it, take it apart, translate it, and summarize it in my own words. I will solve easier problems first and then tackle harder problems.

- **Apply strategies to math and science courses.** What model, formula, drawing, sketch, equation, chart, table, calculation, or particular strategy will help? I choose the most appropriate strategy and outline a step-by-step plan. I show all my work, so I can review.

- **Overcome anxiety for math and science.** If I am anxious about taking math and science courses, I will attempt to maintain a positive attitude, use helpful resources available to me, and take control and focus on the task at hand.

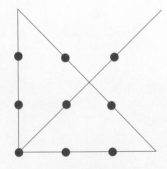

Solution to the Nine-Dot Exercise on Page 267

When confronted with this problem, most people approach it by remaining within the boundaries of the dots. However, when you move outside the confines of the dots and the boundaries are reset, you can easily solve the puzzle. This exercise helps illustrate that some problems cannot be solved with traditional thinking.

Performance Strategies

Following are the top 10 strategies for critical thinking and creative problem solving:

- Define the problem.
- Gather and interpret information.
- Develop and implement a plan of action.
- Evaluate your decisions.
- Ask questions.
- Brainstorm creative options.
- Pay attention to details.
- Consider all sides of an issue.
- Use reasoning and avoid errors in judgment.
- Have a positive attitude.

Tech for Success

Take advantage of the text's Web site at **www.mhhe.com/ferrett7e** for additional study aids, useful forms, and convenient and applicable resources.

- **Work on weak areas.** There are excellent online programs that help you determine the mathematical areas where you need the most work. ALEKS (**www.aleks.com/highered**) is a tutorial program that identifies your less proficient areas, then focuses on improvement through practice and targeted problems.

- **Math at your fingertips.** In your studies, you will come across many standard calculations and formulas, most of which can be found online and downloaded. Although this should not replace working through the formulas yourself to make sure you understand their applications, it does make incorporating math into your everyday life much easier.

Study Team Notes

Creativity at Work

Marina Koshetz and her husband, Josef, have recently opened a small restaurant that serves foods from their homeland of Russia. Starting their restaurant was a great deal of work, requiring getting the correct permits, remodeling an existing building, purchasing equipment, and planning the menu. The couple works long hours, six days a week. Before opening the restaurant at 11 A.M., Marina makes bread while Josef mixes together the traditional dishes they will serve. Then Marina remains in the kitchen to cook and prepare dishes while Josef waits tables and runs the cash register. At the end of the day, the couple washes the dishes and cleans the restaurant together. Although the restaurant is closed on Mondays, Marina and Josef use that day to plan the next week's specials and purchase food and other supplies.

Despite their hard work, the couple has made only enough money to cover costs. On a recent Monday afternoon, the two restaurateurs brainstormed ways to attract more customers. The restaurant is located in a quiet neighborhood on the edge of a district where many Russian immigrants live. So far, almost all of their customers have been Russian. Josef and Marina realized that they needed to do more to attract other residents to their restaurant. They decided to host an open house and invite everyone who lived within a mile radius of the restaurant. Then they decided to add a couple of popular American dishes and began running ads in a local newspaper. Soon their restaurant was attracting more customers, and the business began to show a profit.

Marina and Josef Koshetz
RESTAURANT OWNERS

Related Majors: Restaurant and Food Service Management, Business

CRITICAL THINKING How did Josef and Marina use creativity and critical thinking to improve their business?

Peak Performer
PROFILE

Scott Adams

He's been described as a techie with the "social skills of a mousepad." He's not the sort of fellow you'd expect to attract media attention. However, pick up a newspaper, turn to the comics, and you'll find him. He's Dilbert. Cartoonist Scott Adams created this comic-strip character who daily lampoons corporate America and provides a humorous outlet for employees everywhere.

Though creative at a young age, Adams's artistic endeavors were discouraged early on. The Famous Artists School rejected him at age 11. Years later, he received the lowest grade in a college drawing class. Practicality replaced creativity. In 1979, Adams earned a B.A. in economics from Hartwick College in Oneonta, New York, and, in 1986, an MBA from the University of California at Berkeley. For the next 15 years, Adams settled uncomfortably into a number of jobs that "defied description." Ironically, the frustrations of the work-place—power-driven co-workers, inept bosses, and cell-like cubicles—fueled his imagination. Adams began doodling, and Dilbert was born.

Encouraged by others, Adams submitted his work to United Media, a major cartoon syndicate. He was offered a contract in 1989, and "Dilbert" debuted in 50 national newspapers. Today, "Dilbert" appears in 2,000

newspapers in 65 countries and was the first syndicated cartoon to have its own Web site.

With such mass exposure, coming up with new ideas for cartoons could be a challenge. However, Adams found the perfect source: He has made his e-mail address available. He gets hundreds of messages a day from workers at home and abroad. His hope is that, through his creative invention, solutions will develop for the problems he satirizes.

PERFORMANCE THINKING Of the creative problem-solving strategies on pages 265–274, which one do you think has been most helpful for Scott Adams and why?

CHECK IT OUT According to Scott Adams, "Creativity is allowing yourself to make mistakes. Art is knowing which ones to keep." Adams is no stranger to taking chances and voicing his views on management—both in the workforce and in the government. At **www.dilbert.com,** you can read (and respond to, if you like) the Dilbert.blog written by Adams, and you can sign up to receive the Dilbert Newsletter (a.k.a. the DNRC—the official publication of Dogbert's New Ruling Class). Although it's geared for entertainment, the games section includes a "Mission Statement Generator," which provides a handy list of key words commonly used in drafting mission statements.

Starting Today

At least one strategy I learned in this chapter that I plan to try right away is:

_____

_____

_____

What changes must I make in order for this strategy to be effective?

_____

_____

_____

Review Questions

Based on what you have learned in this chapter, write your answers to the following questions:

1. Name six essential critical thinking skills necessary for success in college.

_____

_____

2. What are the attributes of a critical thinker?

_____

_____

3. What are the four steps of problem solving?

_____

_____

4. Name five strategies for becoming more creative.

_____

_____

5. Name five strategies for problem solving in math and science.

_____

_____

Conquering Fear of Failure

In the Classroom

Gloria Ramone is a single mom who works part-time and lives and attends school in the inner city. She is eager to complete her education, begin her career, and have the opportunity to receive a higher salary. She is an electronics student who wants her classes to be practical and relevant. She is required to take a class in critical thinking, a class she is resisting because she sees no practical application to her job. Her attitude is affecting her attendance and participation.

1. Offer ideas to help Gloria see the importance of critical thinking in decision making.

2. Help her connect decisions in school with job decisions.

In the Workplace

Gloria is now a manager in a small electronics business. She is also taking evening classes, working toward a business degree. She has received promotions quickly on her job, but she knows that she needs further management training. Gloria is very interested in the electronics field and loves to solve problems. On a daily basis, she is faced with issues to solve and has decisions to make. She has lots of practice predicting results and using critical thinking for problem solving. Gloria enjoys most of the business classes, but she doesn't want to take the classes in finance and statistics. Gloria has math anxiety and is dreading the upper-division math and statistics.

3. What strategies in this chapter can help Gloria overcome math anxiety?

4. What are some affirmations Gloria could use to help her develop a positive attitude about math?

Applying the ABC Method of Self-Management

In the Journal Entry on page 255, you were asked to describe a decision you made that cost you a great deal in time, money, or stress. How would using critical thinking and creative problem solving have helped you make better decisions?

_____

_____

_____

Now that you know more strategies for critical thinking and creative problem solving, apply the ABC method to a difficult situation you have encountered, such as a financial dilemma, a rigorous course, or a serious personal crisis. Use your critical thinking skills to work through the situation and arrive at a positive result.

A = Actual event:

B = Beliefs:

C = Challenge:

Use positive visualization and practice deep breathing with your eyes closed for just one minute. See yourself calm, centered, and relaxed, learning formulas, practicing problem solving, and using critical thinking to work through problems. You feel confident about yourself because you have learned to control your anxiety and maintain a positive attitude.

PRACTICE SELF-MANAGEMENT

For more examples of learning how to manage difficult situations, see the "Self-Management Workbook" section of the Online Learning Center Web site at **www.mhhe.com/ferrett7e.**

Apply Bloom's Taxonomy

Different situations call for different levels of thinking. Although many, if not all, these skills are required in every course you take, jot down the classes or situations where you might use a particular thinking skill to a greater degree. For example, if you are in a speech class, you may be asked to evaluate others' speeches.

Critical Thinking Skill	Task	Class or Situation
Knowledge	Recite; recall; recognize	
Comprehension	Restate; explain; state; discuss; summarize	
Application	Apply; prepare; solve a problem; explore a case study	
Analysis	Break ideas apart and relate to other ideas; complete an essay	
Synthesis	Integrate ideas; create new ideas; improve on design	
Evaluate	Critique; evaluate; cite advantages and disadvantages	

Problem Solving

Write three problems you may be experiencing in the workplace or at school. Use critical thinking to find creative solutions to the problems.

PROBLEMS

1. _____
   _____
   _____
2. _____
   _____
   _____
3. _____
   _____
   _____

POSSIBLE SOLUTIONS

1. a. _____
   b. _____
   c. _____
2. a. _____
   b. _____
   c. _____
3. a. _____
   b. _____
   c. _____

Preparing for Critical Thinking

Brainstorm alternative approaches and solutions to the problems that arise in your day-to-day activities. By using critical thinking, you will be able to explore new ideas as you fill in this form.

ISSUES/PROBLEMS IN DAY-TO-DAY ACTIVITIES

_____

_____

_____

_____

_____

SOLUTION #1: _____

Pros	Cons	Potential Consequences	Costs	Timing

SOLUTION #2: _____

Pros	Cons	Potential Consequences	Costs	Timing

SOLUTION #3: _____

Pros	Cons	Potential Consequences	Costs	Timing

You Can Solve the Problem: Sue's Decision

Every day you solve problems. Some problems are easy to solve: *Should I do my shopping now or later?* Some problems are harder: *My car is in the shop. How will I get to work?* Some problems change your life forever: *Can I afford to go to school?*

Every day life brings problems and choices. The kinds of choices you make can make your life easier or harder. Often, you do not know which direction to take. But there are ways to help you be more certain. There are steps you can take. You can look at your choices before you make them. You can see some of the problems you may face. You may find you have other or better choices. Here are some steps to help you make choices:

Step 1 Know what the problem really is. Is it a daily problem? Is it a once-in-a-lifetime problem?
Step 2 List the things you know about the problem. List the things you don't know. Ask questions. Get help and advice.
Step 3 Explore alternate choices.
Step 4 Think about the pros and cons for the other choices. Put them in order from best to worst choice.
Step 5 Pick the choice you feel good about.
Step 6 Study what happens after you have made your choice. Are you happy about the choice? Would you make it again?

Read the following story and apply the steps in the following exercise.

Sue has been diagnosed with cancer. Her doctor has told her that it is in only one place in her body. The doctor wants to operate. He thinks that he will be able to remove all of it, but he still wants Sue to do something else. He wants her to undergo chemotherapy for four months, which will make her feel very sick. It will make her tired, but the medicine can help keep the cancer from coming back.

Sue is not sure what to do. She has two small children who are not in school. Sue's husband works days and cannot help care for the children during the day. Sue's family lives far away, and she cannot afford day care. She asks herself, "How will I be able to care for my children if I am sick?"

The doctor has told Sue that she must make her own choice. Will she take the medicine? Sue must decide. She will talk with her husband, and they will make a choice together.

What is Sue's problem? What are her choices? What would you decide? Apply the six steps to help Sue make a good choice by writing responses to the following questions and statements.

Step 1 The problem is

_____

_____

_____

(continued)

Step 2

a. You know these things about the problem:

_____

_____

_____

b. You don't know these things about the problem:

_____

_____

_____

_____

Step 3 The other choices are

_____

_____

_____

Step 4 Rank the choices, best to worst.

_____

_____

_____

Step 5 Pick a choice the family might feel good about.

_____

_____

_____

Step 6 What might happen to Sue and her family?

_____

_____

_____

_____

You Can Solve the Problem: Casey's Dilemma

You make choices and solve problems every day. Some choices are automatic and don't require much thought, such as stopping a car at a red light or stepping on the gas pedal when the light turns green. Other problems require you to make easy choices, such as which TV show to watch. Other problems are more difficult to solve—for example, what to say to your teenage son when he comes home past curfew, smelling like beer.

In your life, you will face many problems and choices. You might make good or poor choices because you don't always know how a choice will turn out.

There are some steps you can follow to help you make a good choice and solve your problem. These steps can help you think of options and improve your problem-solving skills:

Step 1   Stop and think. Take a deep breath before you say or do something you will regret.

Step 2   Write a problem statement. Be sure to include who has the problem and state it clearly.

Step 3   Write a goal statement. Check to see that it has simple, realistic, and positive words.

Step 4   List all your choices, both the good and the bad choices.

Step 5   Remove choices that don't match your goal, will hurt others, or will cause more problems than they will solve.

Step 6   Make your best choice. Check Step 3 to be sure your choice matches your goal.

Read the following story and apply the steps in the following exercise.

Casey has been divorced for three years, and her children visit their father every other weekend. When he brought the children home this weekend, he told Casey that he was planning to remarry.

Now her children will have a stepmother and Casey is worried how everyone will get along. She wants her children to continue to visit their dad and enjoy the visits.

Can you help Casey solve this problem? Follow the six steps to help Casey make a choice by writing responses to the following questions and statements.

1. What is the first thing Casey should do?

_____

_____

2. Write a problem statement.

_____

_____

3. What is Casey's goal?

_____

_____

(continued)

4. List as many choices as you can for Casey.

_____

_____

_____

5. Which choices should Casey cross off her list?

_____

_____

_____

6. What is the best choice for Casey to make?

_____

_____

_____

7. Does your answer in number 6 match her goal in Step 3?

_____

_____

_____

Assessing and Demonstrating Your Critical Thinking Skills

1. **Looking back:** Review your worksheets to find activities through which you learned to make decisions and solve problems creatively. Jot down examples. Also, look for examples of how you learned to apply critical thinking skills to math and science.

_____

_____

_____

_____

_____

2. **Taking stock:** What are your strengths in making decisions and in using critical thinking? Are you a creative person? What areas would you like to improve?

_____

_____

_____

_____

_____

3. **Looking forward:** How would you demonstrate critical thinking and creative problem-solving skills to an employer?

_____

_____

_____

_____

_____

4. **Documentation:** Include documentation of your critical thinking and creative problem-solving skills. Find an instructor or employer who will write a letter of recommendation. Add this letter to your portfolio.

_____

_____

_____

_____

_____

Add this page to your Career Development Portfolio.

Glossary

A

acronym A word formed from the first letter of a series of other words.

acrostic A made-up sentence in which the first letter of each word stands for something.

affirmation Positive self-talk or internal thoughts that counter self-defeating thought patterns with positive, hopeful, or realistic thoughts.

attentive listening A decision to be fully focused with the intent of understanding the speaker.

B

body smart People who have physical and kinesthetic intelligence; have the ability to understand and control their bodies; and have tactical sensitivity, like movement, and handle objects skillfully.

C

character Attributes or features that make up and distinguish an individual and are considered constant and relatively noncontroversial by most people.

cheating Using or providing unauthorized help.

chunking Breaking up long lists of information or numbers to make it easier to remember.

civility Interacting with others with respect, kindness, good manners, or etiquette.

comprehension Understanding main ideas and details.

convergent The ability to look at several unrelated items and bring order to them.

critical thinking A logical, rational, systematic thought process that is necessary to understand, analyze, and evaluate information in order to solve a problem or situation.

D

decision making Determining or selecting the best or most effective answer or solution.

deductive reasoning Drawing conclusions based on going from the general to the specific.

directors People who are dependable, self-directed, conscientious, efficient, decisive, and results-orientated.

divergent The ability to break apart an idea into many different ideas.

E

emotional intelligence The ability to understand and manage oneself and relate effectively to others.

empathy Understanding and having compassion for others.

ethics The principles of conduct that govern a group or society.

external locus of control The belief that success or failure is due to outside influences such as fate, luck, or other people.

extrovert A person who is outgoing, social, optimistic, and often uncomfortable with being alone.

F–I

feeler A person who is sensitive to the concerns and feelings of others, values harmony, and dislikes creating conflict.

formal outline A traditional outline that uses Roman numerals and capital letters to highlight main points.

important priorities Essential tasks or activities that support a person's goals and can be scheduled with some flexibility.

informal outline A free form of outline that uses dashes and indenting to highlight main points.

internal locus of control The belief that control over life is due to behavior choices, character, and effort.

interpreting Developing ideas and being able to summarize the material.

introvert A person who tends to like time alone, solitude, and reflection, and prefers the world of ideas and thoughts.

intuitive People who are more comfortable with theories, abstraction, imagination, and speculation.

J–L

judgers A person who prefers orderly, planned, and structured learning and working environments.

logic smart People who have logical/mathematical intelligence; like numbers, puzzles, and logic; and have the ability to reason, solve problems, create hypotheses, and think in terms of cause and effect.

M

maturity The ability to control impulses, to think beyond the moment, and to consider how words and actions affect others.

mind map A visual, holistic form of note taking that starts with the main idea placed in the center of a page and branches out with subtopics through associations and patterns.

mindfulness The state of being totally in the moment and part of the process.

motivation An inner drive that moves a person to action.

music smart People who have rhythm and melody intelligence; the ability to appreciate, perceive, and produce rhythms.

N

note taking A method of creating order and arranging thoughts and materials to help retain information.

O

ongoing activities Necessary "maintenance" tasks that should be carefully managed so they don't take up too much time.

outdoor smart People who have environmental intelligence and are good at measuring, charting, and observing animals and plants.

P

people smart People who have interpersonal intelligence; like to talk and work with people, join groups, and solve problems as part of a team; and have the ability to work with and understand people, as well as to perceive and be responsive to the moods, intentions, and desires of other people.

perceiver A person who prefers flexibility and spontaneity, and likes to allow life to unfold.

picture smart People who have spatial intelligence; like to draw, sketch, and visualize information; and have the ability to perceive in three-dimensional space and re-create various aspects of the visual world.

plagiarism To steal and pass off the ideas or words of another as one's own.

problem solving Creating or identifying potential answers or solutions to a problem or situation.

procrastination Deliberately putting off tasks.

R

recall The transfer of information from long-term memory into short-term memory.

reflect To think about something in a purposeful way with the intention of creating new meaning.

reframing Choosing to see a situation in a new way.

retention The process of storing information.

S

self smart People who have interpersonal and inner intelligence; have the ability to be contemplative, self-disciplined, and introspective.

self-assessment The recognition of the need to learn new tasks and subjects, relate more effectively with others, set goals, manage time and stress, and create a balanced and productive life.

self-management A thought process that involves techniques you can utilize to help you manage your thoughts and behaviors, and keep you focused, overcome obstacles, and succeed.

sensors People who learn best from their senses and feel comfortable with facts and concrete data.

T

thinker A person who likes to analyze problems with facts, rational logic, and analysis.

trivial activities Nonessential activities that are completely discretionary and do not directly support a person's goals.

U–W

urgent priorities Tasks or activities that support a person's goals and must be accomplished by a specified date or time to avoid negative consequences.

word smart People who have verbal/linguistic intelligence; like to read, talk, and write about information; and have the ability to argue, persuade, entertain, and teach with words.

Additional Credits

Features Guide

Worksheets

Career Development Portfolio

Index